Skiing in the Catskill Region

On the Front Cover: Norway Ski Club member Harold Johansen sails off the ski jump like a bird in flight in East White Plains, New York, on January 16, 1938. At the bottom of the run, there was still a small stream to cross among the spectators. Johansen placed third in this Class A competition. (Courtesy of the author.)

On the Back Cover: A group of happy skiers at Plattekill Mountain in the mid-1960s demonstrates the domino theory on skis. (Courtesy of Gary Hinkley.)

Skiing in the Catskill Region

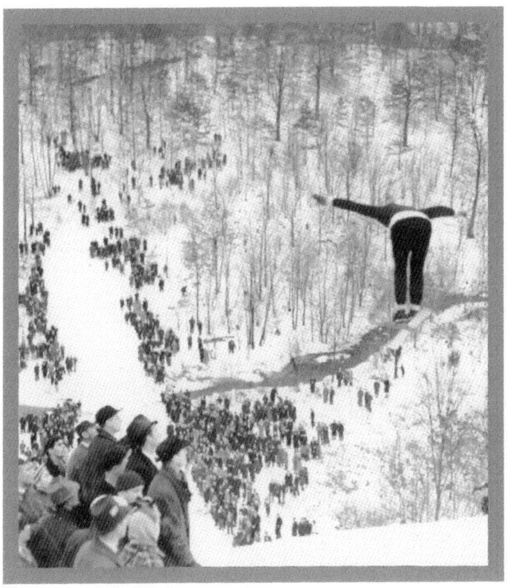

George V. Quinn

Arcadia Publishing

ISBN 978-1-4671-2054-8

Published by Arcadia Publishing
Charleston, South Carolina

Printed in the United States of America

Library of Congress Control Number: 2013937263

For all general information, please contact Arcadia Publishing:
Telephone 843-853-2070
Fax 843-853-0044
E-mail sales@arcadiapublishing.com
For customer service and orders:
Toll-Free 1-888-313-2665

Visit us on the Internet at www.arcadiapublishing.com

To my father, Vincent Quinn, a true pioneer in the ski business

CONTENTS

Acknowledgments 6

Introduction 7

1. The Early Years and Ski Jumping 9

2. Getting Slopeside Was Half the Fun 19

3. Fashion, Style, and Flair 27

4. Food, Entertainment, and Rest 37

5. Ski Clubs and Organizations 49

6. The Great Northern Catskills 59

7. Belleayre Mountain and Points South 81

8. Gone Home 109

ACKNOWLEDGMENTS

I would like to show my gratitude to the following ski resorts and organizations that helped in the creation of this book: Holiday Mountain, Hunter Mountain, Belleayre Mountain, Rip Van Winkle Ski Club, Woodstock Historical Society, and Norway Ski Club.

I am also grateful to the many individuals who shared their lives and photographic archives: John M. Ham, Edith Brody, Joe Strauss, Karl and Margot Plattner, Phil and Anne Davenport, Robert and Valerie Konefal, Steve Witte, Dean Schambach, Laura Kluthe Iwanski, Howard and Elinor Lindemann, Jerry Fielding, Bonnie Hinkley, Gary Hinkley, Bea Hinkley, Carol Tomesetti, Breeda O'Callaghan, Nell Boucher, Hermann Amsz, Anthony and Lynette Liberetore, Richard Heppner, Milo Stewart Jr., David Slutzky, Rick Barthel, Jerry Fielding.

I especially want to thank Bernadette Quinn and Ilene Mark for their hard work and encouragement.

A special thanks goes to Mohonk Mountain House Archives, which will be referred to in the caption credits as MMHA. Unless otherwise noted, all images appear courtesy of the Quinn collection.

INTRODUCTION

The Catskill region was a bustling place at the end of the 19th century. Many large hotels were built, and most were accessible by train from New York City. This provided employment for local residents in the summer; however, winters months were tough to get through. Logging and farming were some of the main occupations in the area. In the late 19th century, Scandinavian immigrants brought skiing skills with them from the old countries, which proved useful in getting around in the winter months on farms and traveling between the small towns that dotted the region. By the 1920s, most people had access to skis, and they could be ordered from department stores by mail. Folks in the Catskill region could climb up a hill and ski down—always a good, healthy exercise. Cross-country skiing, although not as popular as downhill, has always been present. With the advent of waxless skis and improved bindings, the sport grew tremendously in the 1970s, and ski areas catering to all the new skiers began to appear.

The Winter Olympics at Lake Placid in 1932 gave skiing a much-needed boost. Until then, ski jumping had been the biggest winter spectator sport, drawing thousands to events mostly in the Hudson Valley region. For many, ski jumping was synonymous with skiing. The central Catskills, where the big mountains were, never had any large ski jumps. Most were located in the Hudson Valley or the southern New York region, closer to the population centers. The Norway Ski Club started building jumps and promoting the sport from the 1920s on. Events at these locations drew many thousands of spectators, elevating the champion ski jumpers to a kind of rock-star status. On Joppenbergh Mountain, overlooking the village of Rosendale below, a jump was created in 1937, designed by Harold Schelderup of Norway, and it lasted until 1971. The sport was so popular that ski jumping was held in the summer for exhibition purposes and still could draw many thousands. Borax, pine needles, and straw were spread over carpets to create a landing area.

With railroad service already in place in the Catskills, it was only logical for skiers to follow along those same lines. Only they needed somewhere to ski, and Phoenicia offered them a place in 1935 at the Simpson Memorial Ski Center. Phoenicia was already a train hub with a branch going north to the Hunter-Tannersville region, and there were many older hotels and rooming houses to lodge the skiers. Ski trains from New York City could park beside the slope at Simpsons for the day, awaiting skiers for the return trip. After the lull period of World War II, other ski areas opened near the train line, trying to keep up with the demand for the sport. Highmount Ski Center, opened in 1947 by the Davenport family, proved very popular. Belleayre Ski Center, developed by the State of New York, soon followed. At one time in the 1950s, there were eight ski areas on or at the base of this miles-long ridge above 3,000 feet in elevation. By now, most skiers came by automobile, and passenger service on the trains stopped by the 1950s. The status quo of skiing changed radically in the late 1950s with the beginning of Hunter Mountain. James Hammerstein, son of Broadway legend Oscar Hammerstein II, and a group of celebrity investors that included the Slutzky brothers formed the Hunter Mountain Development Corporation to develop the area. After three seasons, the corporation went bankrupt, and the Slutzky brothers took full control. It was a period of exponential growth for Hunter and other fledgling ski areas, such as Windham, over the hill to the northwest. At Hunter, Austrian ski instructor Karl Plattner headed a large ski school. Celebrity skiers such as Larry Hagman, Kim Novak, and Mitch Miller gave the area a much-needed publicity boost. By the mid-1960s, summer skiing on tiny plastic chips was happening under the B-chairlift, although this lasted only for a few seasons since it was just a little too slow for most people. Of course, snowmaking was important to the success of any area, and the Slutzky brothers insisted on having it early at the slopes of Hunter Mountain. Belleayre and Highmount, at higher base elevations with more consistent natural snow, followed much later after some poor seasons in the 1970s.

All this growth in downhill skiing was not without controversy. While most residents welcomed any kind of new commerce to the region, there were others who could see that it was changing a rural way of life in certain communities. The skiers' fast-paced lives were a contrast to the slower lifestyle of the locals. Generally, things worked out.

Competition among the areas has sometimes been fierce. The most outstanding example has pitted the New York State–run Belleayre Mountain against all the other privately run areas of the Catskills, which claim that Belleayre has an unfair competitive advantage. This conflict has endured for over four decades and has shown no abatement since the New York State Olympic Regional Development Authority (ORDA) took over Belleayre in 2012.

The final chapter of this book will journey down memory lane to some of the lost ski areas that time has forgotten. In the era before the big corporate development of the mountains, the skiing was not necessarily better; lifts, equipment, and bindings broke frequently, and skiers may have had to pack their own ski trails. Even getting to the slopes—traveling on a county road without four-wheel drive—could be difficult. But there was an ambience of personal connection that is not found on the large mountains of today. People in the rural communities had the idea of just putting up a single rope tow on a hill to entertain the locals during the bleak winter months. If that drew enough people, maybe a T-bar was added and a heated warming hut with an outhouse, or even running water with toilets. Many areas were joint efforts run by extended families, with everyone contributing his or her innate skills. As you gaze through the photographs of the book, you can see where skiing has taken the Catskill region, for better or worse.

1

THE EARLY YEARS AND SKI JUMPING

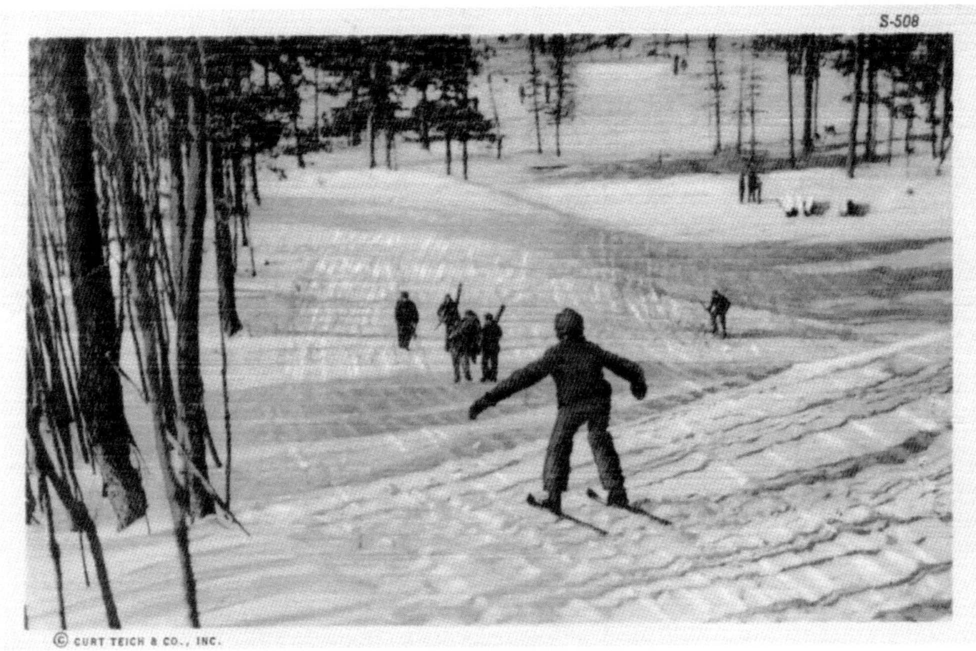

As seen in this 1920s Catskill postcard, in order to ski down the mountain, one had to hike up it. Scandinavian immigrants brought with them the skis and skiing ability in late 1800s. Skiing then was partly utilitarian, facilitating work around the farm or travel to rural villages in deep snow.

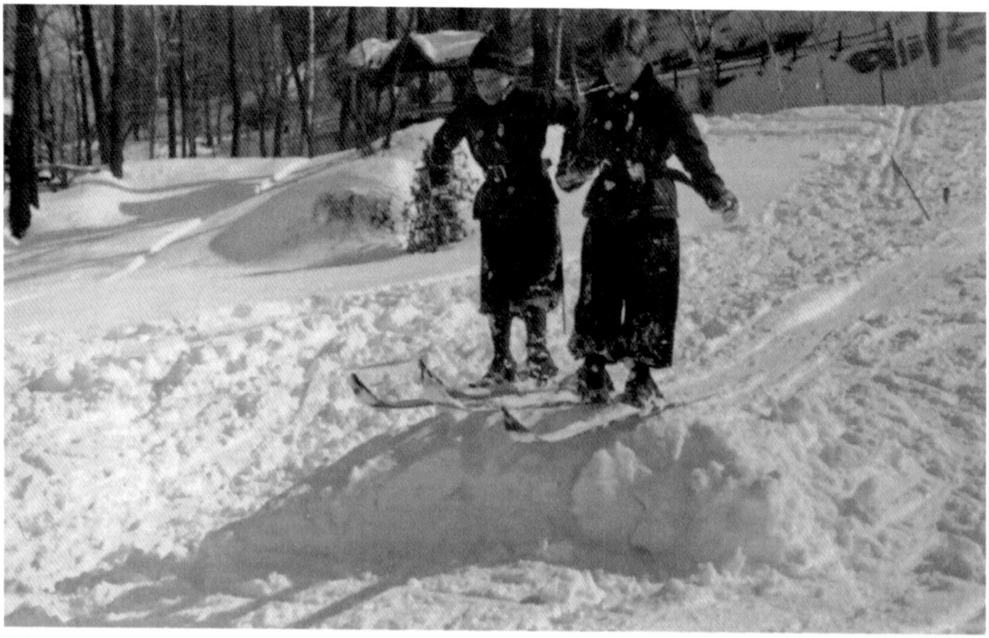

These Mohonk schoolboys are pictured on Garden Hill ski jump near Mohonk Mountain House in 1935. (Courtesy of MMHA.)

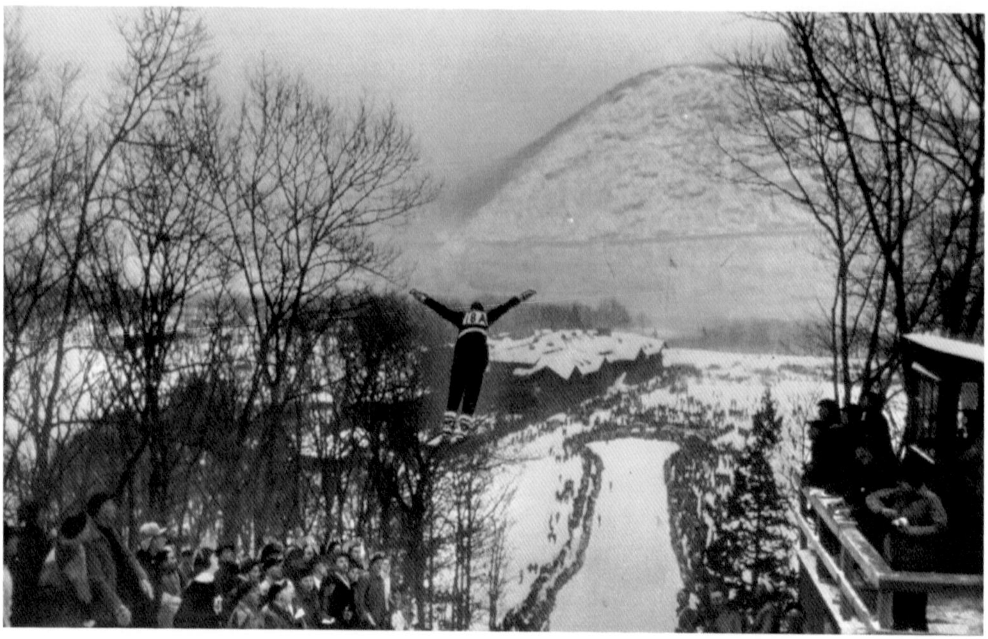

Ski jumper Odd Hirsheim takes off from the ramp at Bear Mountain State Park. Ski jumping was held nearly every Saturday and Sunday afternoon during winter months. There was no need to wait for natural snow as ground-up ice was used as an alternative. From the 1920s through the 1950s, ski jumping events drew many thousands of spectators.

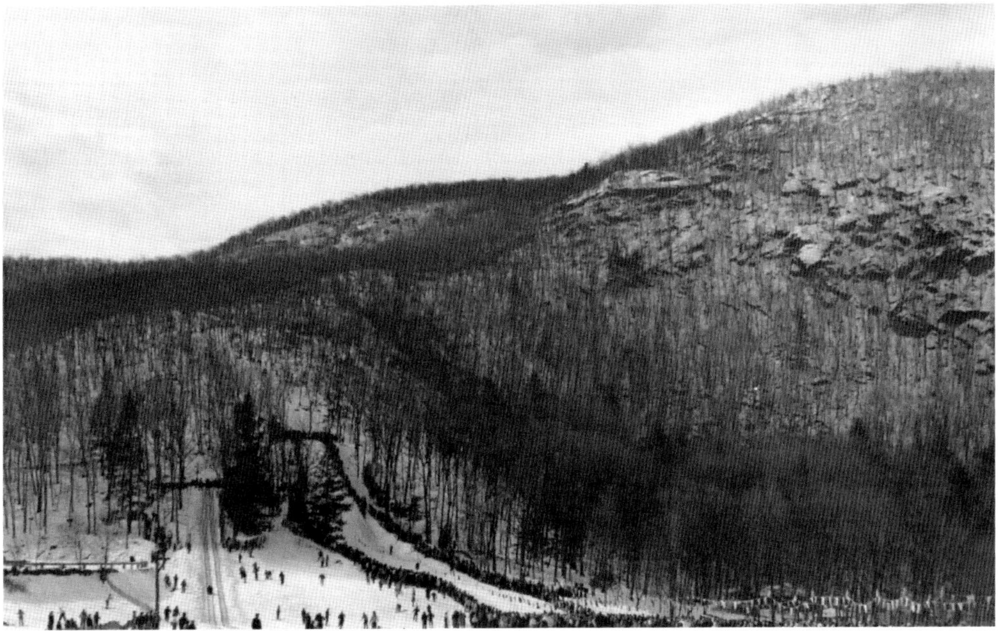

A large crowd is gathered along the ski jump to the right at Bear Mountain State Park at the Ski Jamboree on January 28, 1945. To the left on the hill is a toboggan run.

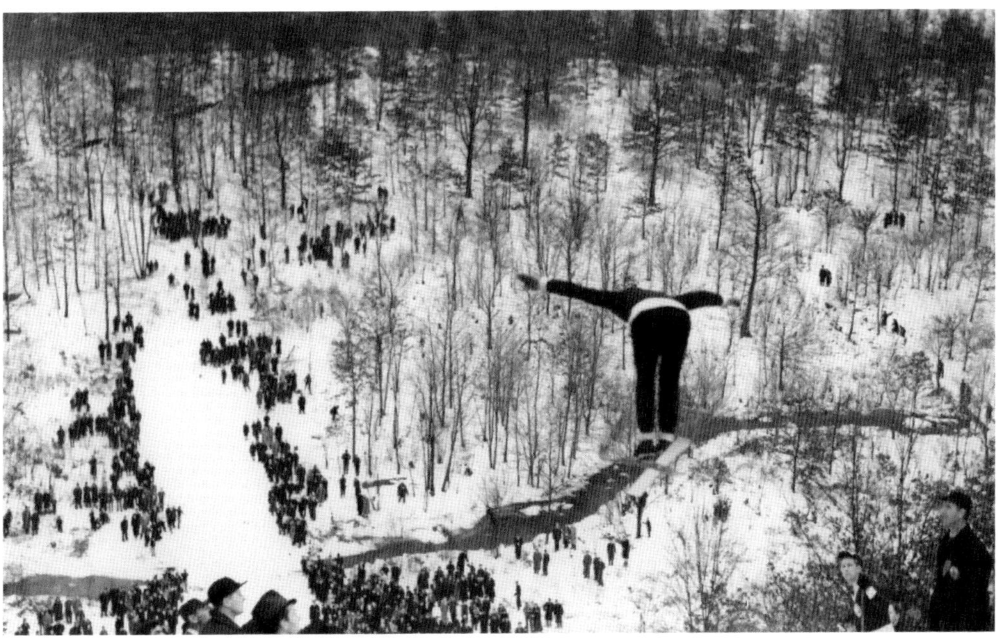

After clearing the jump and landing safely, ski jumper Harold Johansen still has a small stream to cross in the valley below. This jump is at Silverlake in East White Plains. After the abandonment of this jump, the Norway Ski Club built several jumps downstate and in Connecticut before settling at Bear Mountain State Park in the late 1930s.

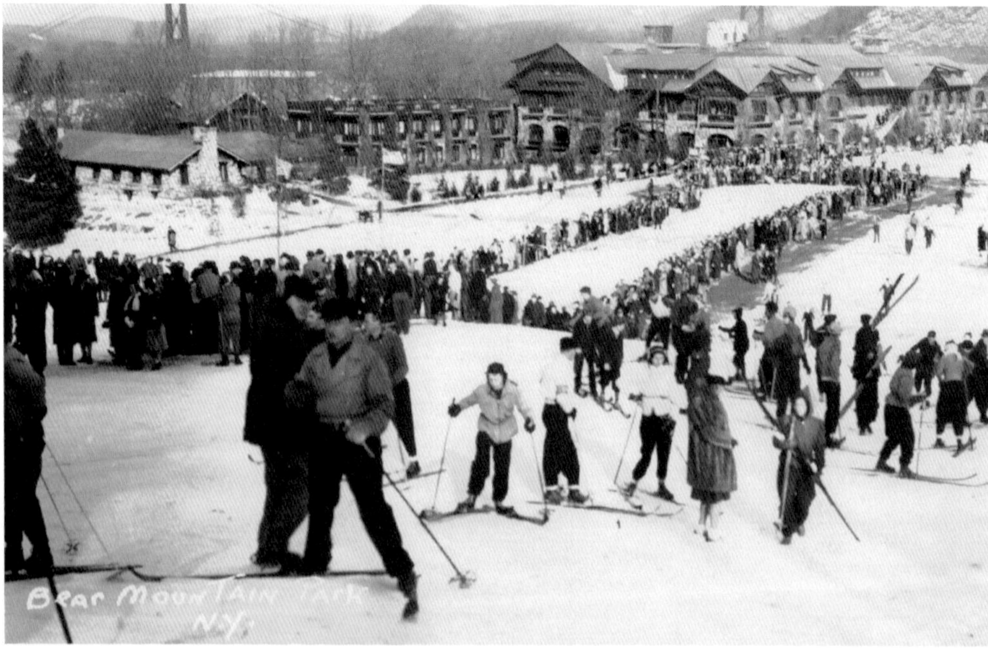

This late-1930s view from the hill at Bear Mountain looks down at the main lodge complex. In the background is Bear Mountain Bridge crossing the Hudson River.

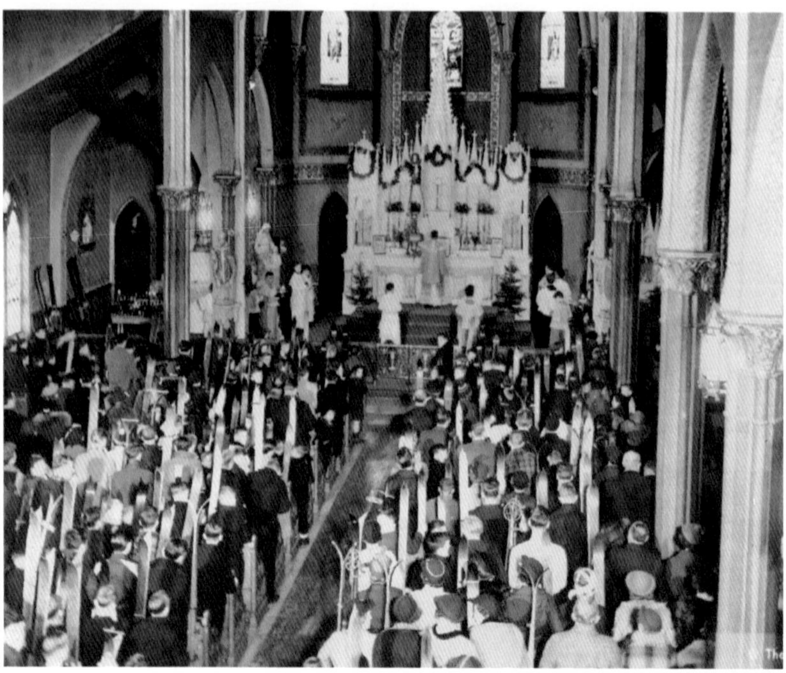

Ski enthusiasts, accompanied by their skis, attend special Mass held for them in 1937. Scenes like this became common before skiers headed to the slopes and on Saturday evenings in the Catskills.

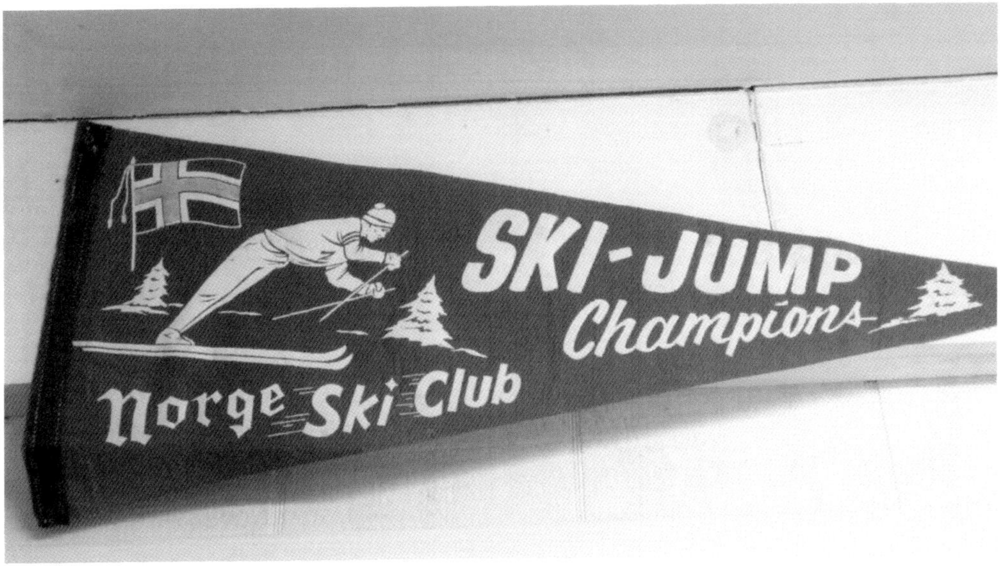

A ski pennant for the Norge, or "Norway," Ski Club tells the story of its many successes at winning competitive ski-jumping events.

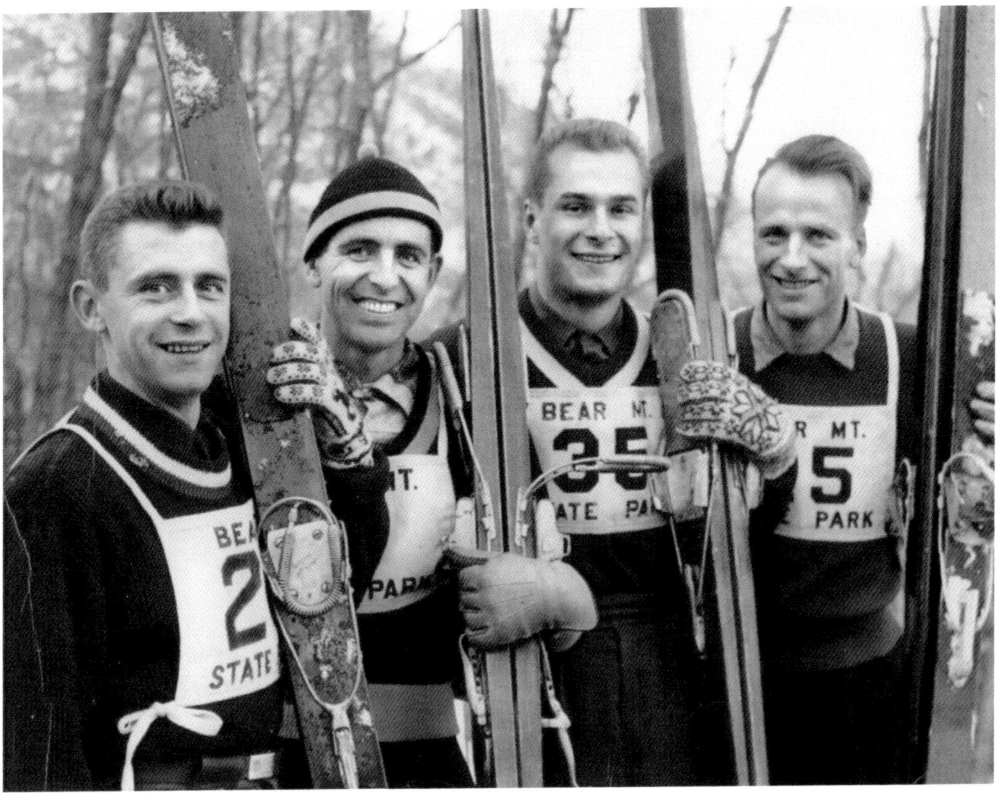

Beaming ski jumpers are lined up at a tournament at Bear Mountain on January 12, 1958. They are, from left to right, Charles Tremblay, Doug Schmaltz, Elinar Dohlen, and Bern Blikstad.

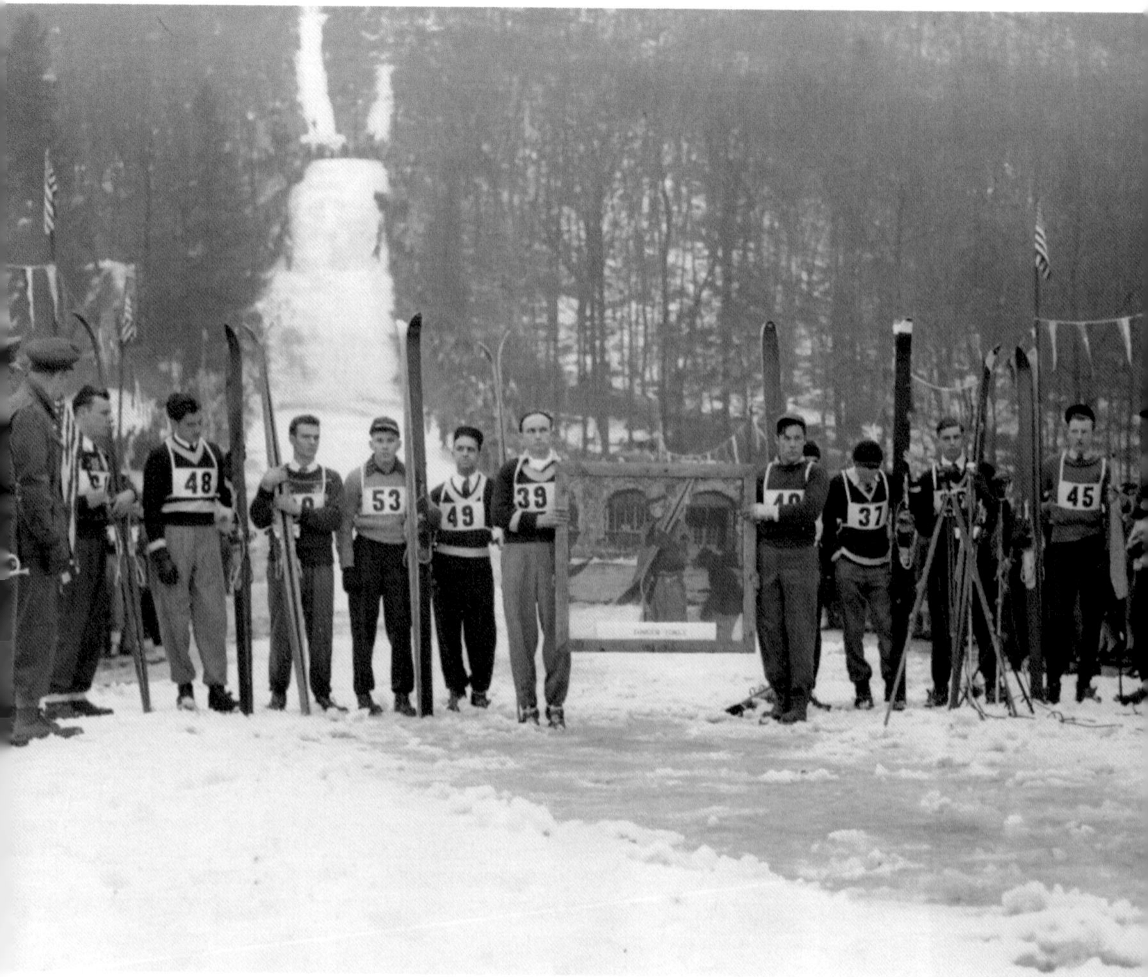

Fellow ski jumpers hold a large picture of Torger Tokle at a memorial jump named for him at Bear Mountain State Park. Torger joined the Army in October 1942 and trained with the 86th Mountain Division at Camp Hale, Colorado, high in the Rockies. There was no more jumping on tremendous hills to ovations; instead, he marched long miles with a gun and a heavy pack on his shoulders. The troops spent weeks at a time training at high altitudes and camping in snow caves to build stamina needed for combat readiness. In the spring of 1945, while leading his men at Monte Terracia, Italy, Torger was hit by shrapnel and died on the battlefield.

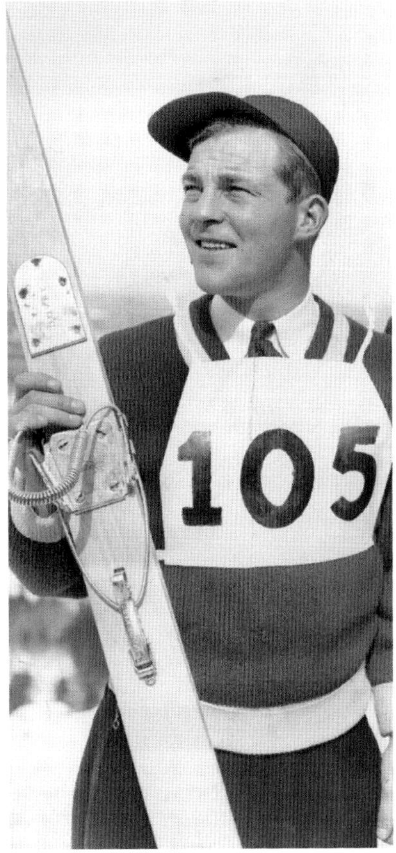

Norway Ski Club member Torger Tokle appears to touch the tops of the trees in this record hill jump of 180 feet at Bear Mountain State Park on February 12, 1941. By 1940, Torger was established as the greatest ski jumper in America. That season, he made a jump on the 288-foot mark in Hyak, Washington, setting a new American record before a record crowd of 25,000 spectators. A multitude of people swarmed around him, virtually tearing his clothes off for souvenirs.

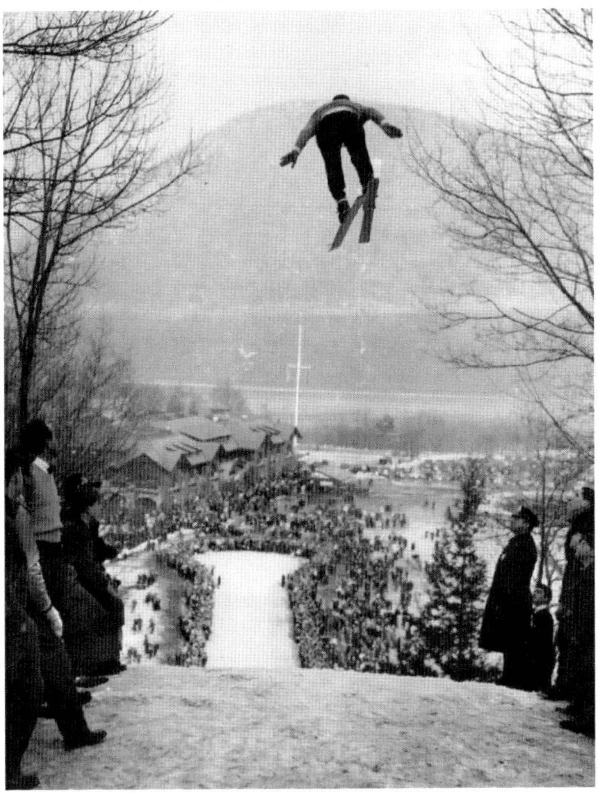

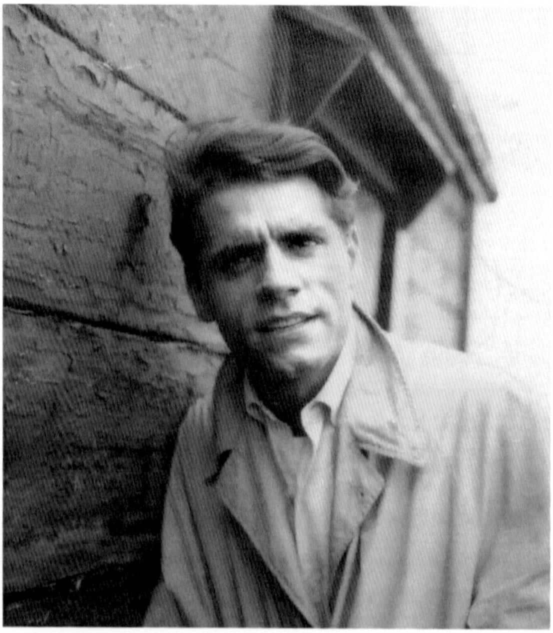

Dean Schambach, nationally recognized Class A ski jumper as well as a poet, actor, philosopher, and carpenter, made his home in the Catskill region. He ski jumped from 1954 to 1973. (Courtesy of Dean Schambach.)

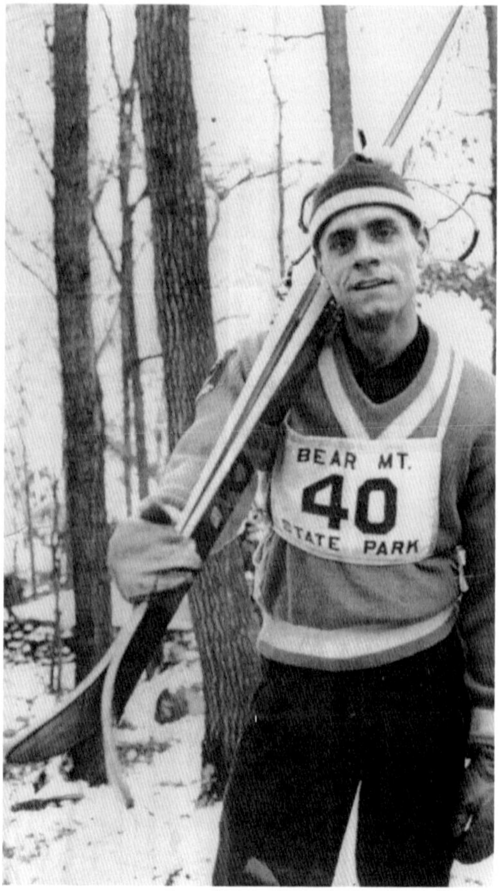

Dean Schambach is shown carrying his skis at an event at Bear Mountain State Park. A review in a local newspaper said, "Schambach is known in the sport as a reckless youth who always will take a chance—glad to sacrifice a few form points for the long jump." (Courtesy of Dean Schambach.)

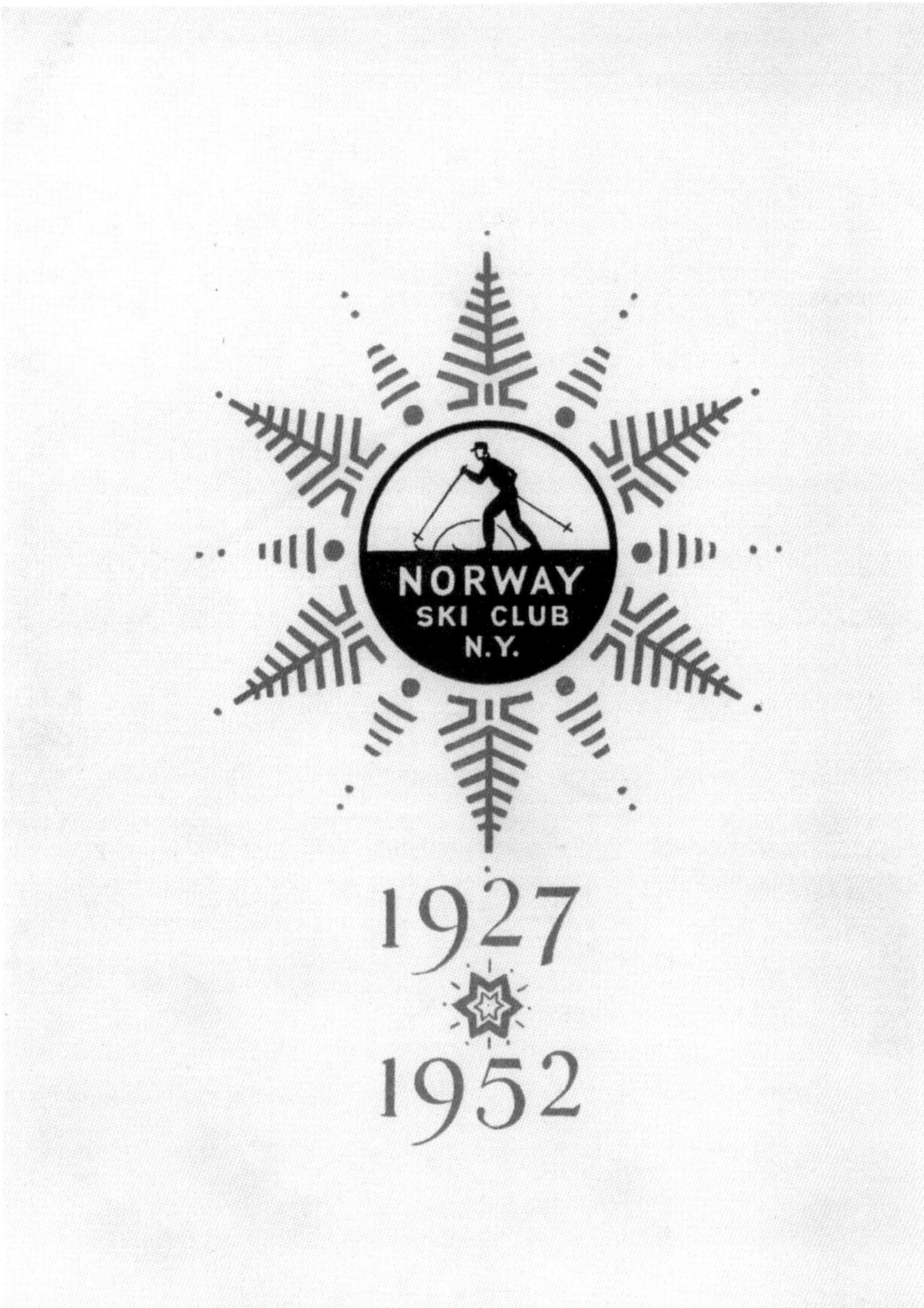

A booklet commemorating the first 25 years of the Norway Ski Club was issued at a club dinner in 1952. Started by Norwegian immigrants in 1927, the group was instrumental in promoting ski jumping in the Hudson Valley and the Catskills.

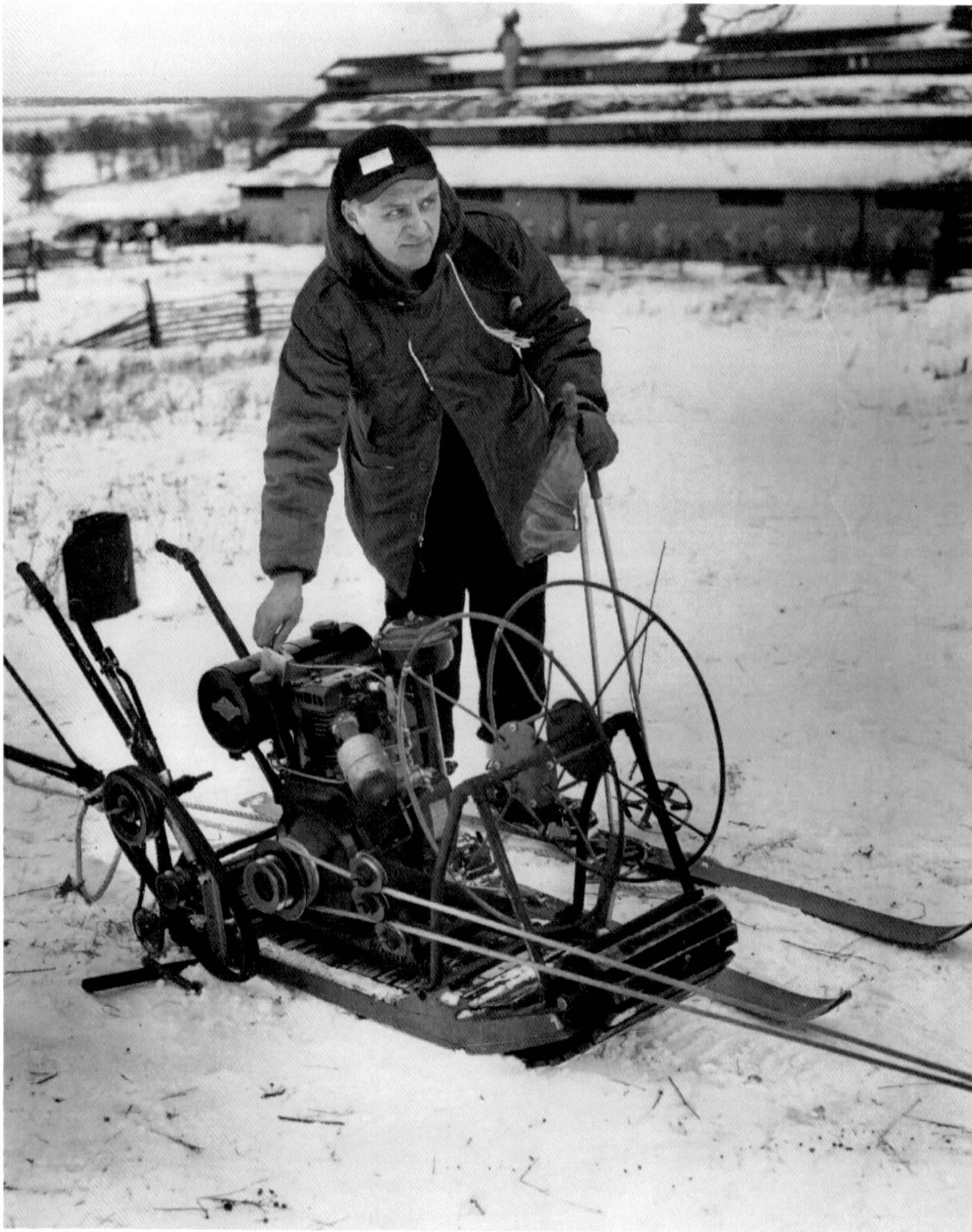

Shown here is an example of one of the first portable tows. Standing in skis with bear-trap bindings, the inventor fires up his contraption on a Catskill hillside.

2

Getting Slopeside Was Half the Fun

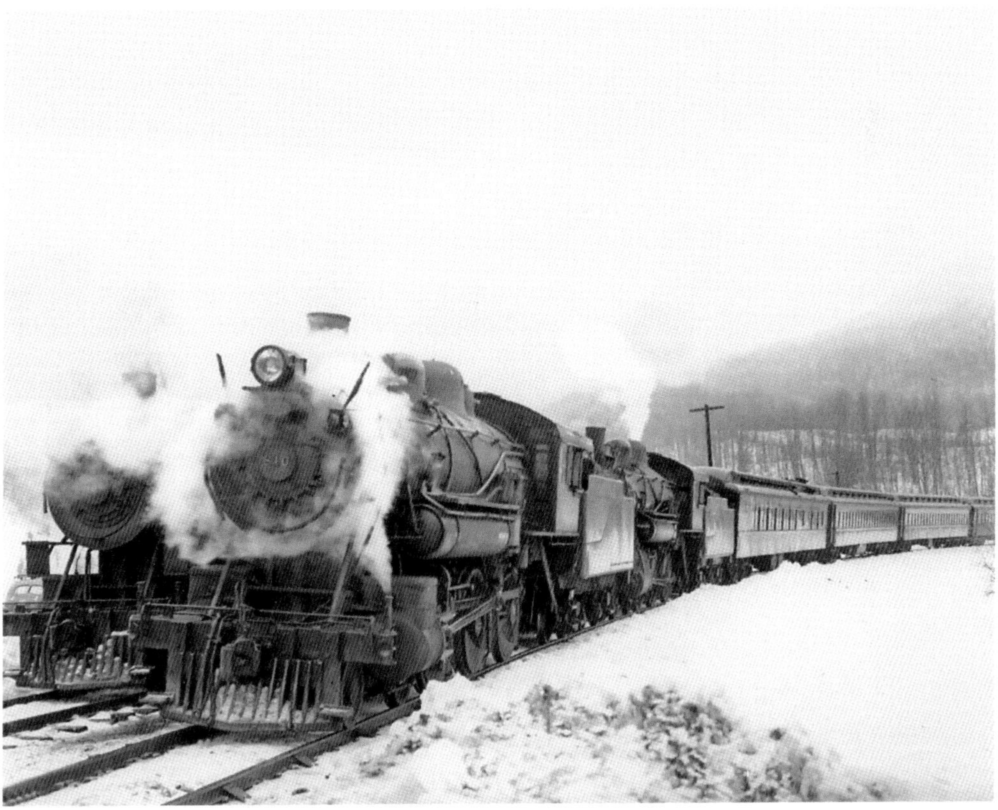

Two steam locomotives are parked slopeside at Simpson Memorial Ski Slope in Phoenicia, New York, waiting for skiers to return to New York City. These trains would deliver more than 1,400 skiers for a day on the slopes and return in late the afternoon to New York City, where the journey had begun. (Courtesy of John M. Ham.)

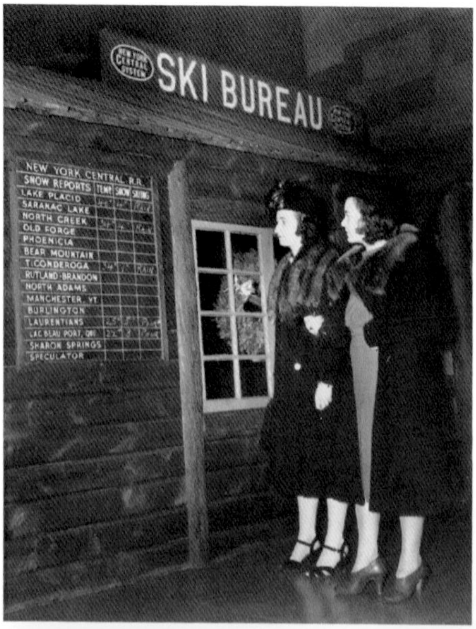

A log cabin Ski Bureau was located in a corner of Grand Central Terminal. Ski trains operated every weekend during the season. The two women are looking at rather bleak skiing conditions for the Northeast in February 1940. The areas open were far to the north. Phoenicia was the only area serviced by the New York Central Railroad in the Catskills.

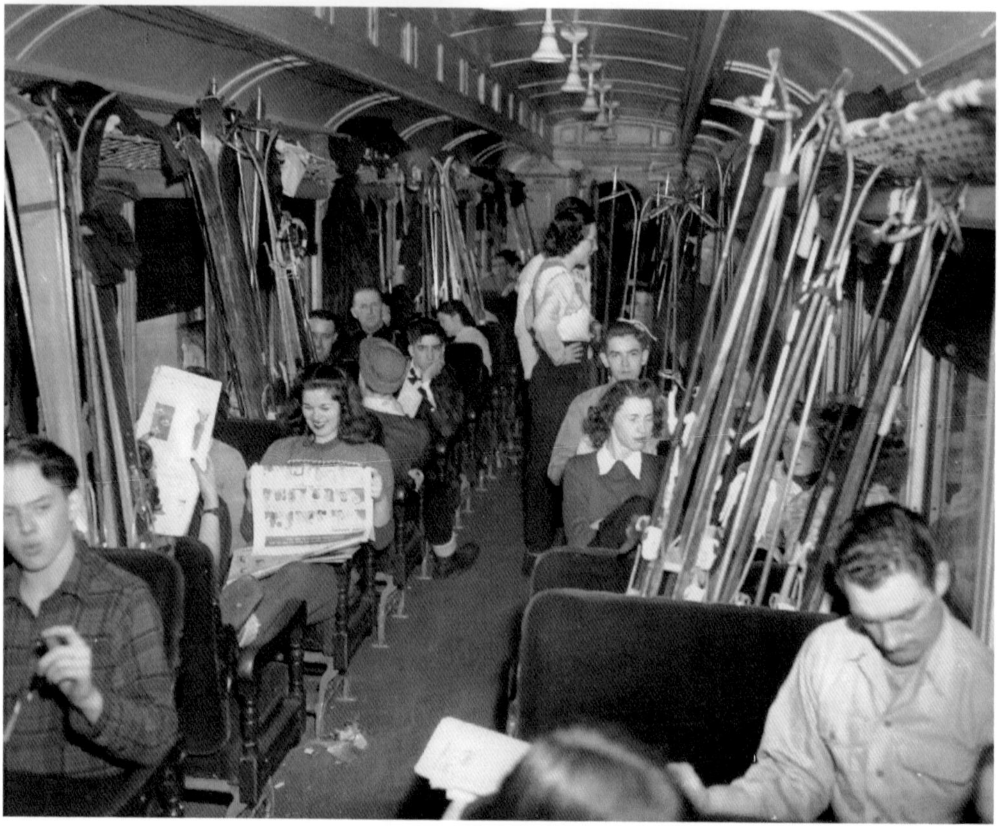

A leisurely ride by train was the easiest way to get to the ski slopes in the 1930s. At this time, there was no New York State Thruway to whisk automobiles quickly to the Catskills. Snow trains were suspended for periods during World War II.

Two trains are stopped at Phoenicia Station. On the back of the passenger car, a sign indicates that it is a Catskill Mountain Snow Train. Barely seen on the left is the train station, which is still in use today as a train museum and concert hall. Since 1996, major floods have left the tracks in constant need of repair. (Courtesy of John M. Ham.)

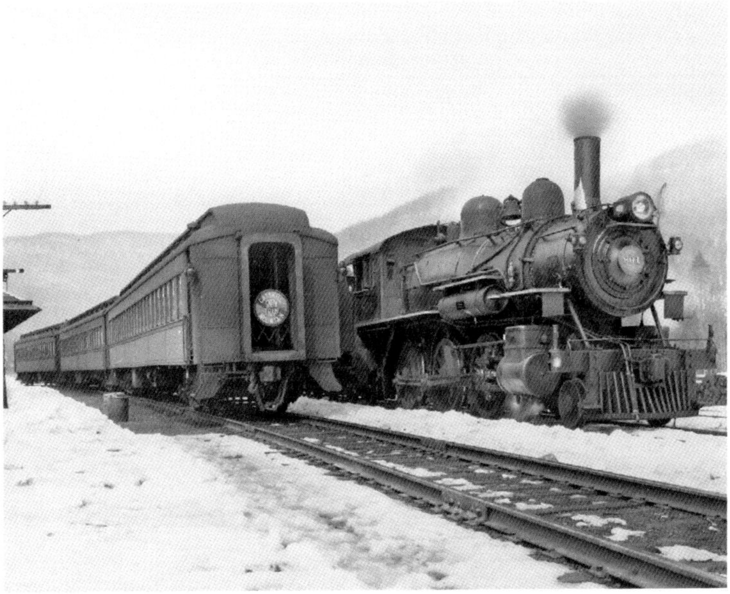

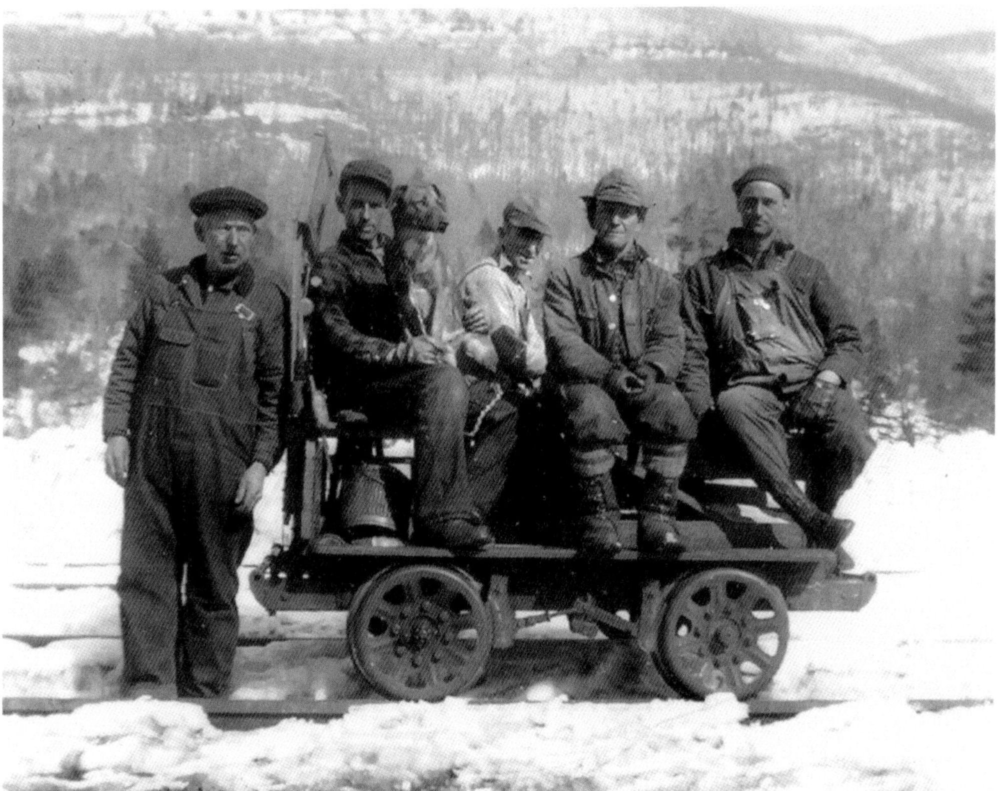

Wally Winchell's Section Gang awaits the ski train near the Phoenicia depot. In the background is part of the ridge that leads up Mount Tremper, which overlooks the Phoenicia valley. (Courtesy of John M. Ham.)

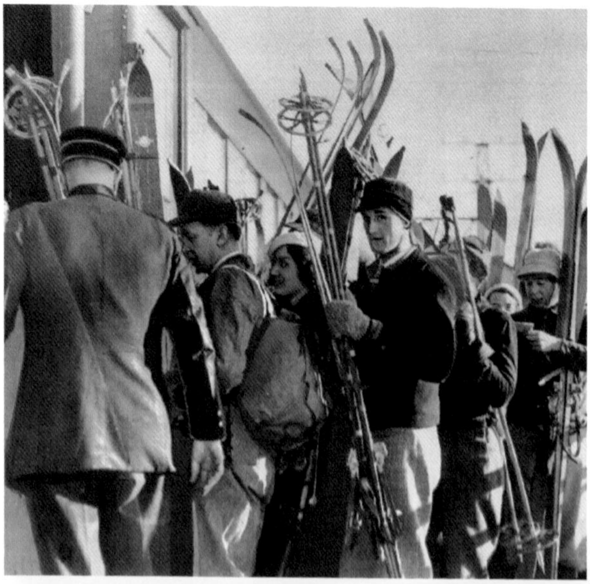

Skiers with long wood skis and spear-tip poles are anxiously waiting to board the trains north to the ski regions of New York in the Catskills and the Adirondacks.

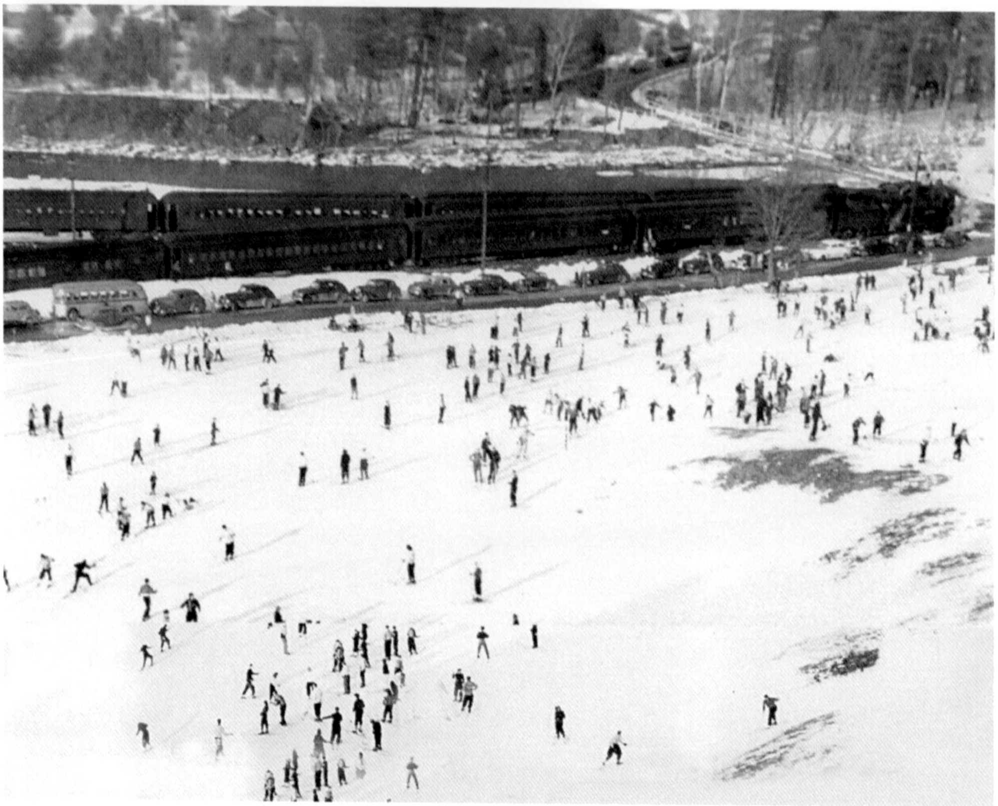

The view here is from Simpson Memorial Ski Slope looking to the Esopus Creek beyond the parked ski trains. The cars and buses are parked along High Street in Phoenicia, near the entrance to Woodland Valley. Most road traffic passed through Phoenicia on Old Route 28, which made the town a bustling place. (Courtesy of John M. Ham.)

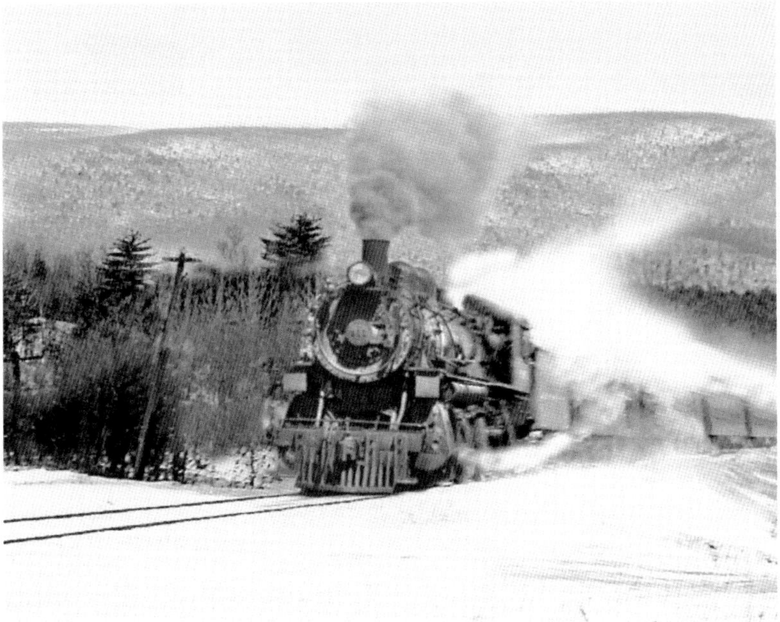

Here is another great wintry scene in the 1930s of the snow train steaming up the tracks near the Phoenicia Train Station. Passenger service on the trains was discontinued by the 1950s as automobile travel became more prevalent with improved roads. (Courtesy of John M. Ham.)

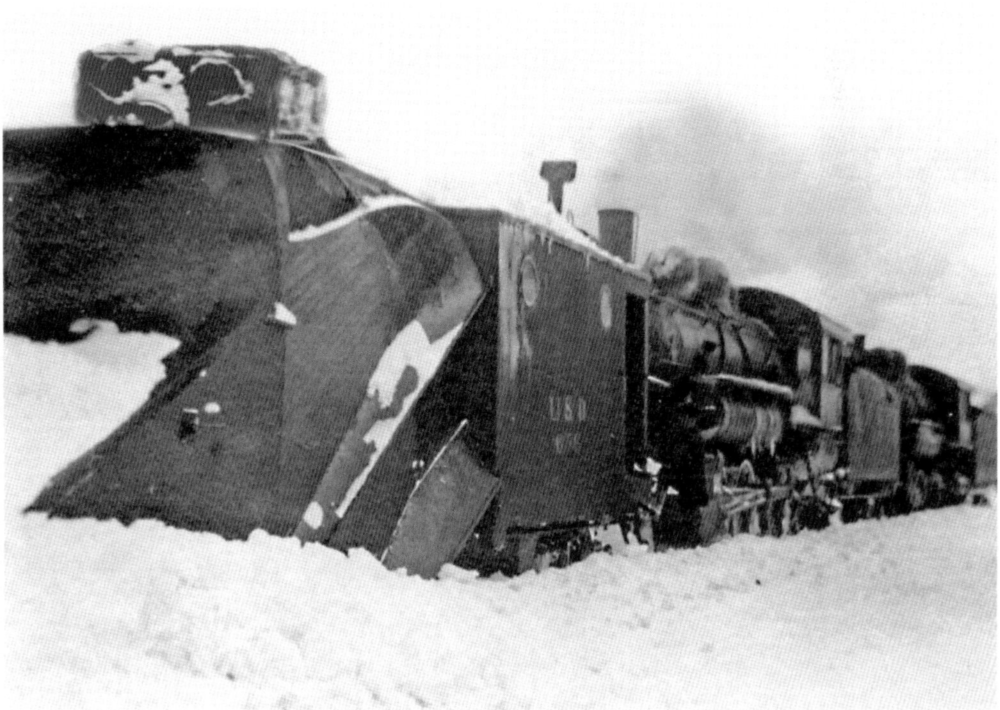

An engine plow clears the tracks for skiers near Phoenicia. The Simpson Memorial Ski Slope was located on the northwest side of Romer Mountain. A land donation by the Simpson family led to the Civilian Conservation Corps clearing trees on six acres of land for the development of a ski slope in 1935. The land around it was cleared further as it was transformed into a larger ski area. A ski jump was planned but never made it to the building stage. (Courtesy of John M. Ham.)

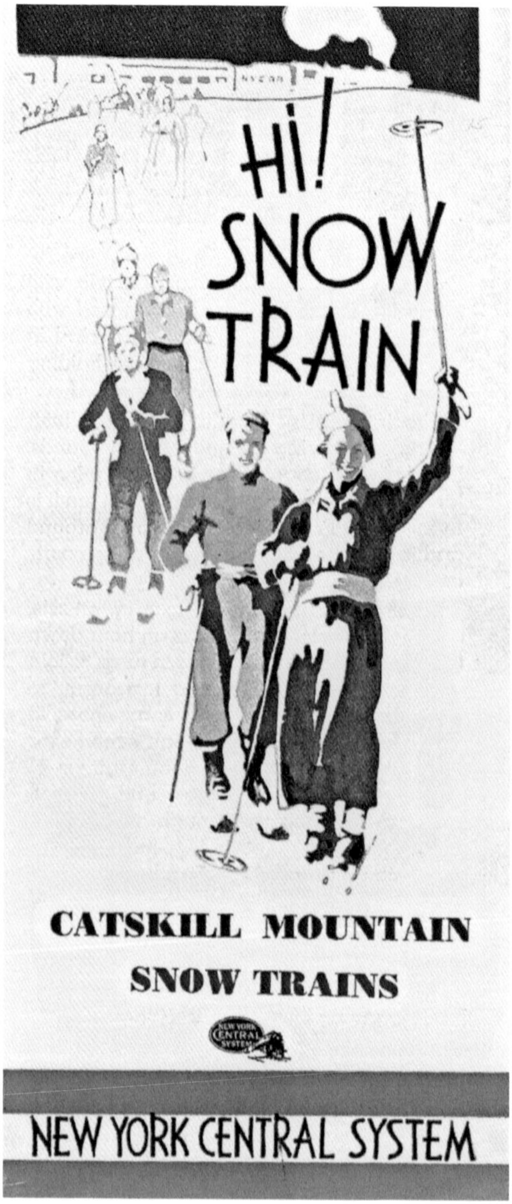

Two posters from the late 1930s advertise the snow trains to the Catskill region and beyond on the New York Central System. Included in the list of destinations is Bear Mountain, the shortest ride from New York City where ski jumping could be observed. (Both, courtesy of John M. Ham)

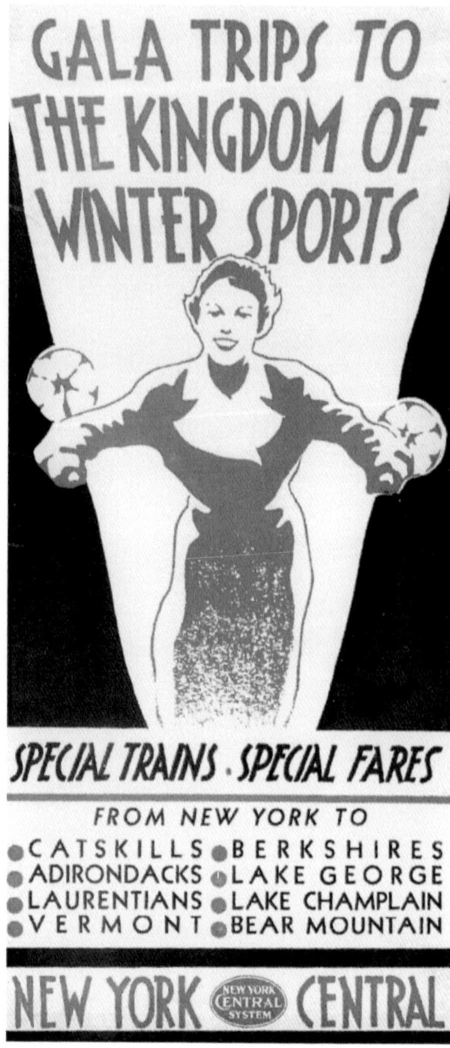

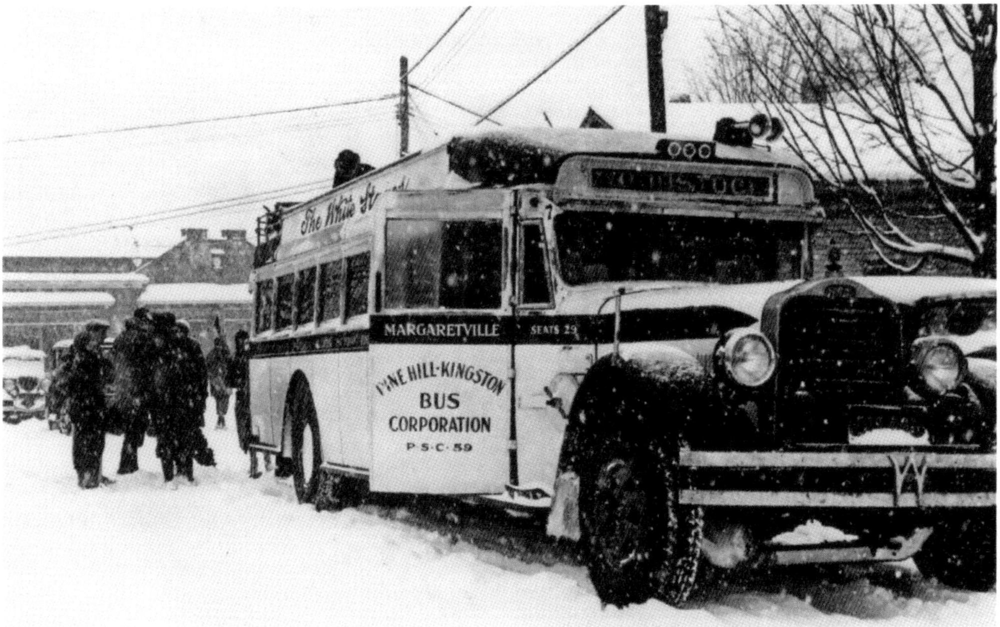

The bus driver on the White Stages Bus Line unloads skis and other baggage from the top of the vehicle. This 1938 scene is on the Village Green in the town of Woodstock. Skiers would board the bus in Kingston or at the nearby train stop in West Hurley. The building in the left background is the still-standing Longyear Building. (Courtesy of the Woodstock Historical Society.)

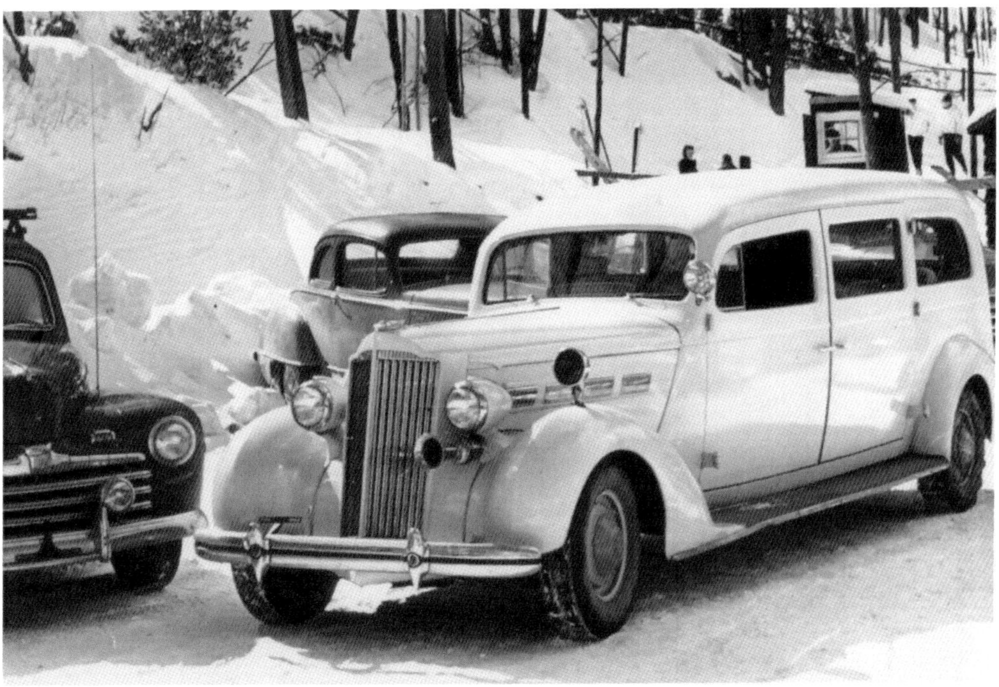

The distinguished 1940s Packard ambulance, parked near the base of the Highmount slopes, gave skiers assurance of a secure ride to a nearby hospital if needed. (Courtesy of Phil Davenport.)

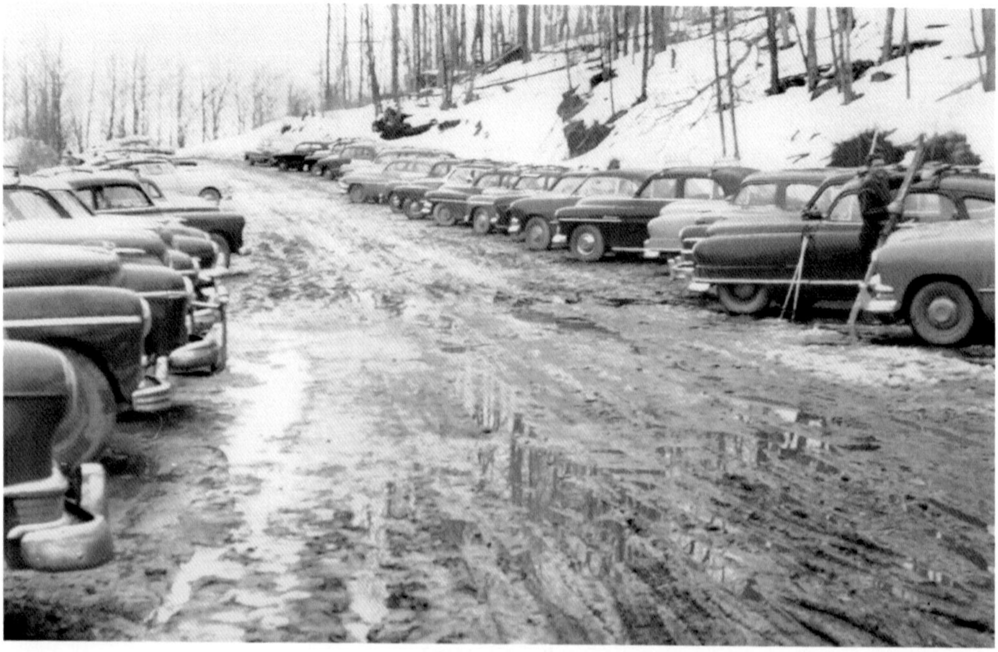

The county road below the Highmount Ski Lodge was yet to be paved in the early 1950s. Light-colored ski pants were avoided in anticipation of trudging through the muddy road during winter and springtime thaws. This was a typical scene at most fledgling ski areas. (Courtesy of Phil Davenport.)

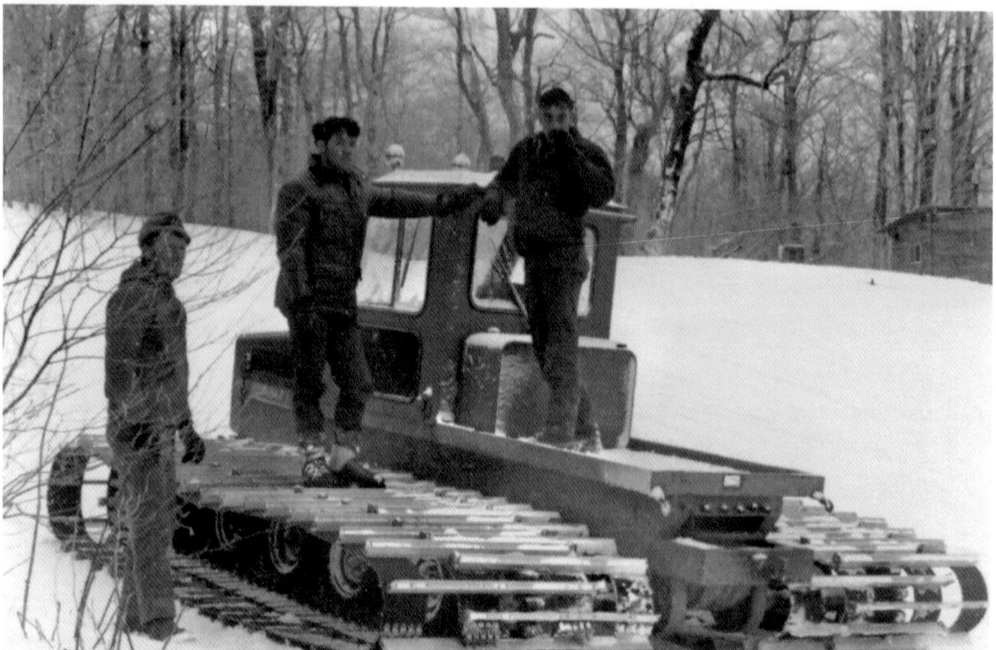

There is more tread than machine on this Tycol 2100-B, the first modern packer, shown here at Plattekill Mountain. (Courtesy of Gary Hinkley.)

3

Fashion, Style, and Flair

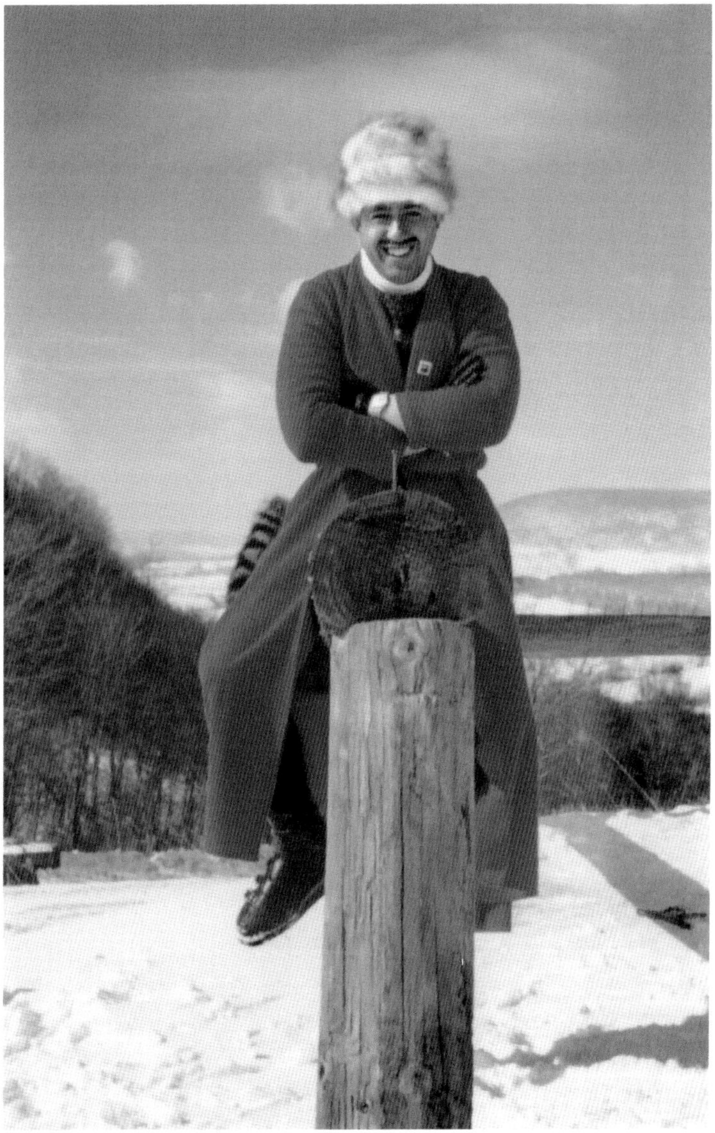

Hermann Amsz is perched on a wooden fence at Big Bear Ski Bowl in the Denver-Vega Valley of Roxbury, New York. Hermann was head instructor at this remote ski area on the back side of Bearpen Mountain, previously known as Roxbury Ski Center. Billboards along the highway to reach it alluded to a chic scene awaiting the skier. (Courtesy of Hermann Amsz.)

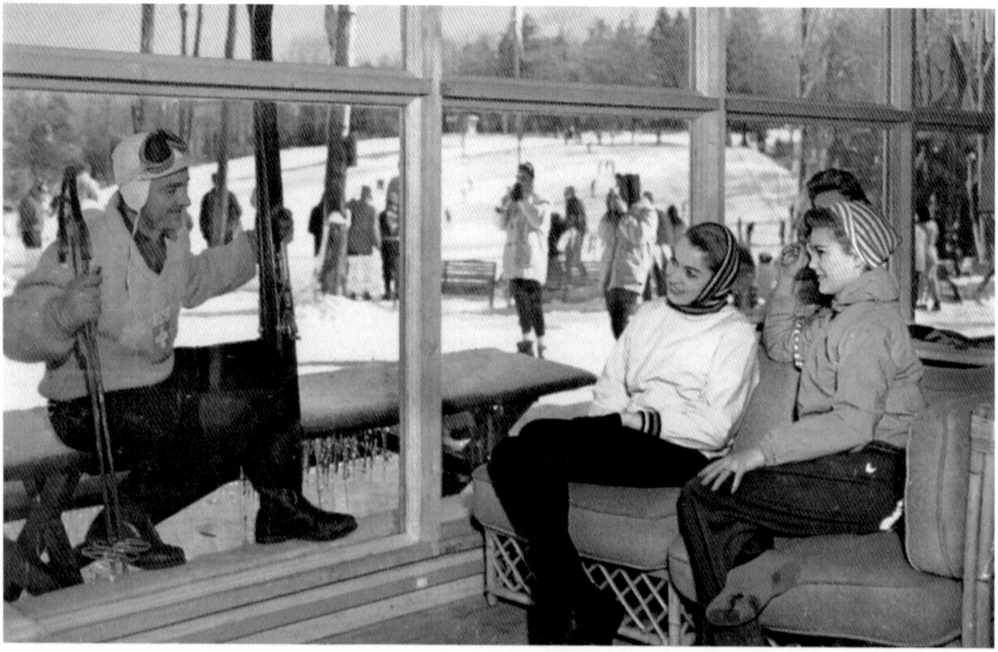

An avid skier looks through the window at two women après-ski lounging at the Concord ski area in the 1950s. The Catskill Mountains become less steep as one gets near the New York Route 17 corridor, where many of the hotels were located. This made the area ideal for novice skiers.

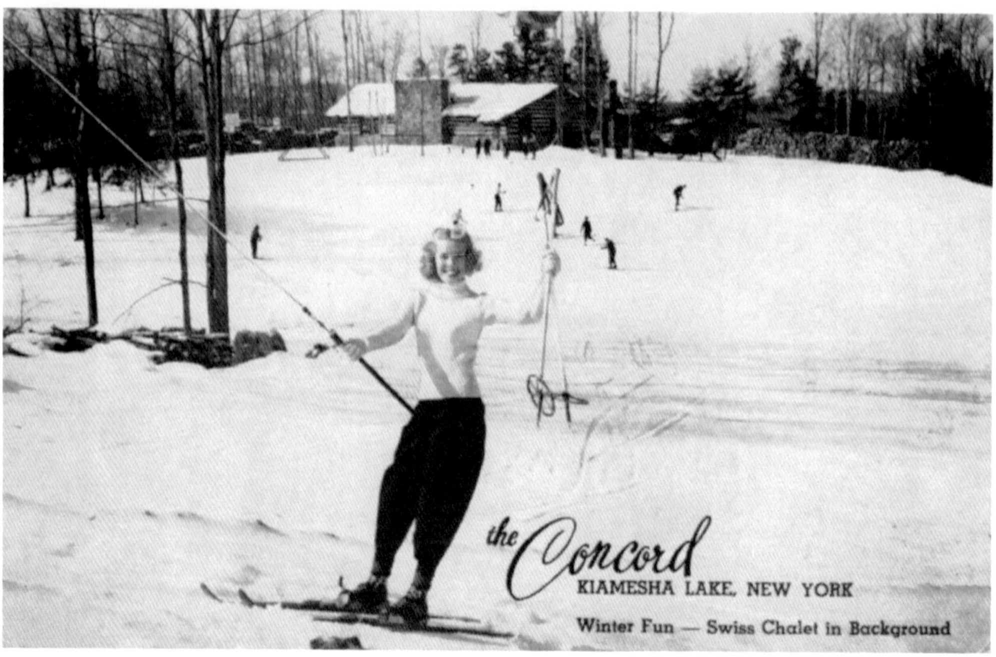

A beautiful woman beckons visitors to come and ski at the Concord Hotel in Kiamesha Lake. She appears to be riding a Poma lift, with the Swiss chalet lodge in the background.

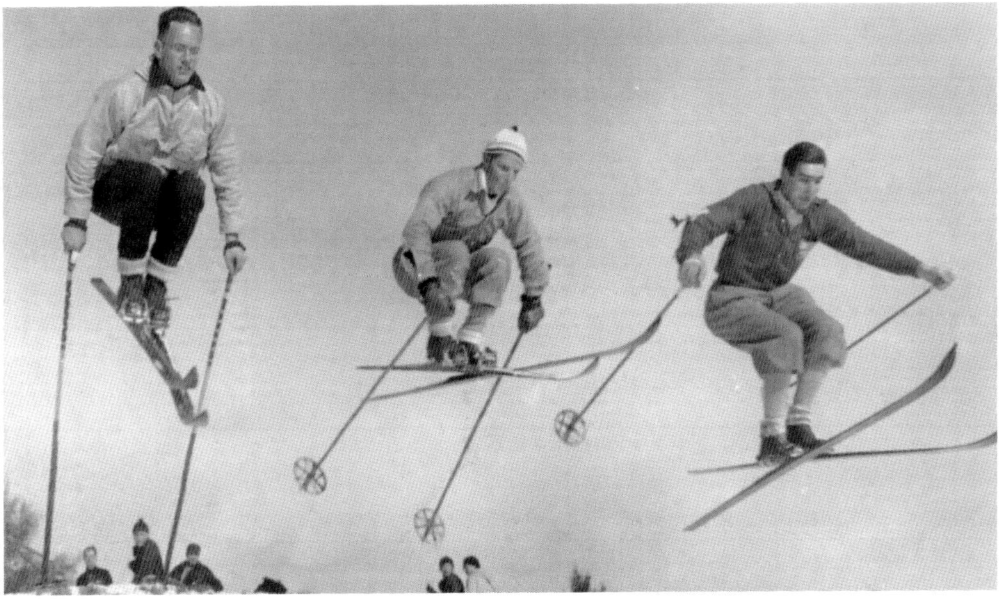

Geländesprung (from the German for "field jumping") is demonstrated here by three skiers clearing small obstacles that appear while zooming down the slopes on a Catskill hillside in 1933. European skiers brought with them many skills to spread throughout the Catskill region.

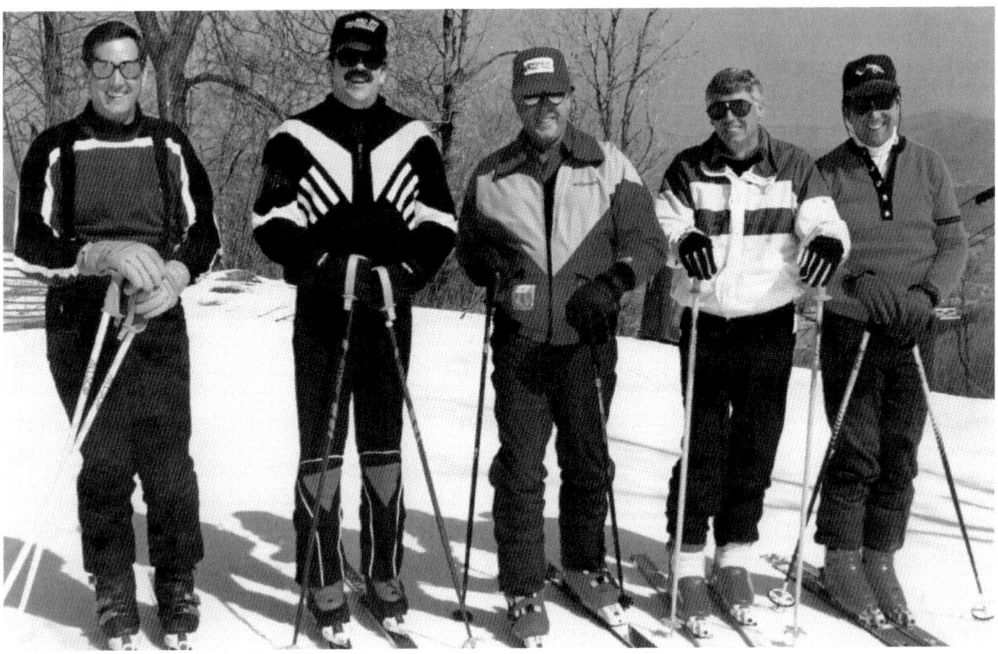

Five local personalities with long ties to Catskill skiing pose on a sunny March day in the mid-1980s, wearing the latest ski sweaters. They are, from left to right, Bob Barthel, James McGrath, John Johnson, Jerry Fielding, and Fred Barthel. McGrath owns the Belleayre Ski Shop in Highmount. Johnson was the superintendent of Belleayre Mountain from the late 1970s into the 1980s. (Courtesy of James McGrath.)

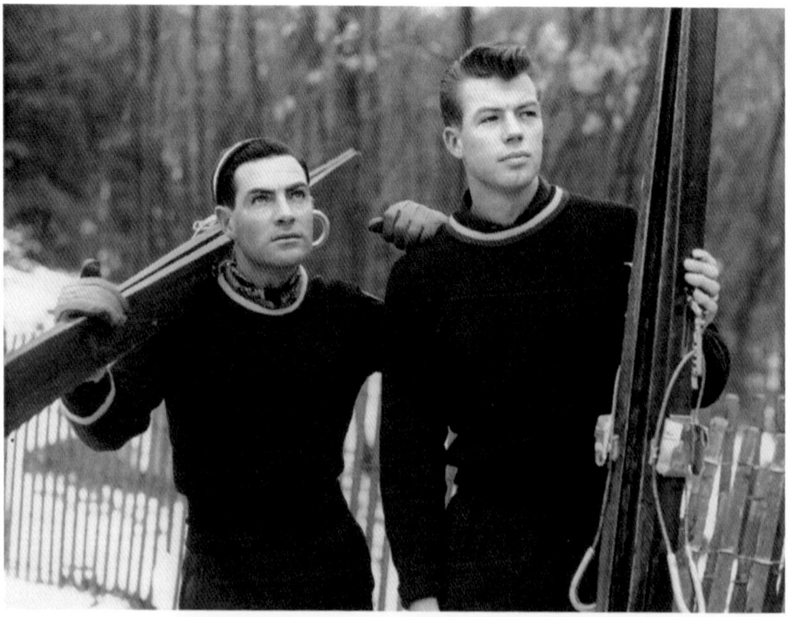

Champion ski jumpers Art Devlin (left) and Keith Wegeman pose for the camera at a Bear Mountain State Park tournament on January 10, 1954. (Courtesy of Norway Ski Club.)

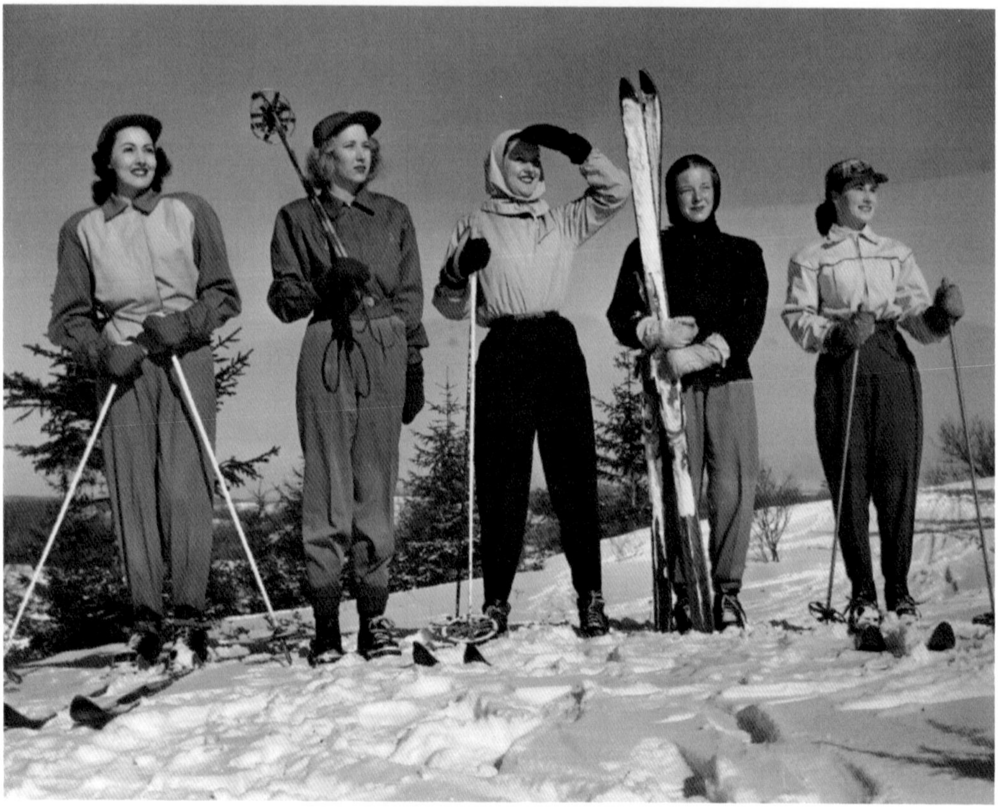

A collection of late-1940s ski fashions is on display on a Catskill hillside. All the women are wearing stirrup pants, a very popular style that tucked into their ski boots.

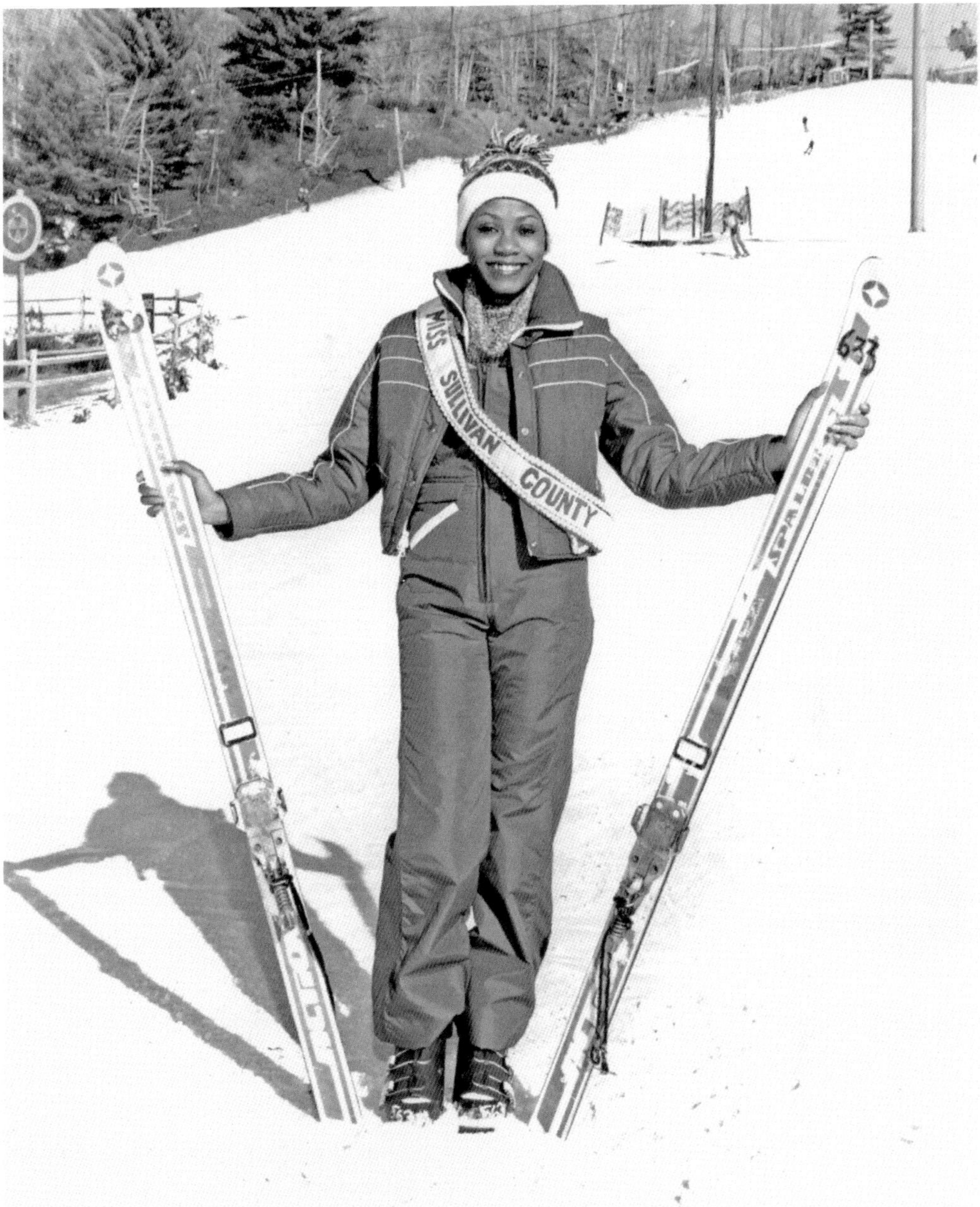

A jubilant Miss Sullivan County is pictured in a stylish ski outfit at Holiday Mountain in 1973. She is posing with a pair of rental skis with the toeless Spademan binding, a very expensive binding at the time that required a side plate mounted on the boot. (Courtesy of Holiday Mountain.)

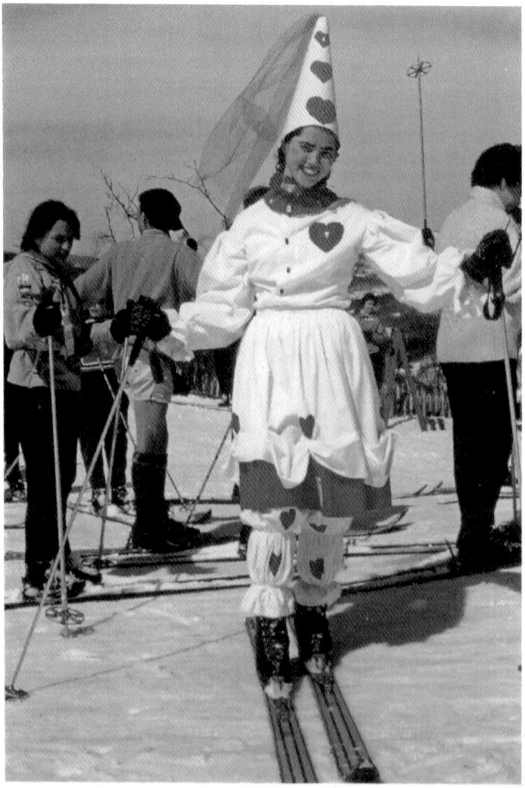

Costumes in the 1960 Easter parade at Highmount were nothing short of outrageous. In the rather macabre scene pictured below, a woman is serving the man's head on a platter—all on skis, of course. For many years, cans of beer were hidden with the eggs for the Easter egg hunt. Scenes like this were lost as ski areas supersized in the 1970s. (Courtesy of Howard Lindemann.)

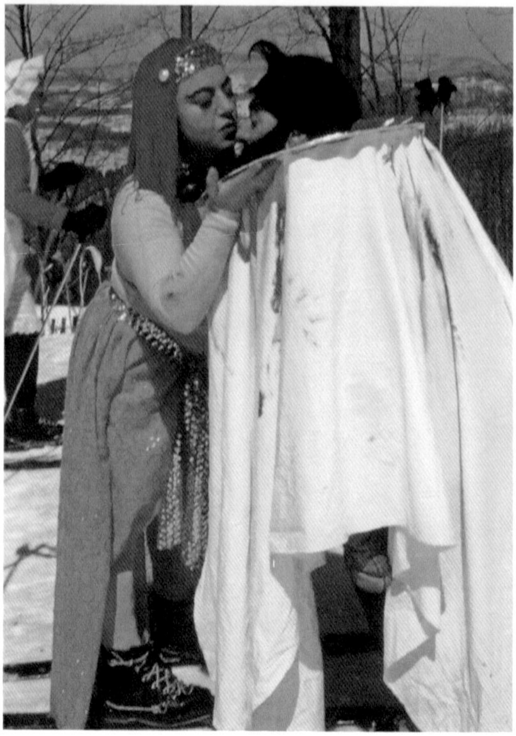

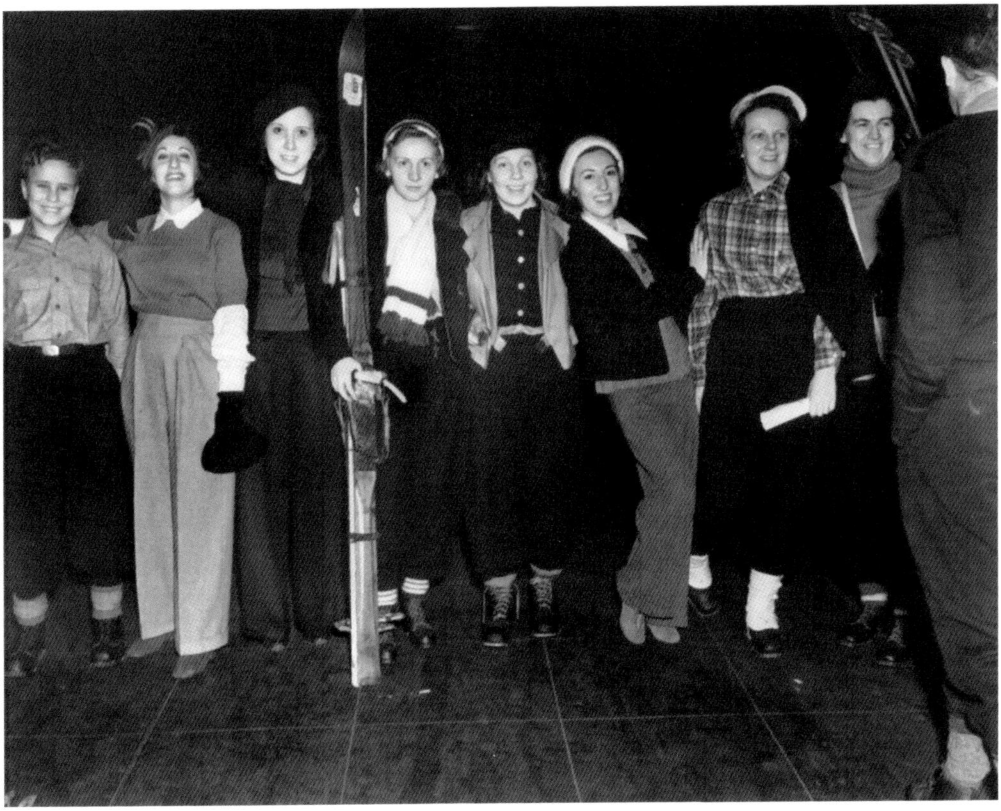

This is part of a large group of skiers waiting to board the Snow Train at Penn Station in Manhattan in 1938. While waiting, they discuss their assortment of variegated ski suits.

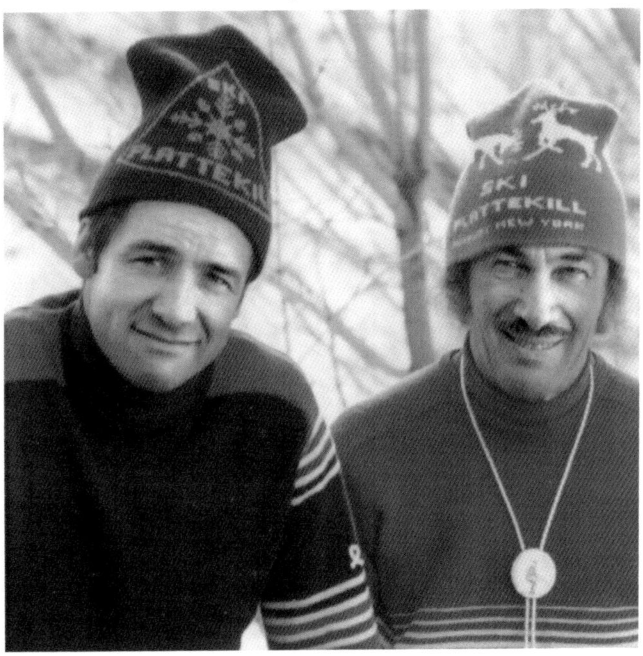

Gary Hinkley (left) and Hal Friedman show off their very sharp peak-style hats at Plattekill Mountain in this 1960s photograph. (Courtesy Gary Hinkley.)

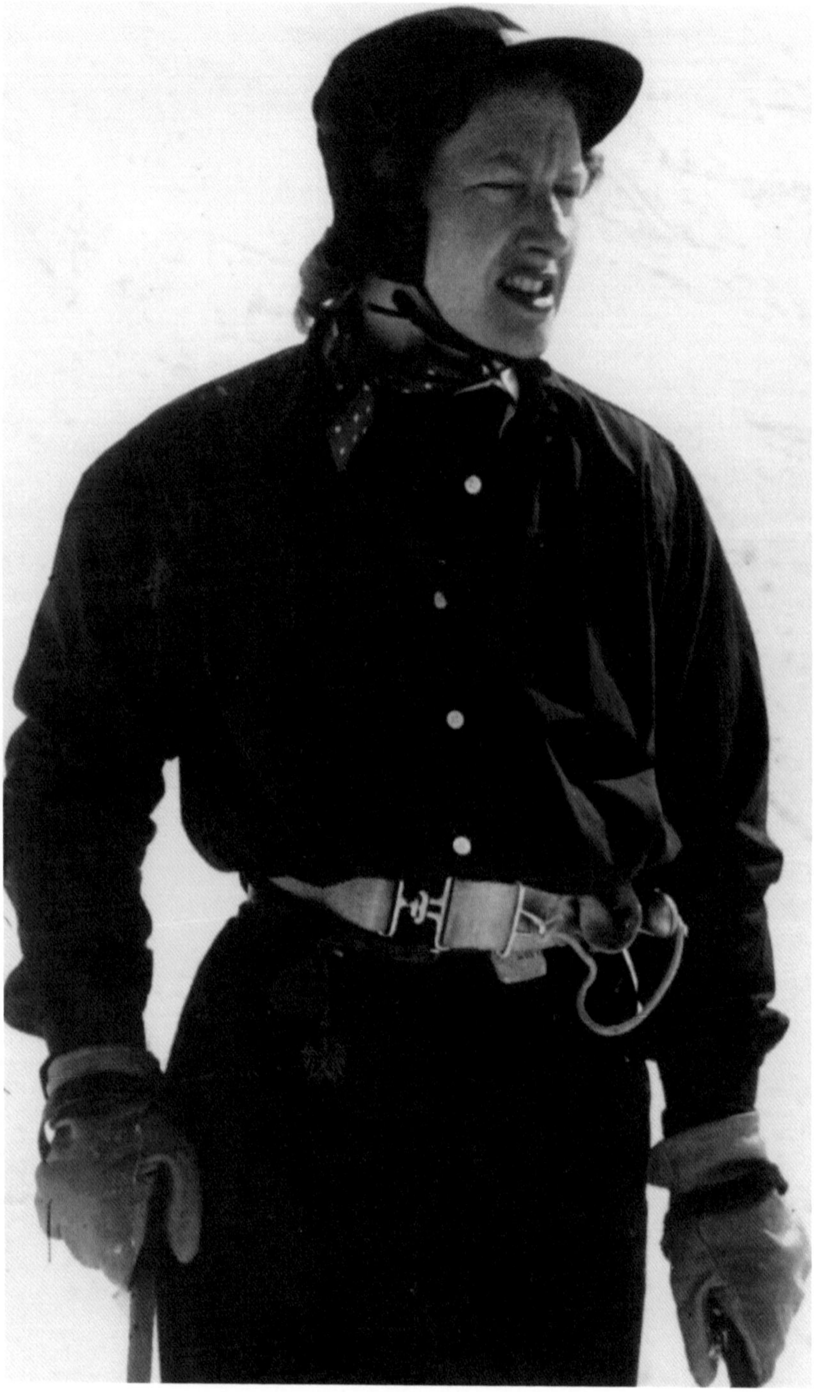

As rope tows became more common and steeper in grade, ski-tow belts like the one around this woman's waist became part of the garb. By putting the pressure of tow riding around the waist, it eliminated the strain on the arms and shoulders, thereby allowing a more pleasurable ride. Wearing all-dark clothing would naturally keep skiers warmer on a sunny, cold winter day.

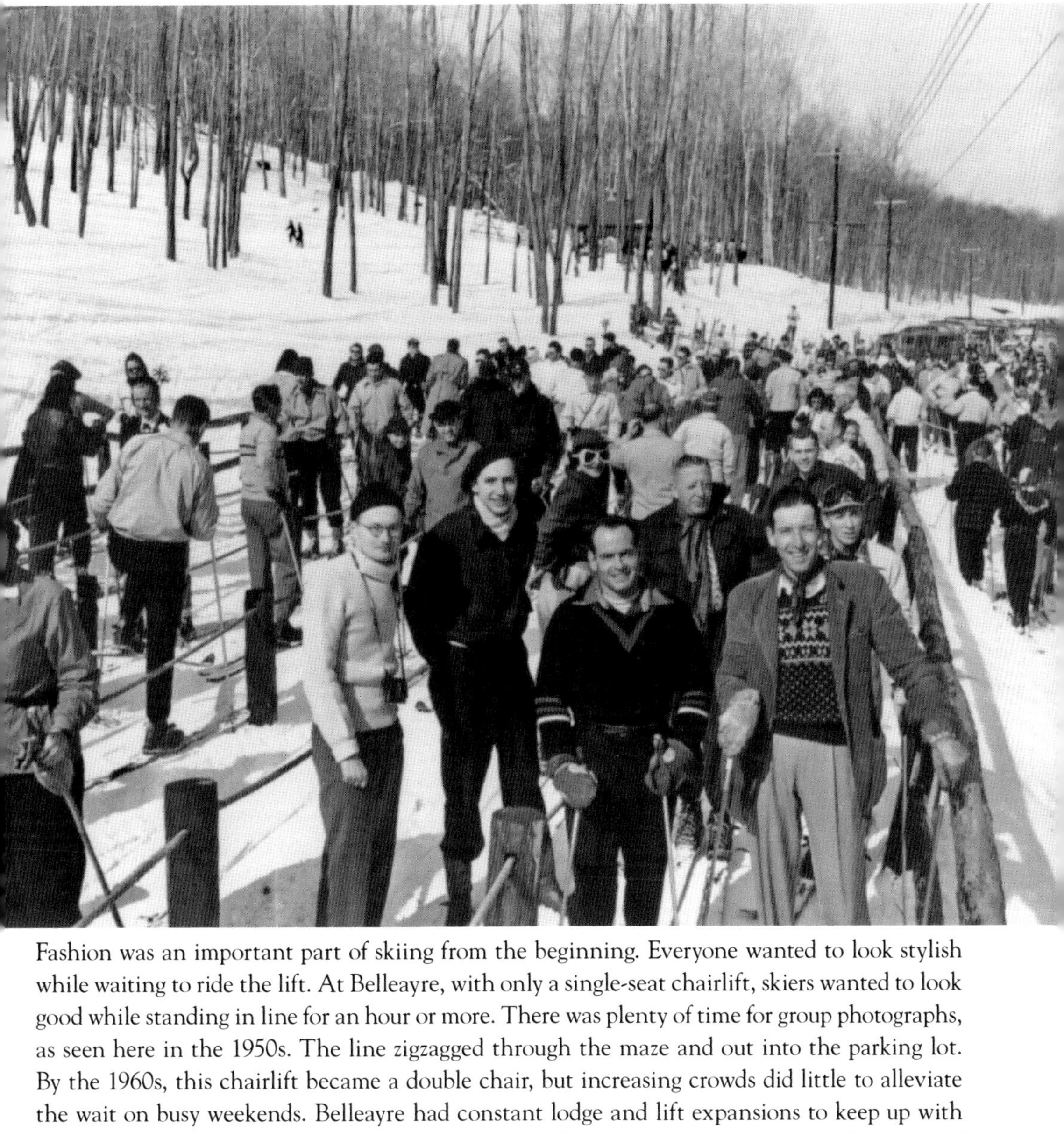

Fashion was an important part of skiing from the beginning. Everyone wanted to look stylish while waiting to ride the lift. At Belleayre, with only a single-seat chairlift, skiers wanted to look good while standing in line for an hour or more. There was plenty of time for group photographs, as seen here in the 1950s. The line zigzagged through the maze and out into the parking lot. By the 1960s, this chairlift became a double chair, but increasing crowds did little to alleviate the wait on busy weekends. Belleayre had constant lodge and lift expansions to keep up with the masses, which mostly came from the nearby New York City metropolitan area. (Courtesy of Belleayre Mountain.)

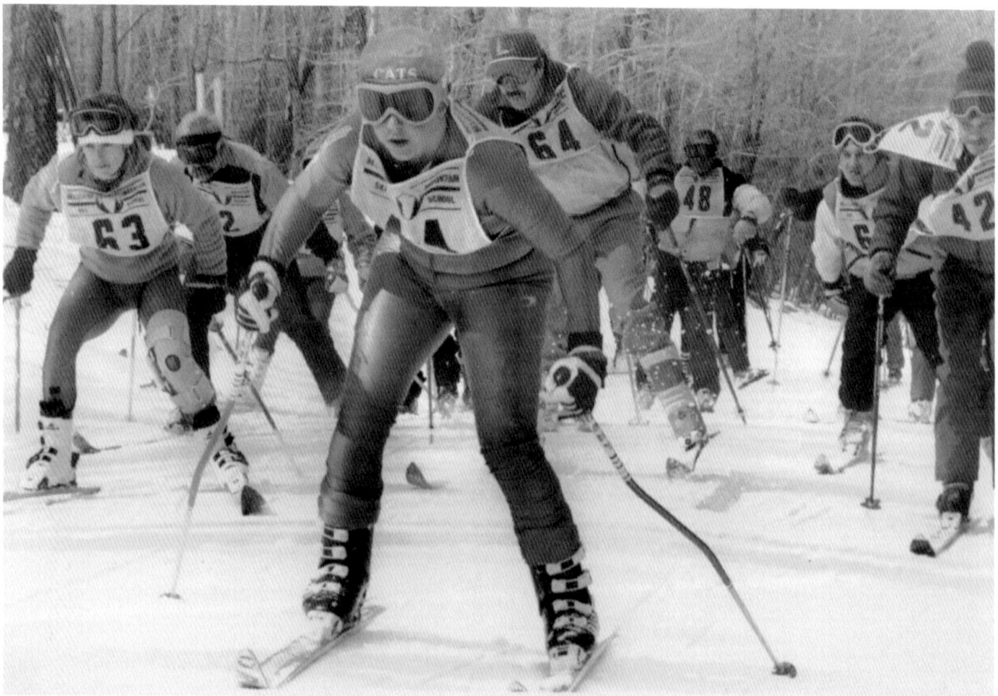

The Pine Hill Arms Triathlon Race, pictured here in the mid-1990s, begins on top of Belleayre Mountain in March. For many years the annual event had racers skiing, running, and biking. It would wind up at the Pine Hill Arms for an evening celebration. (Courtesy of Belleayre Mountain.)

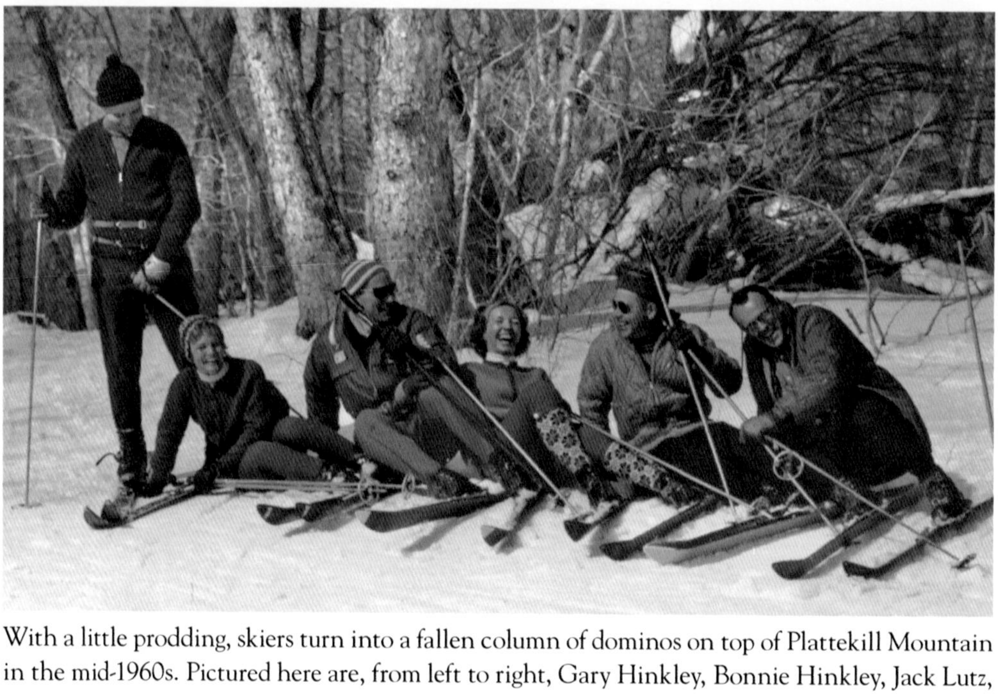

With a little prodding, skiers turn into a fallen column of dominos on top of Plattekill Mountain in the mid-1960s. Pictured here are, from left to right, Gary Hinkley, Bonnie Hinkley, Jack Lutz, Kay Lutz, Andrew "Jun" Schuman, and Milton Slauso. (Courtesy of Gary Hinkley.)

4

Food, Entertainment, and Rest

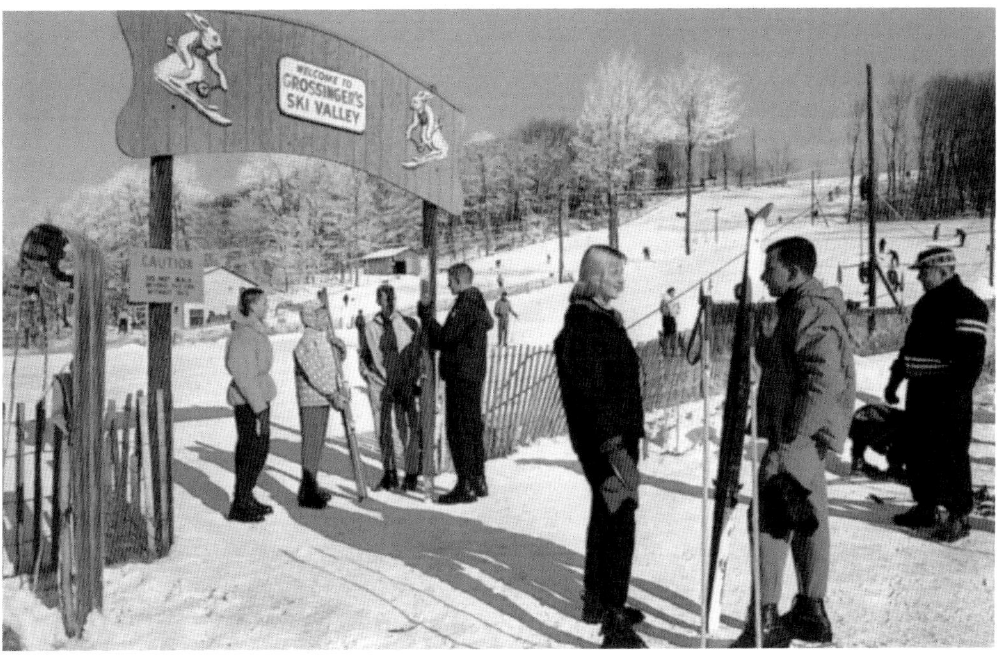

The entrance to the ski slope at the Grossinger's Resort complex, near Liberty, is shown here in the 1950s. Like the nearby Concord Hotel, Grossinger's was among the first to develop snowmaking to ensure white slopes for its legions of guests. The slopes were gentle in grade, catering mainly to the novice skier.

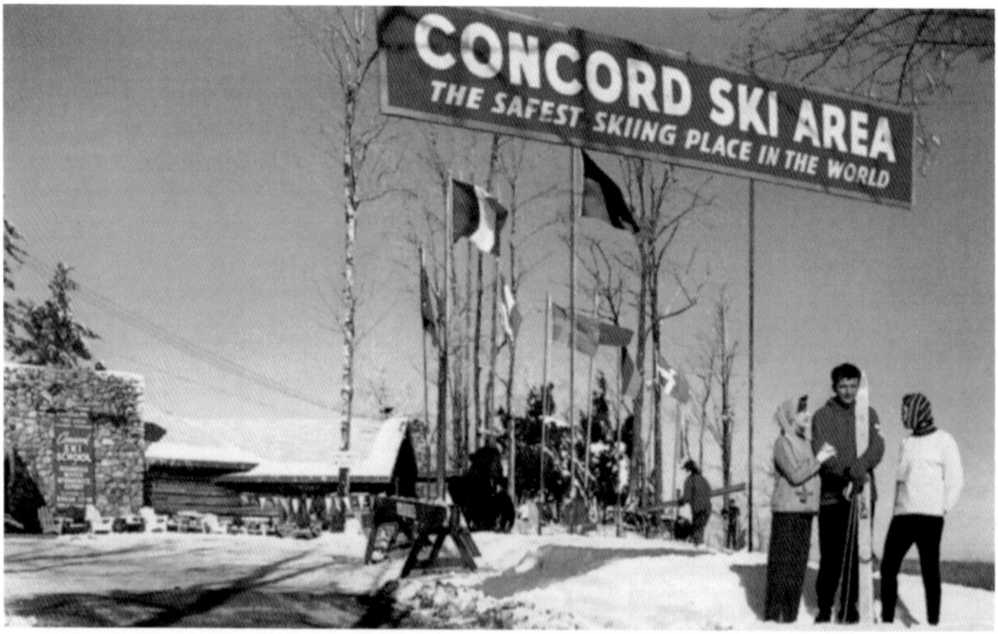

This was quite a claim from the Concord Hotel ski area. A relatively short ride from the New York City metropolitan region brought many overnight guests to the southern Catskill region. As big-hill resorts and better highways to points north were developed, these large hotels began to lose their appeal as ski destinations in the late 20th century.

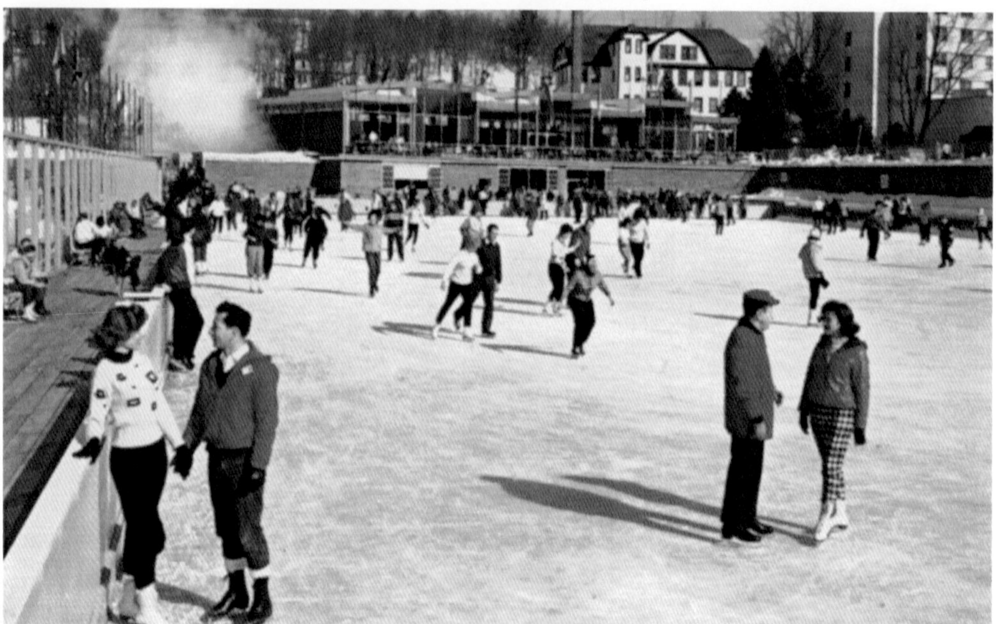

To keep up with the nearby competition, hotels like the Concord, pictured here, had to offer many winter recreational activities, such as Olympic-sized skating rinks, indoor and outdoor heated pools, and sledding runs.

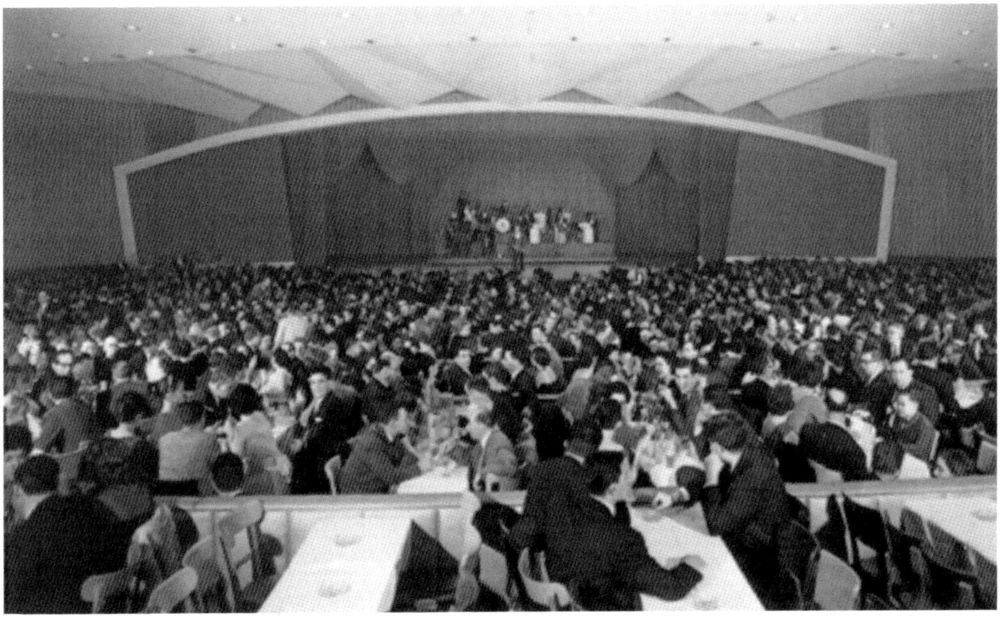

After a day of skiing, a fine show with a band would be enjoyed in the main ballroom by guests in semiformal attire. This scene is from the showroom of the Concord Hotel in the mid-1950s. This was all part of the southern Catskills, or Borscht Belt, experience.

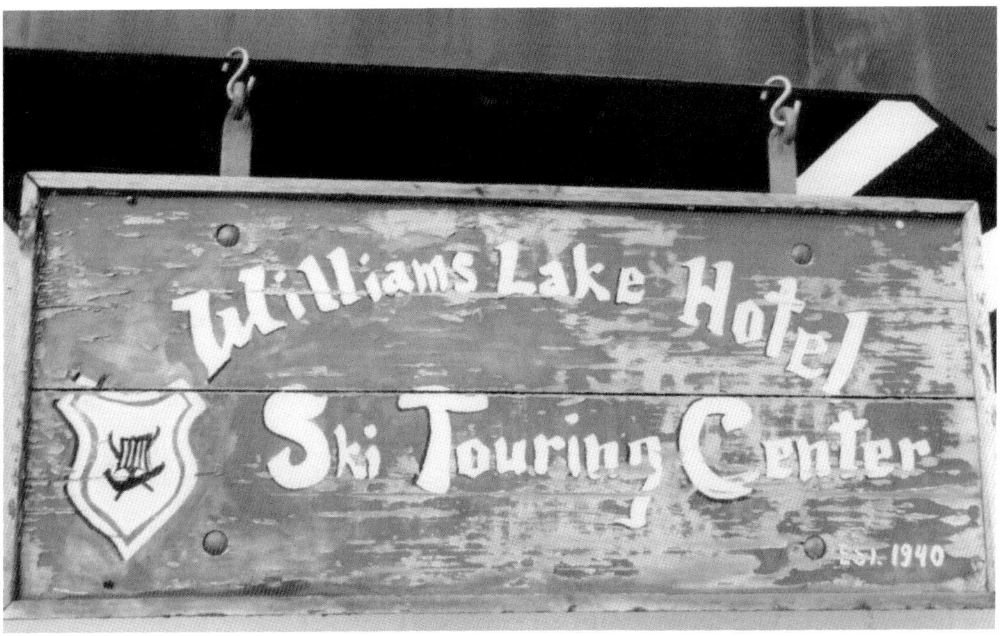

A sign from Williams Lake Hotel signifies better days from the past. A ski-touring center was located at this hotel with a beautiful lake in front of it. It lasted as a cross-country–ski area until 2006, when the Williams family sold the business. Several miles south of the hotel on Joppenbergh Mountain was a major ski jump. The Rosendale jump was one of the largest in the Catskill region and drew many thousands to events from the late 1930s to 1971.

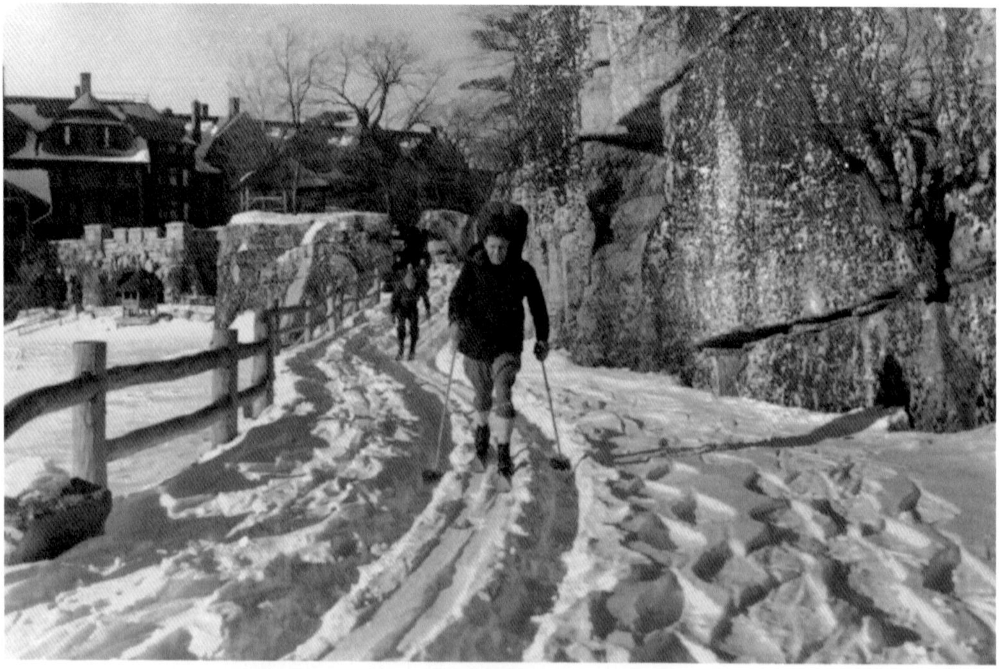

Cross-country skiers depart from Mohonk Mountain House after a fresh snowfall in 1935. (Photograph by Daniel Smiley Jr., courtesy of MMHA.)

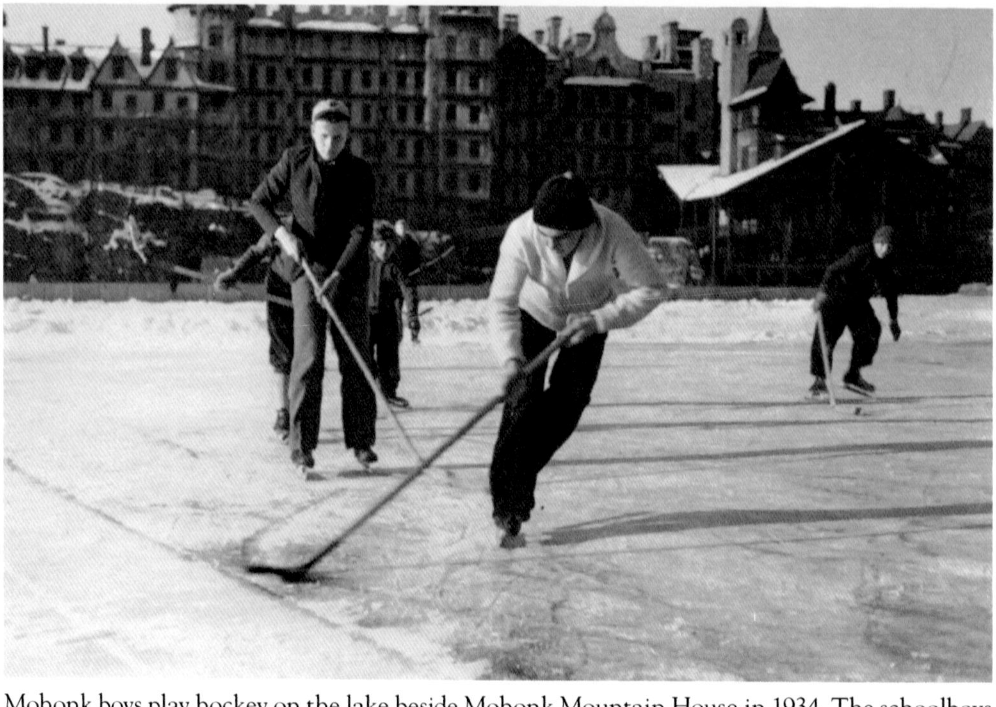

Mohonk boys play hockey on the lake beside Mohonk Mountain House in 1934. The schoolboys were required to participate in hockey as part of their physical education programs. (Photograph by Daniel Smiley Jr., courtesy of MMHA.)

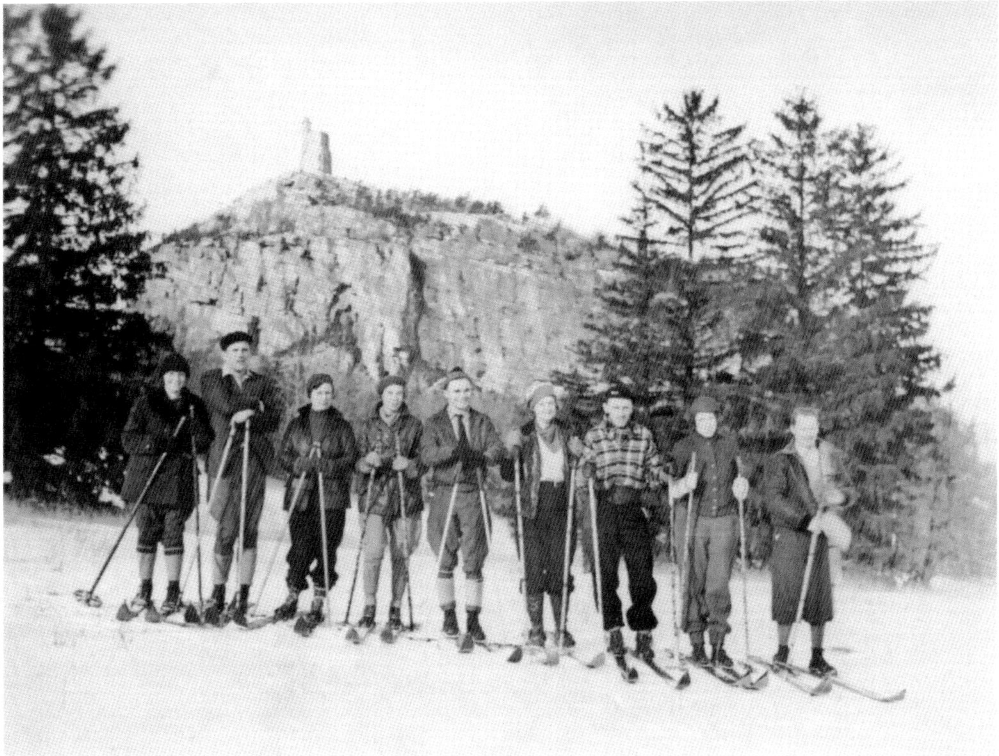

These Members of the Adirondack Mountain Club are pictured on a visit to Mohonk in 1935. Here they are at Home Farm below Sky Top Tower. (Photograph by Daniel Smiley Jr., courtesy of MMHA.)

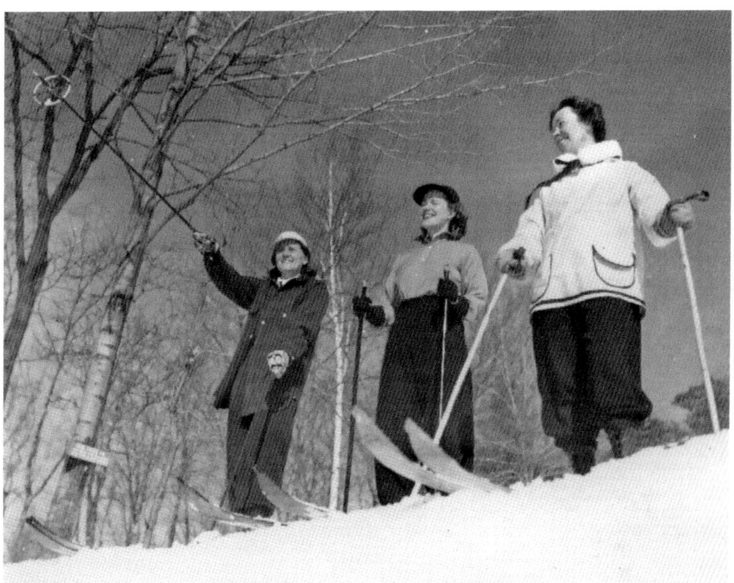

In this 1940s image, Smiley family members and a friend are seen at the top of a slope. Ruth H. Smiley (left) points to their destination, while Rachel O. Smiley (right) smiles in agreement. (Photograph by Daniel Smiley Jr., courtesy of MMHA.)

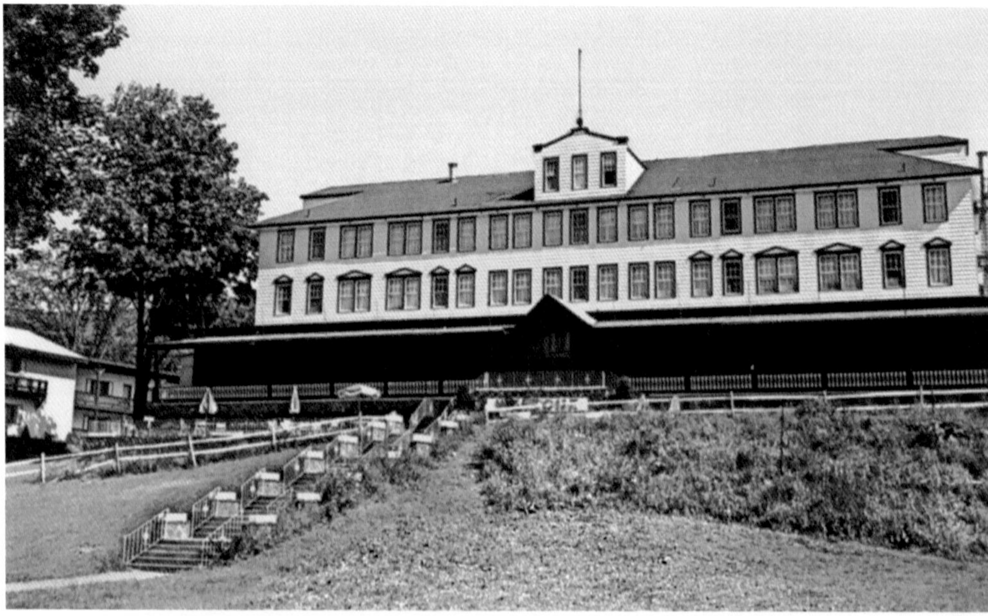

The Hunter House, located on New York Route 23A in the village of Hunter, became a popular ski hotel before succumbing to fire in the early 21st century. In the mid-1960s, it advertised in magazines as having a Snowbunny Lounge and Entertainment a Go-Go. (Courtesy of John M. Ham.)

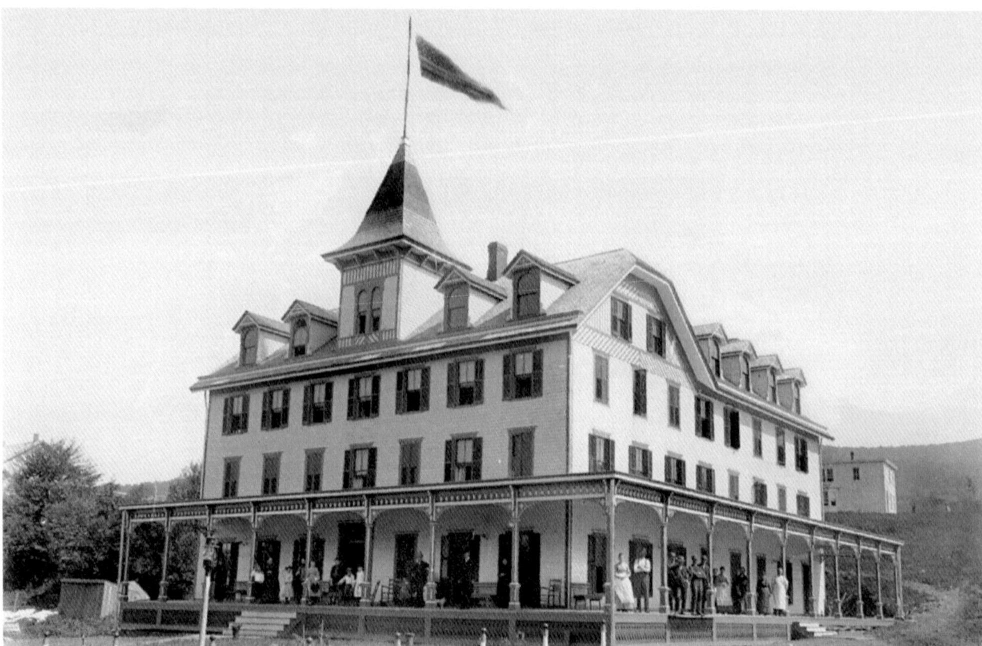

The West End Hotel is pictured in the late 19th century. It later became Addo's and then the Ritz, housing skiers and ski-industry workers alike in the early Hunter Mountain days. (Courtesy of John M. Ham.)

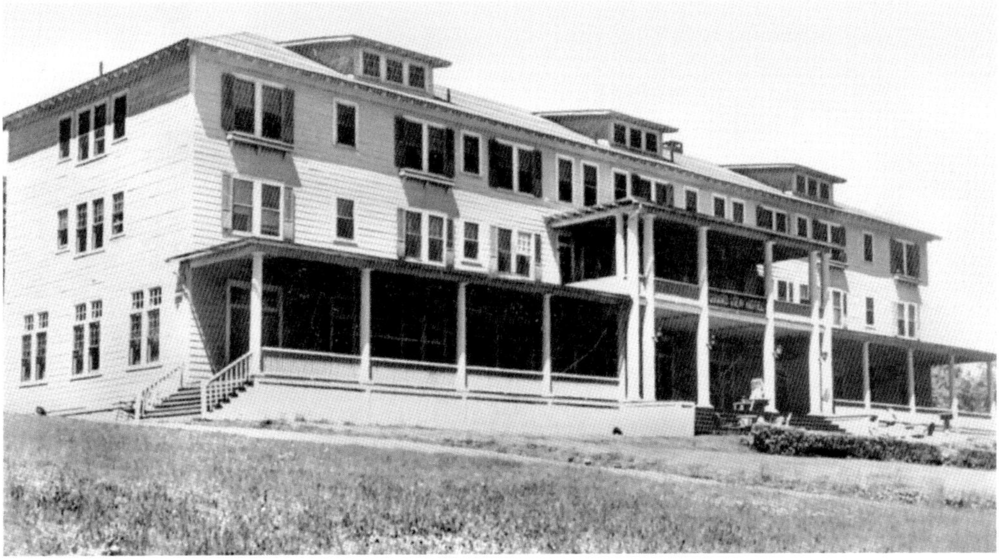

The Grand View Hotel—also known later as the Colonel's Table Inn, O'Sheas, and, finally, Ski Bowl Lodge—was located on what is now Ski Run Road near Hunter Mountain. This lodge served as a hotel and large après-ski lounge for skiers in the area. What happened here was typical of most of the grand, late-19th-century hotels and rooming houses that dotted the Mountain Top area around Hunter and Tannersville: They were built for summer visitors and train travelers, making the transition to the ski crowd difficult, although they served their purposes until new hotels could be constructed. The picture below is from one of the last days of the Ski Bowl Lodge before it was torn down in 2012. Many others had burned to the ground much sooner.

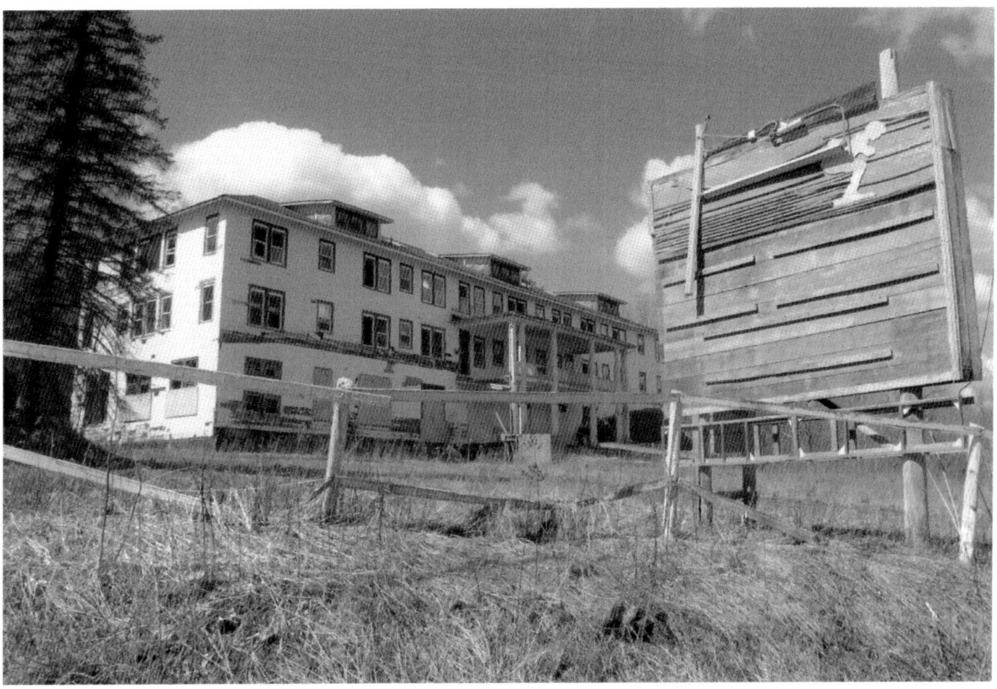

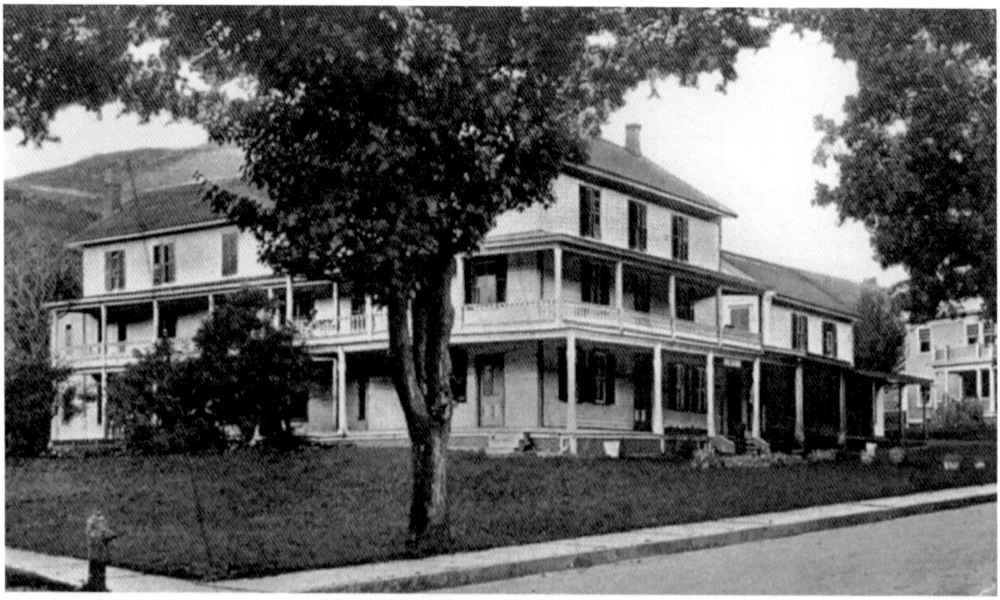

Pictured here is an early-20th-century view of the Colonial Inn on Main Street in Pine Hill. A small tow installed behind the lodge proved very popular in the late 1940s into the 1950s. The town thrived thanks to the nearby train tracks that brought hordes of visitors in the late 19th century. New York Route 28, the main thoroughfare through the central Catskills, brought increasing amounts of automobile traffic to the village center. Later, the village was bypassed when the main road moved across the valley in the early 1960s. (Courtesy of John M. Ham.)

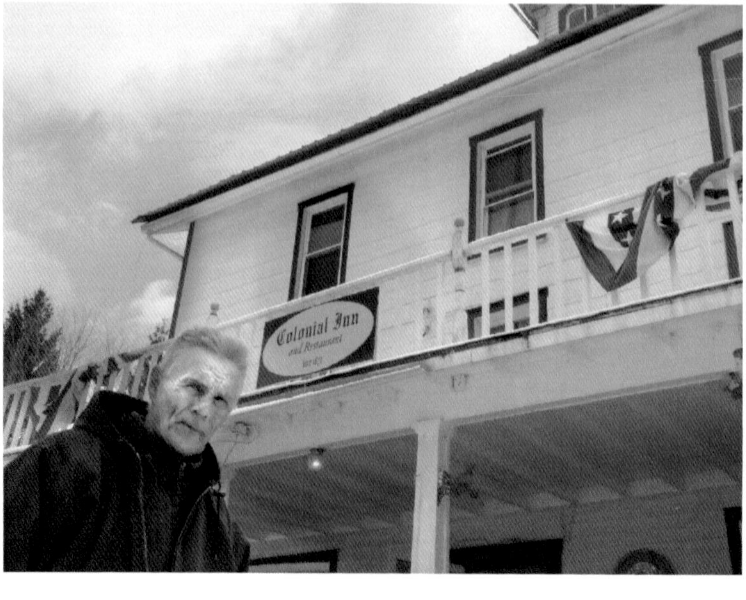

Steve Witte is pictured in front of the Colonial Inn, which opened in 1870. Beginning in the 1970s, he and his family toiled through long hours to save this large building from an uncertain fate. The inn still serves skiers and summer visitors alike with a famous Saturday-night buffet.

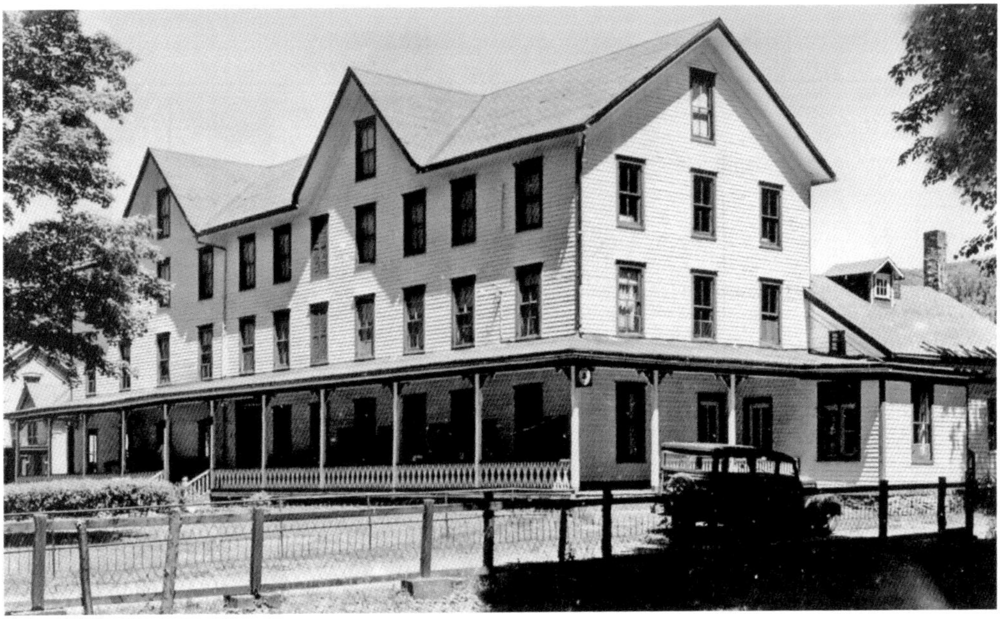

The Villa Rex Hotel became the Hunter Village Inn around the time Hunter Mountain Ski Bowl opened in the early 1960s. The location was ideal as skiers poured into the large bar and après-ski lounge on New York Route 23A, near the entrance way to Hunter Mountain, after the lifts closed. It survived to the 21st century before going up in flames. (Courtesy of John M. Ham.)

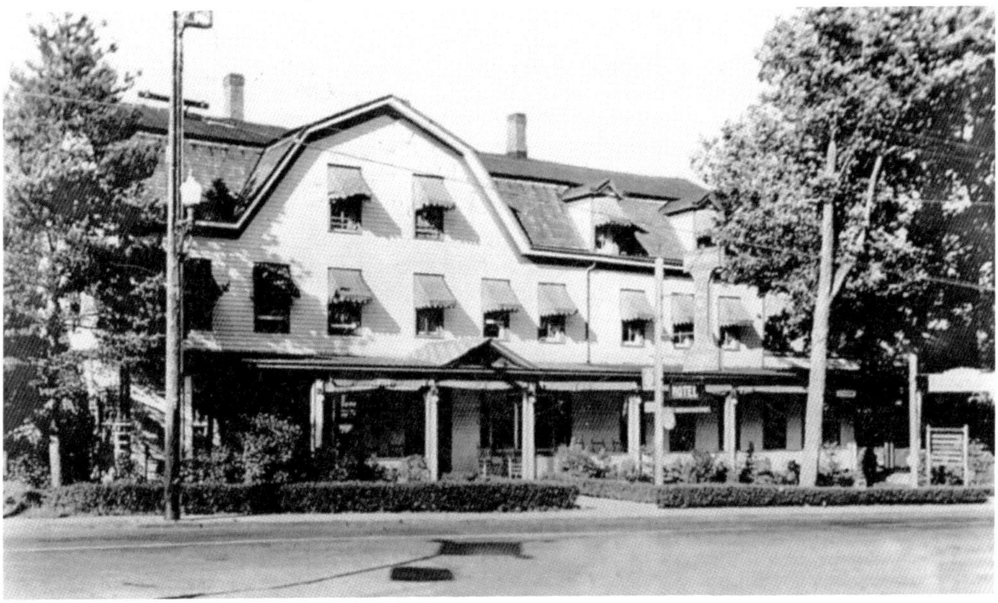

The Pine Hill Arms, originally called the Avon Inn, was built during the heyday of the late-19th-century tourist-train era. Robert and Valerie Konefal purchased the hotel in 1973 and started a long renovation project. It has become a mainstay of the community, sponsoring many local functions and ski events even as other businesses in the village have closed. (Courtesy of Valerie Konefal.)

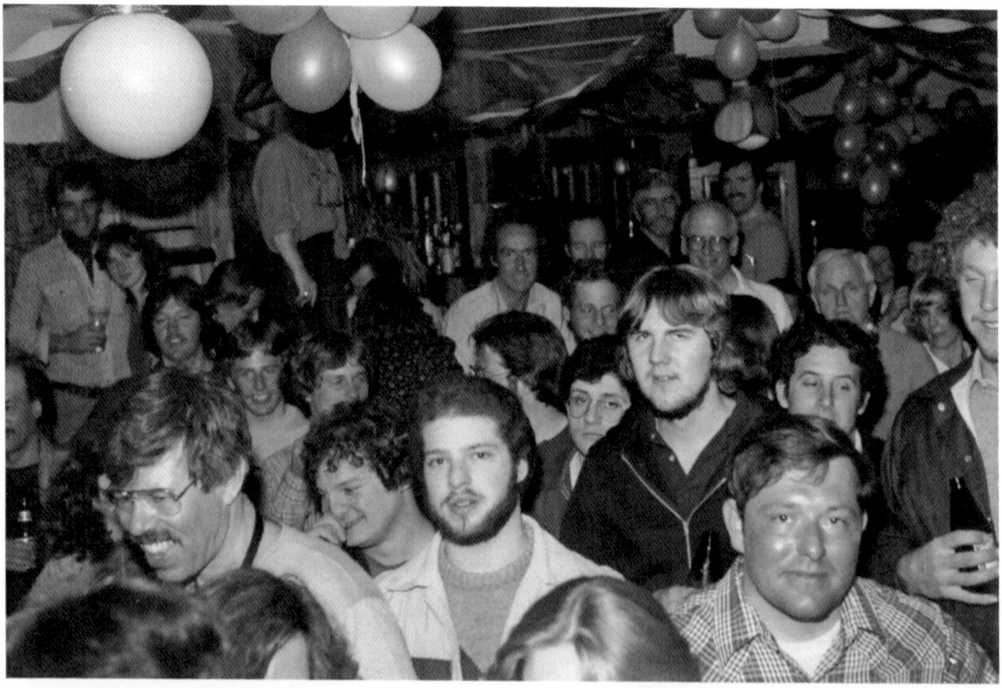

Revelers celebrate the 100th anniversary of the Pine Hill Arms (1882–1982) in a scene that is replicated often on cold, winter weekends during ski season. As a host to ski clubs and organizations, the Pine Arms has thrived with its personal, family-run atmosphere. (Courtesy of Valerie Konefal.)

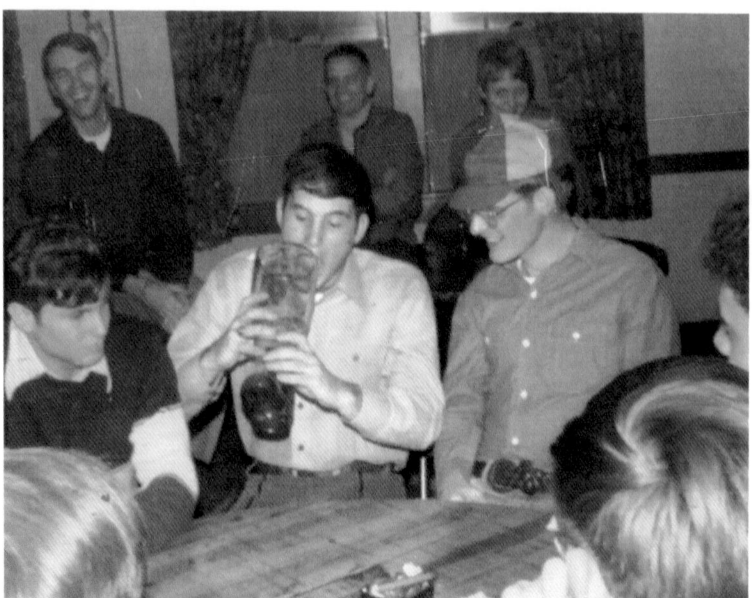

This West Point cadet, pictured with his fellow mates at the Pine Hill Arms in 1975, would get quite a "kickback" from drinking too fast from his large, boot-shaped mug. The cadets and other member clubs were frequent visitors to the hotel during ski season. (Courtesy of Valerie Konafal.)

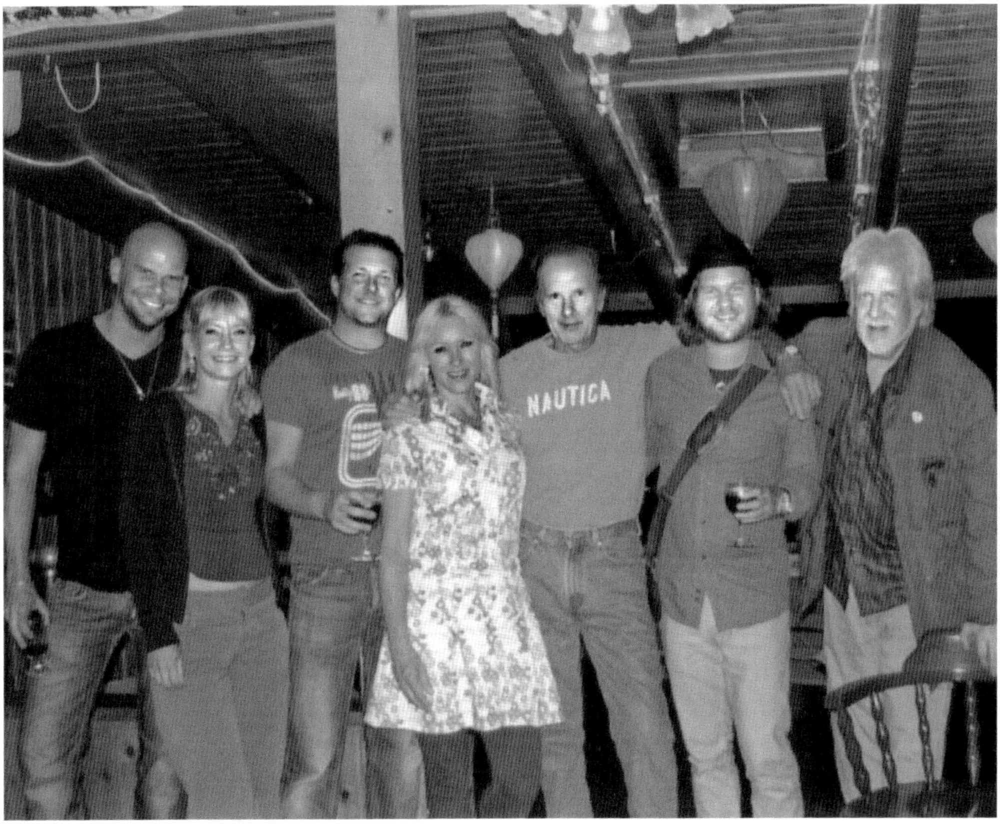

Members of the rock group ABBA, and their backing musicians, pose with Pine Hill Arms proprietor Robert Konefal (third from right). Groups from the nearby Belleayre Music Festival often visit or stay at the hotel as part of their tour. (Courtesy of Valerie Konefal.)

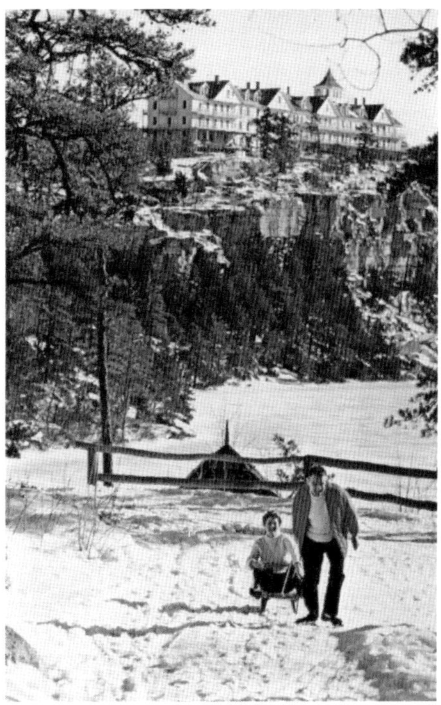

A man pulls a woman on a sled by the shores of Lake Minnewaska. Above the majestic cliffs next to the lake stands the Cliff House, part of the same resort. Opened in 1879, it lasted for almost a century until fire engulfed it in January 1978. The Wildmere lasted a while longer before it too burned. The hotel area became part of Minnewaska State Park despite attempts at further commercial development. Cross-country skiing is very popular here today, and the area features an extensive trail system.

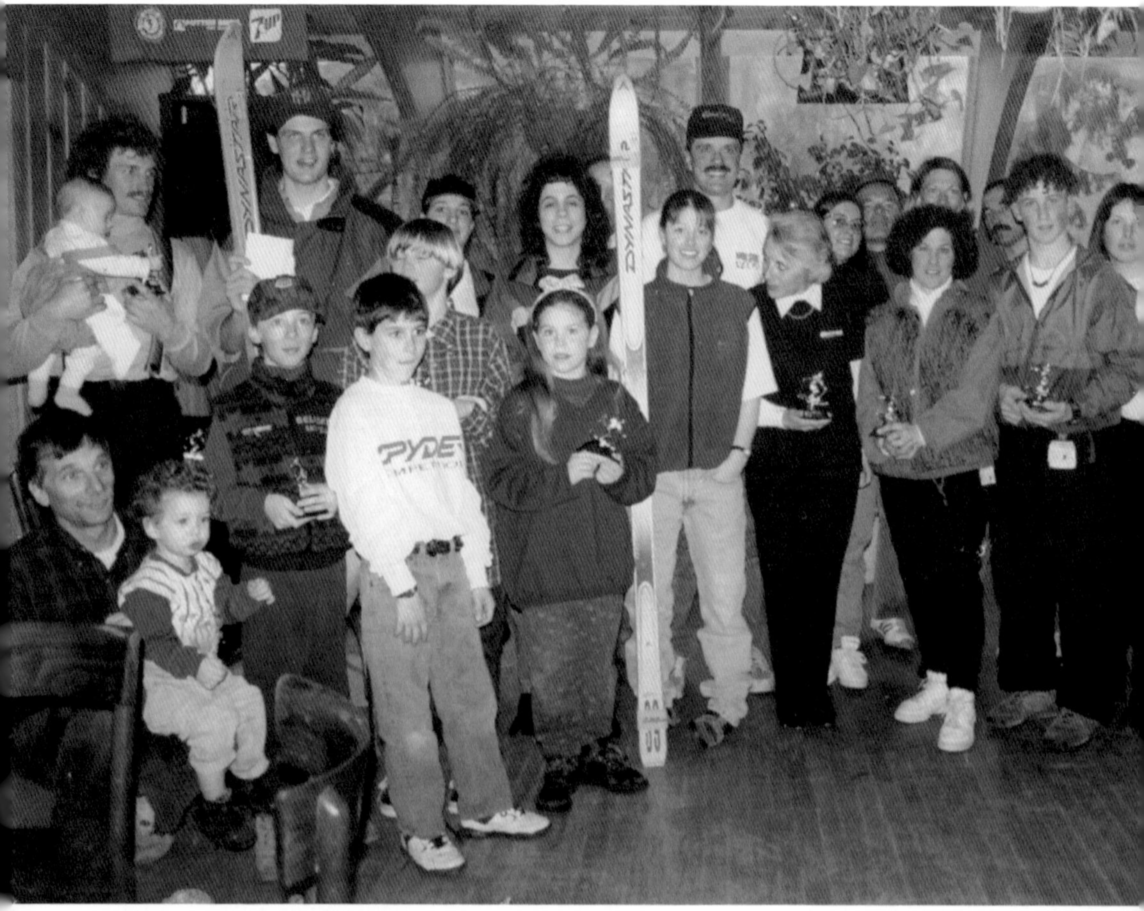

Ben Davenport and Jennifer Konefal are pictured holding their newly won Dynastar skis. Standing around them are all the other winners in the Pine Hill Arms Cup Race, which was held at Highmount Ski Center for many years. A young Brian "Rocket" Perez (front row, fourth from left, in white shirt) went on to win local and state championship races. In addition to sponsoring this race, the hotel also held mid-week races at Belleayre Mountain. It did help that both the owners, Bob and Valerie Konefal, were avid skiers known to sneak out during business hours to catch a few runs. (Courtesy of Valerie Konefal.)

5

Ski Clubs and Organizations

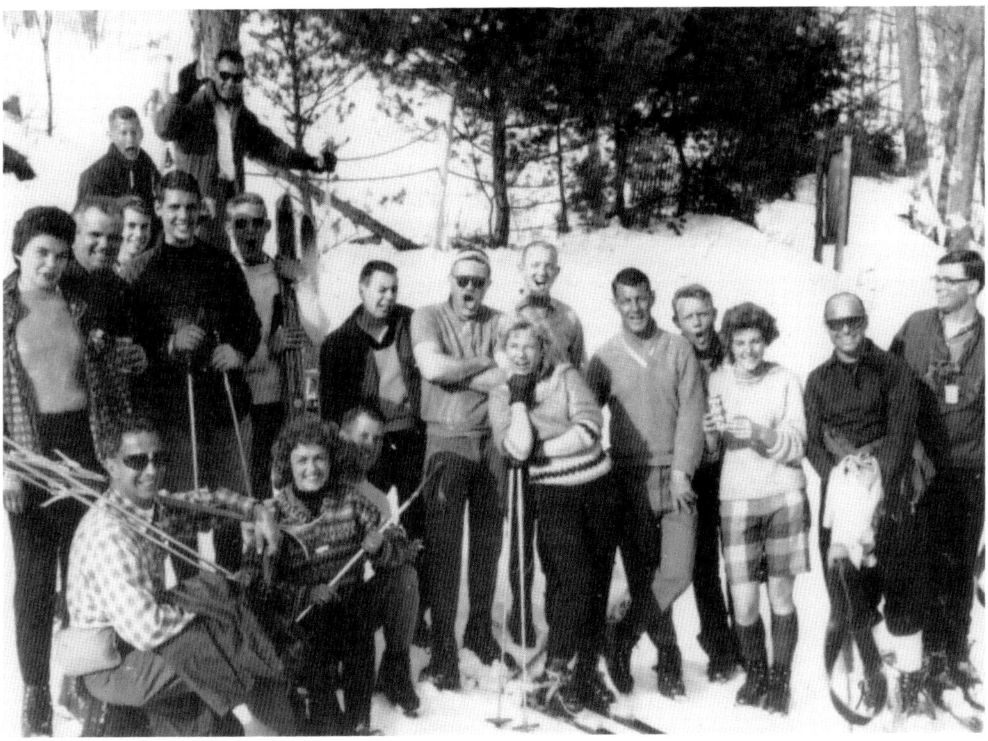

Exuberant members of Trailsweepers Ski Club pose for a group picture at the Highmount ski area after a race in the early 1950s. Groups such as this became tight-knit year-round social clubs, and bus excursions out of the Hudson Valley region traveled throughout the Northeast on a regular basis. (Courtesy of Trailsweepers.)

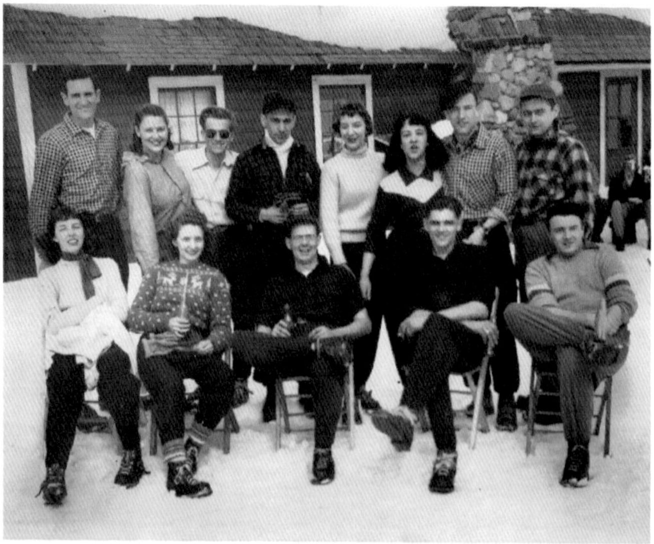

Members of Trailsweepers Ski Club pose in front of the Phoenicia ski area lodge in February 1950. Pictured are, from left to right, (first row) Alice Cerasaro, Chris Cook, Bert Cook, unidentified, and Jim Clancy; (second row) John Cerasaro, Noni Van Steenberg, Joan Van Steenberg, Dan Morehouse, Joan Ballard, Audrey Sheriff, Bense Roger, and Rudy Kaiser. (Courtesy of Trailsweepers.)

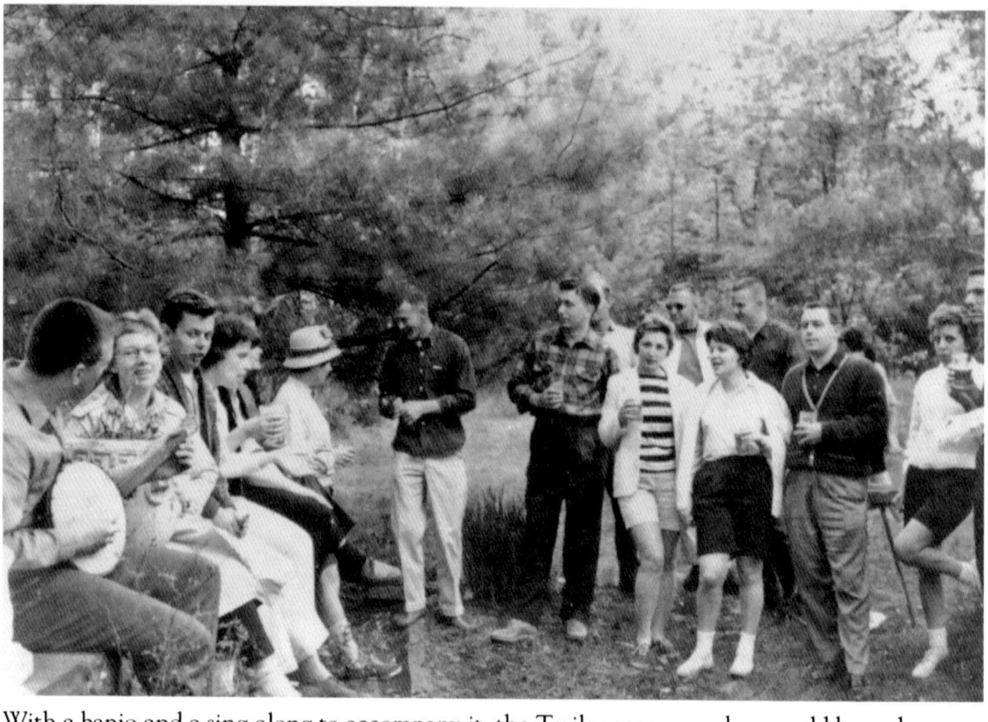

With a banjo and a sing-along to accompany it, the Trailsweeper members could keep the party going through the long summer months as they awaited the return of the snows. The group here is gathered in 1950. (Courtesy of Trailsweepers.)

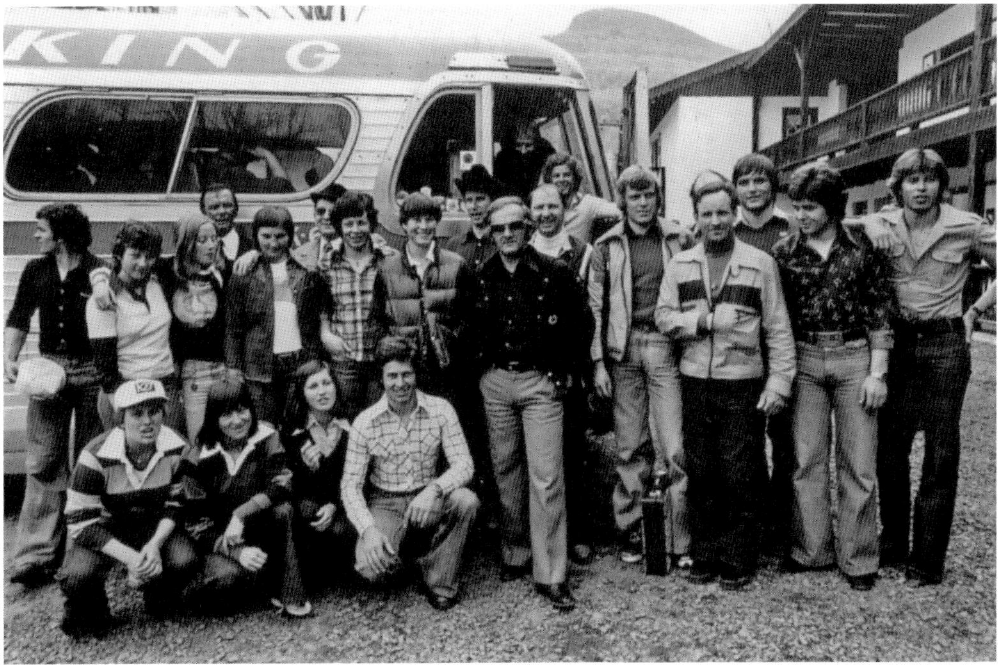

Members of the Austrian National Ski Team visit Hunter Mountain as part of their training for the World Cup. In the center, with the dark jacket and sunglasses, is head coach Karl Karr. To Karr's right, with his hand in his jacket, is Hunter Mountain Ski School director and host Karl Plattner, also of Austrian descent. (Courtesy of Karl Plattner.)

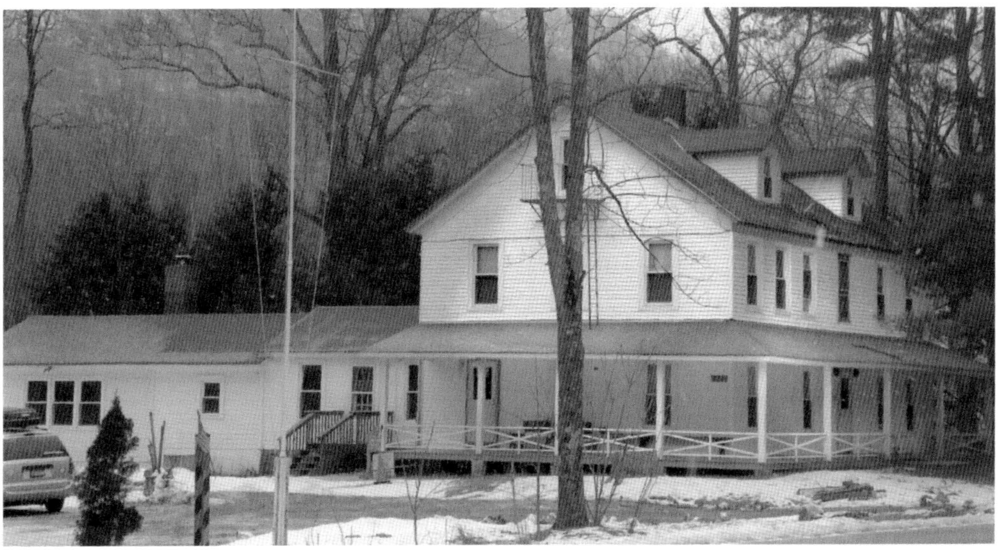

Nestled deep in the Upper Esopus Valley on New York Route 28 in Shandaken is the Catskill home of the Norway Ski Club, located here in 1959. The club was started in 1927 in Mamaroneck, New York, by a small group of Norwegian immigrants, many of them from Brooklyn. Busy days followed as ski jumps were constructed in different locations almost yearly. They finally settled at Bear Mountain State Park, holding sanctioned tournaments in the late 1930s.

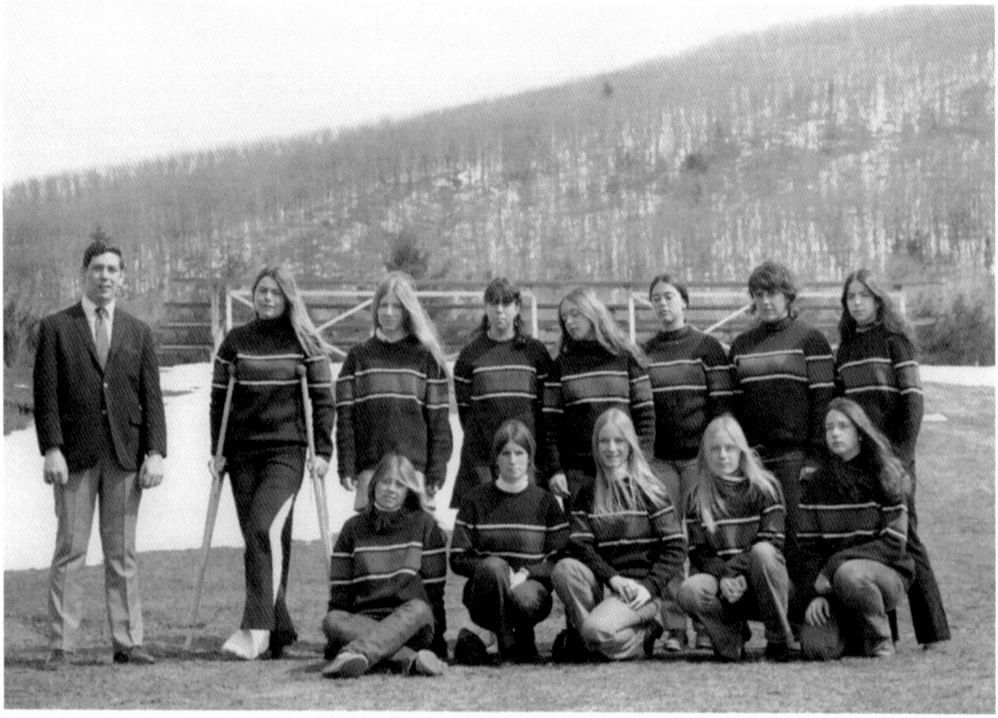

Members of the Onteora Girls Ski Team assemble for a group photograph behind the high school in Boiceville in 1970. Pictured are, from left to right, (first row) Nickie Desy, Derby Moyer, Robin McFadden, Karen Jensen, and Anna McGrath; (second row) coach Rick Barthel, Judy Hevesi, Jesse Craig, Sue Wallace, Bridget Sweeny, Kathy Wallace, Sue France, and Mary McGrath. (Courtesy of Rick Barthel.)

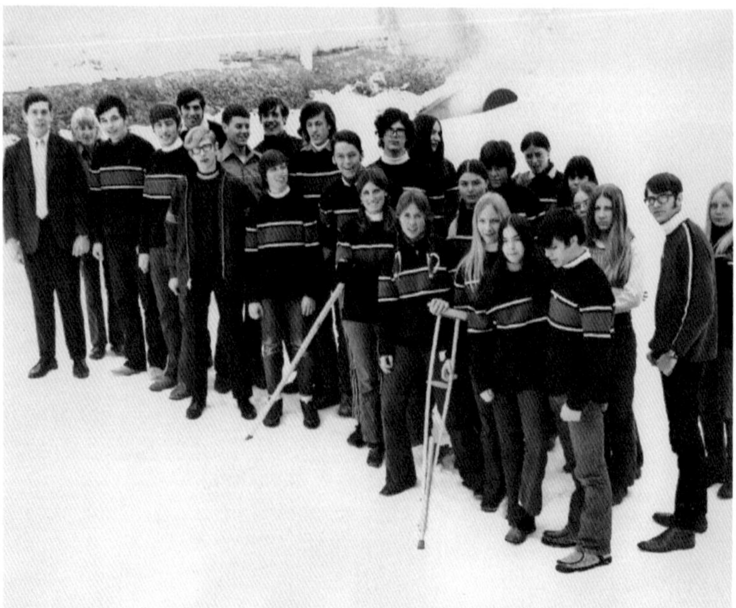

The full Onteora Ski Team poses for the camera in 1971. Growing up in proximity to so many ski areas gave these skiers a little edge in training. They were Section IX champions for many years straight. The genial head coach, Rick Barthel, stands to the far left. (Courtesy of Rick Barthel.)

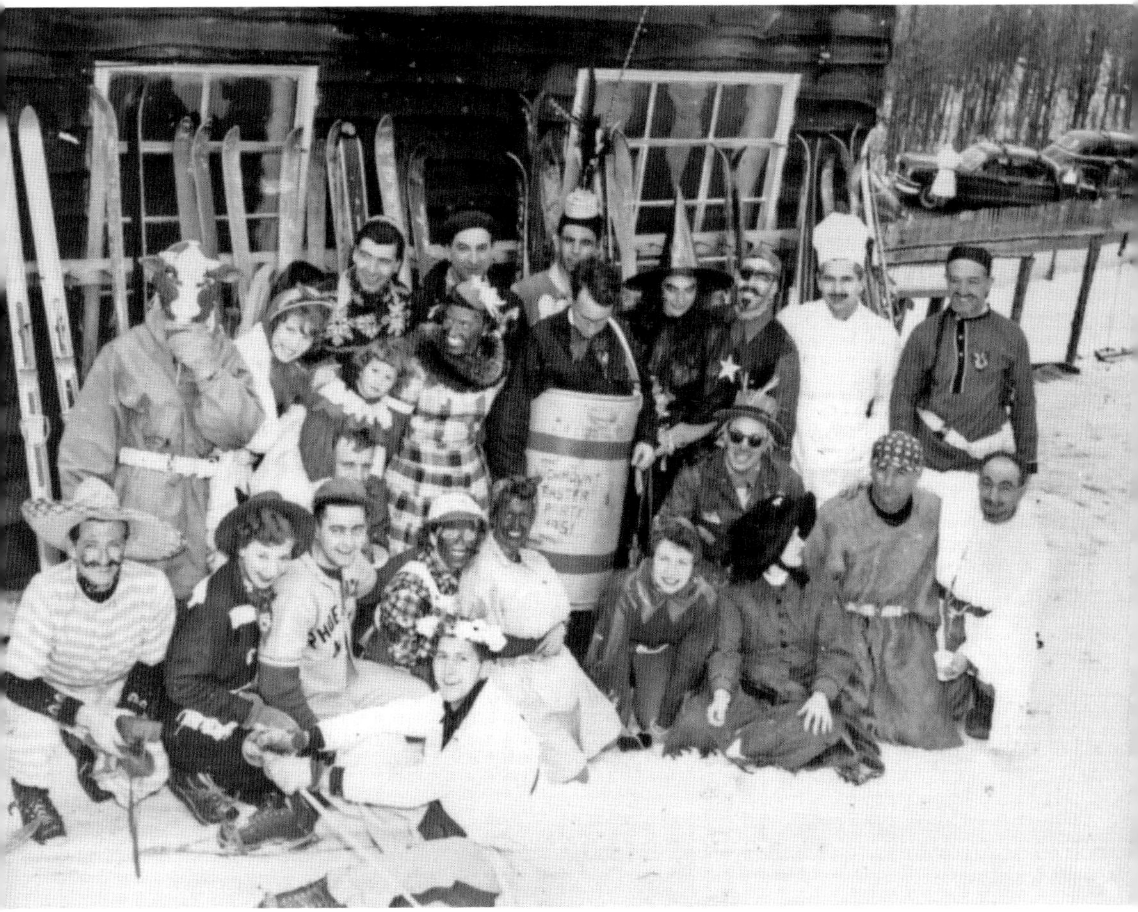

Members of Trailsweepers Ski Club are pictured in front of Highmount Ski Lodge after the Easter parade in 1951. On bottom right wearing a polka-dot bandana is Francis Davenport, and to his left, in a black bonnet, is his wife, Blanche. Francis started Highmount in 1947 with his brother Maurice (to his right, in white) and Lincoln Christensen (behind him). Operations began with narrow trails and little snow, but as snow conditions improved, Highmount slowly expanded into a premier resort in the Catskills. (Courtesy of Trailsweepers.)

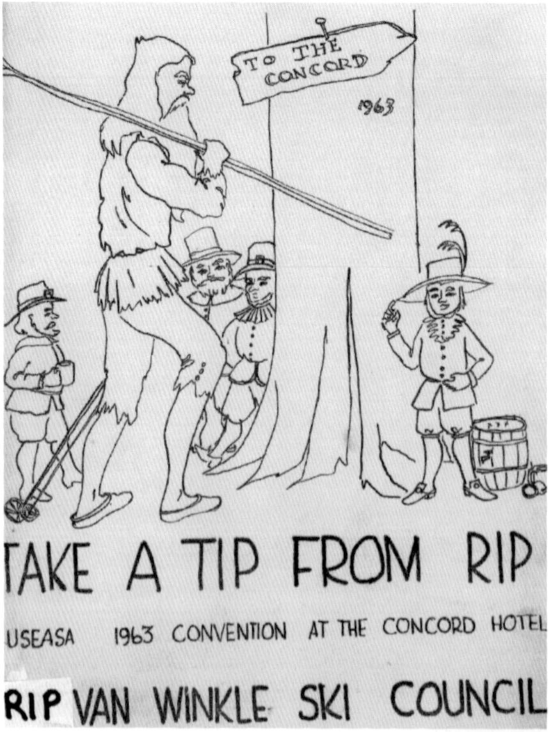

In this poster from 1963, local folk character Rip Van Winkle is hauling his skis to the Concord Hotel for the 1963 United States Eastern Amateur Ski Association (USEASA) convention. A conglomeration of clubs from the Catskills and beyond, the Rip Van Winkle Ski Council sponsored clinics in the latest ski techniques—from snowplowing to wedeln—and continues to sponsor ski races to this day. (Courtesy of Trailsweepers.)

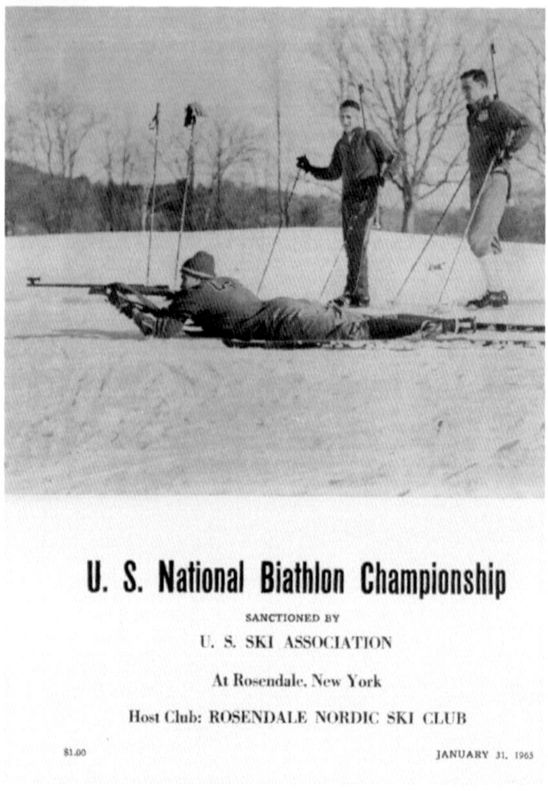

The Rosendale area was a center of ski activity in the 1960s. With the Rosendale ski jump right above town and Williams Lake ski touring up the road, the US National Ski Association felt the area was suitable to host the US National Biathlon Championship in 1966. Shown here is the cover of a booklet for the event.

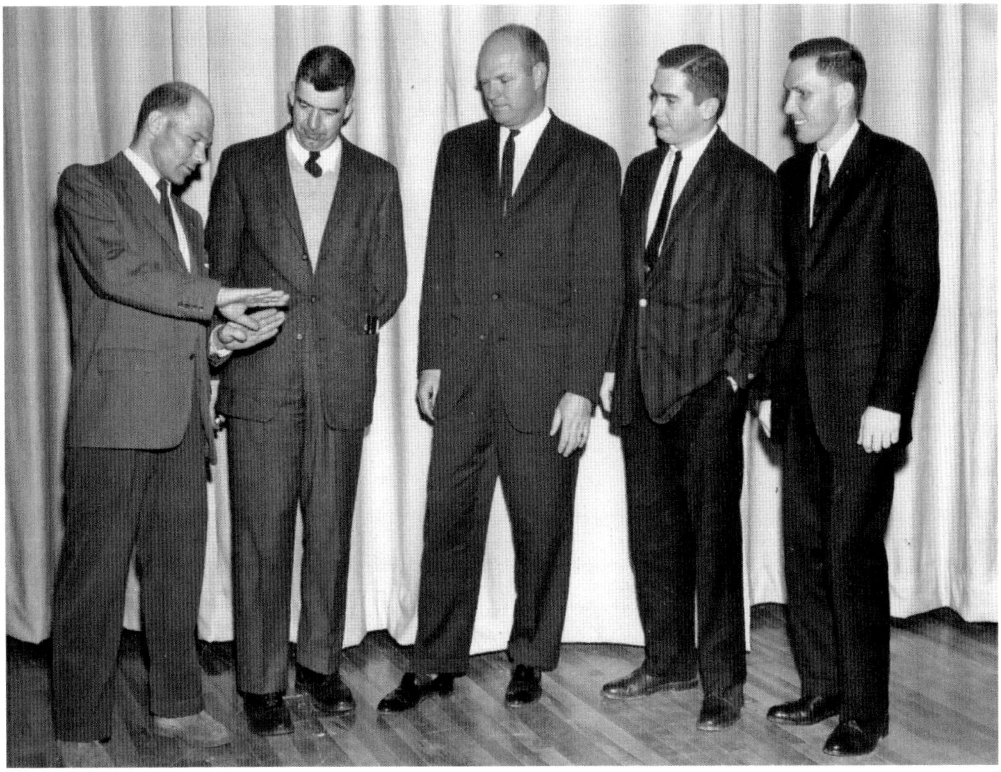

The best way to promote the sport of skiing in the 1950s was to have a group lecture on the subject, such as this one sponsored by Trailsweepers. Pictured are, from left to right, Jim Andres, John McGrath, Warren Miller, Jim Fuller, and Irv Wisneski. McGrath was head ski instructor at Highmount and later ran the ski shops on Main Street and in Scandinavian Village in Phoenicia. Warren Miller, originally a ski bum from Sun Valley, Idaho, went on to astound the world with his ski films and left an indelible mark in ski history. (Courtesy of Trailsweepers.)

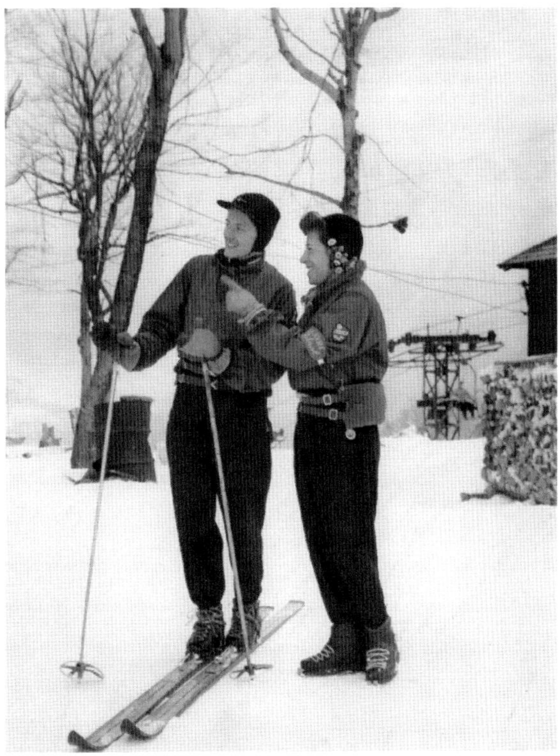

Two members of the Belleayre Ski Patrol in their 1950s attire point to the west on the summit. At the time, they were identified by a loose armband. (Courtesy of Belleayre Mountain.)

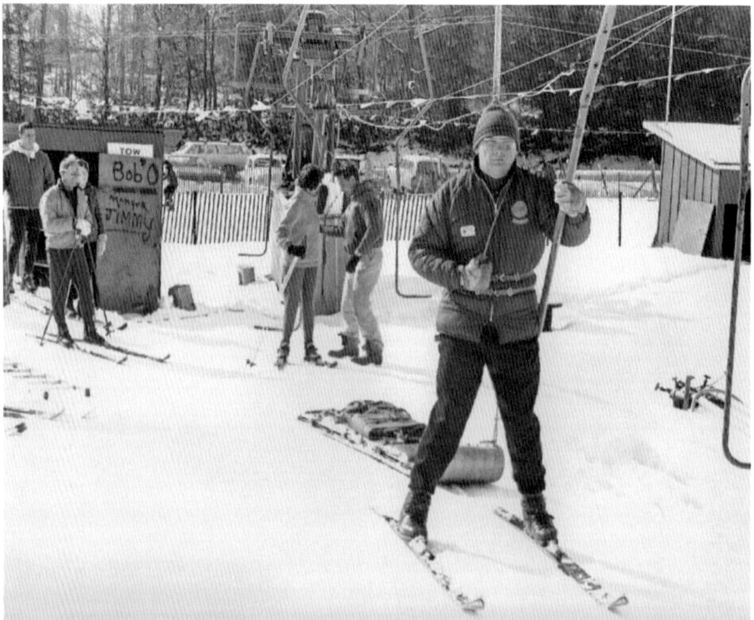

The head ski patrolman at Holiday Mountain, Stu Jones, heads uphill on the J-bar in the mid-1960s. Being towed behind him is the small wood toboggan that was used to haul injured skiers off the slopes. (Courtesy of Holiday Mountain.)

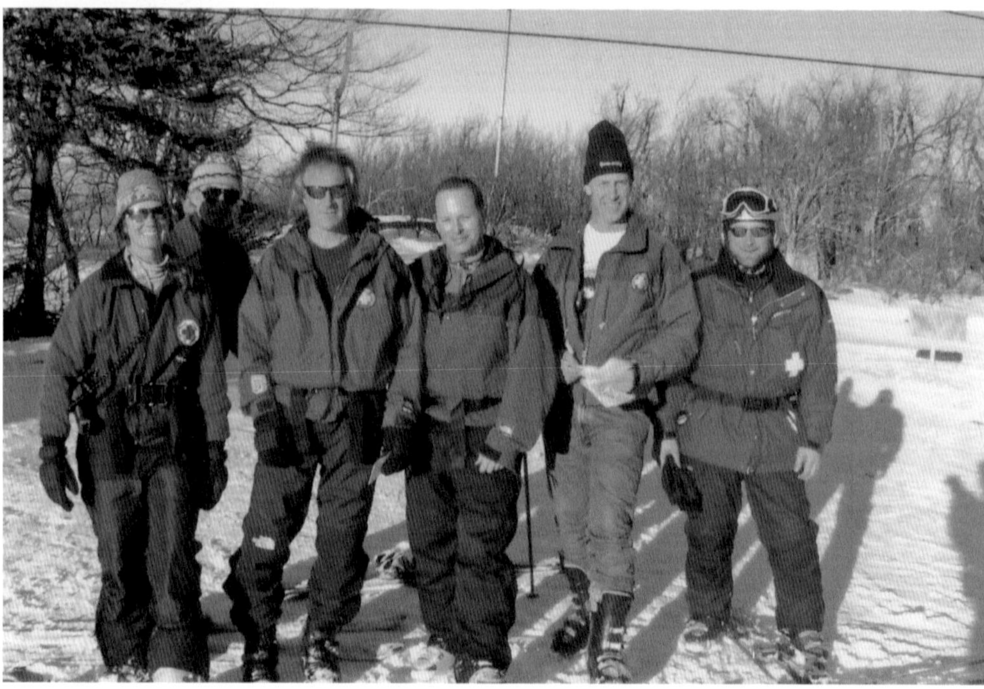

The small, tight-knit ski patrol is standing on the top of the Bobcat ski area. Behind them is the long T-bar that lasted throughout the existence of this enchanted ski area, which closed around 2005. Pictured are, from left to right, Lynne Brittian, Peter Brittian, Dave Gile, Matt Dreyfus, Don Trelease, and Mike Cipperly. (Courtesy of Lynne Brittian.)

Three jubilant winning racers are holding their trophies at Holiday Mountain in February 1977. They are, from left to right, Bucky Laufeesweiber, David Kent (from Whiteface Mountain), and Peter Dill. Despite having a small vertical drop, Holiday Mountain has hosted many regional races over the years. (Courtesy of Holiday Mountain.)

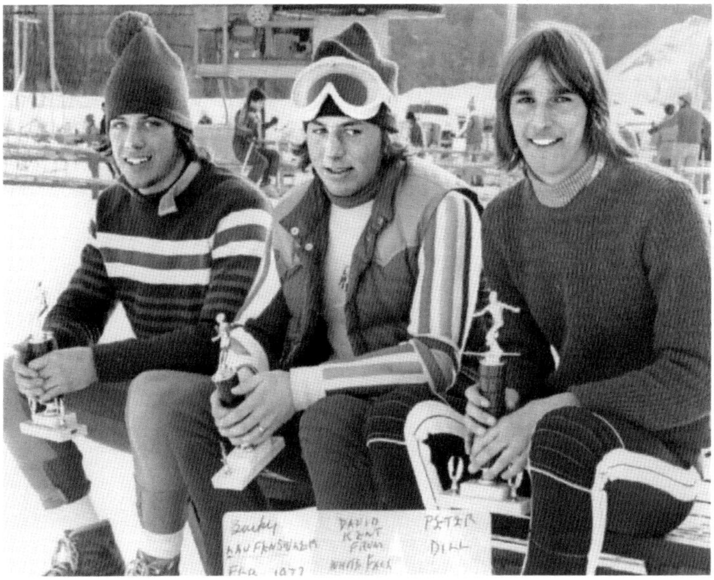

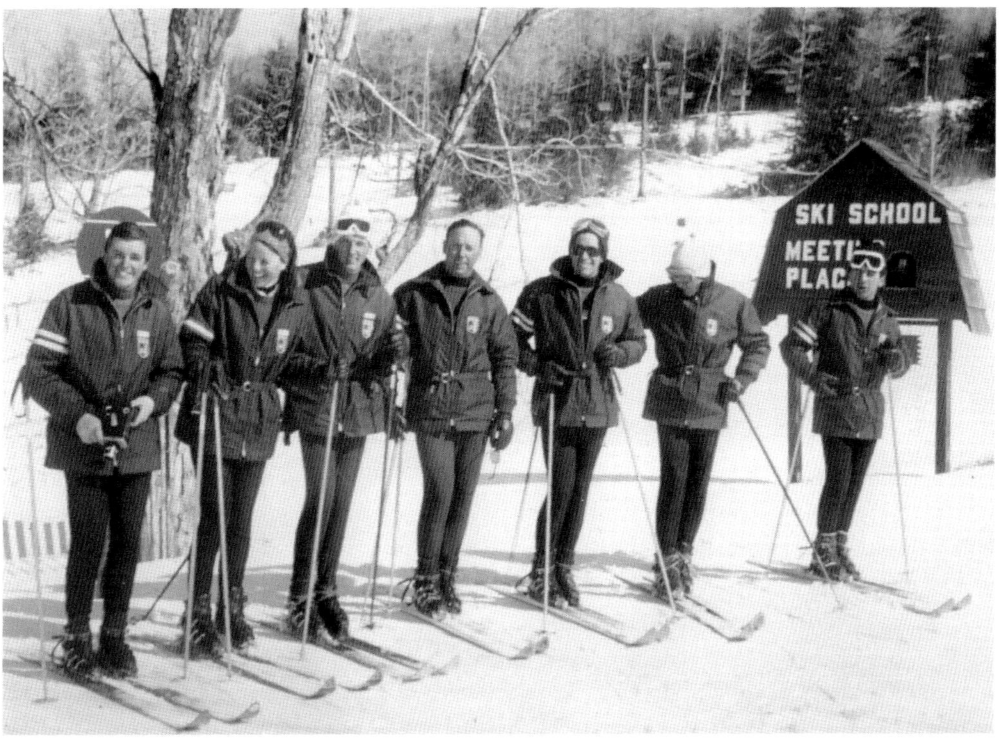

A cheery Windham Mountain Ski School is ready to teach in 1966. Pictured here are, from left to right, Osvaldo Runge (Argentina), Edith Brody (Austria), Ray Melz (Austria), Martin Jareb (Austria), Fito Lopez (Argentina), Seppand Linher (Austria), and Julio Fernandez (Argentina). (Courtesy of Edith Brody.)

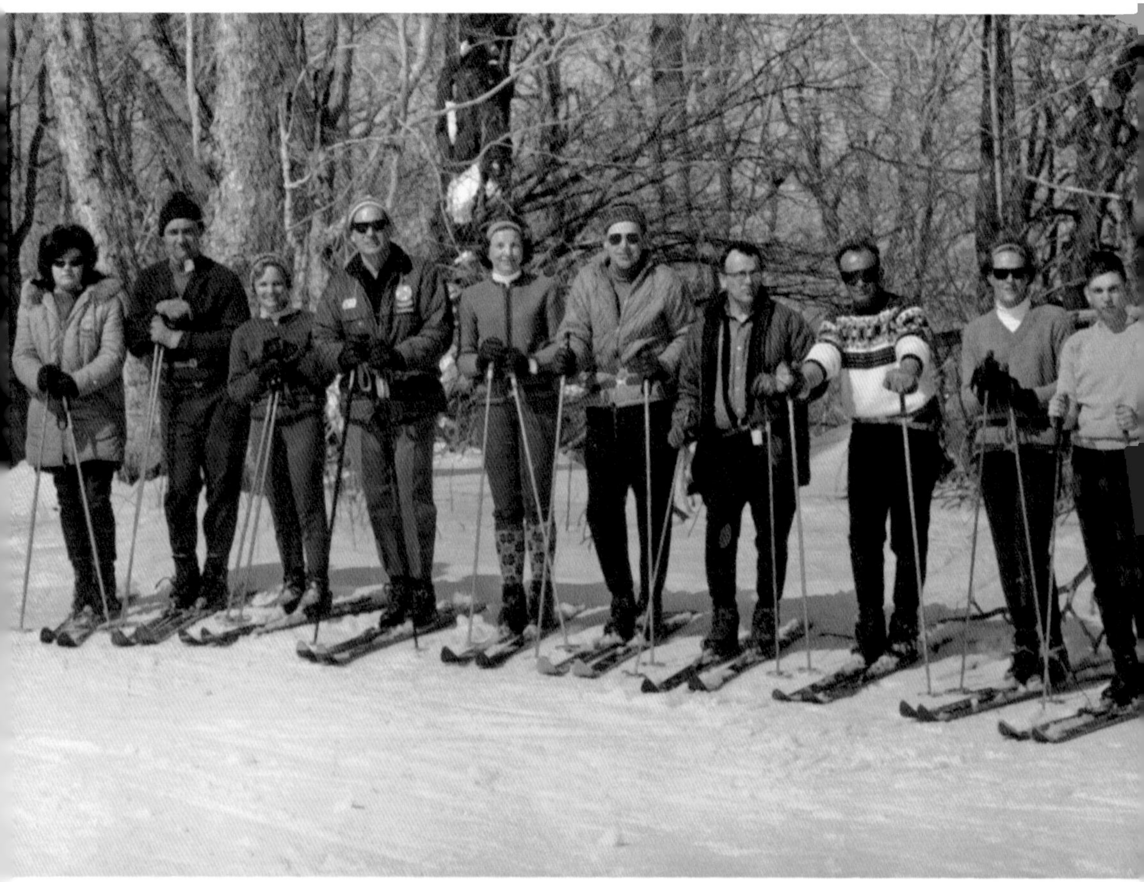

A group of ski patrollers, ski school instructors, and friends lines up on a sunny day on top of Plattekill Mountain in the mid-1960s. Pictured are, from left to right, Carol Morse, Gary Hinkley, Bonnie Hinkley, Jack Lutz, Kay Lutz, Andrew "Jun" Schuman, Milton Slauso, Charlie Faraci, Sylvia Lutz, and Tom Schumann. (Courtesy of Gary Hinkley.)

6

THE GREAT NORTHERN CATSKILLS

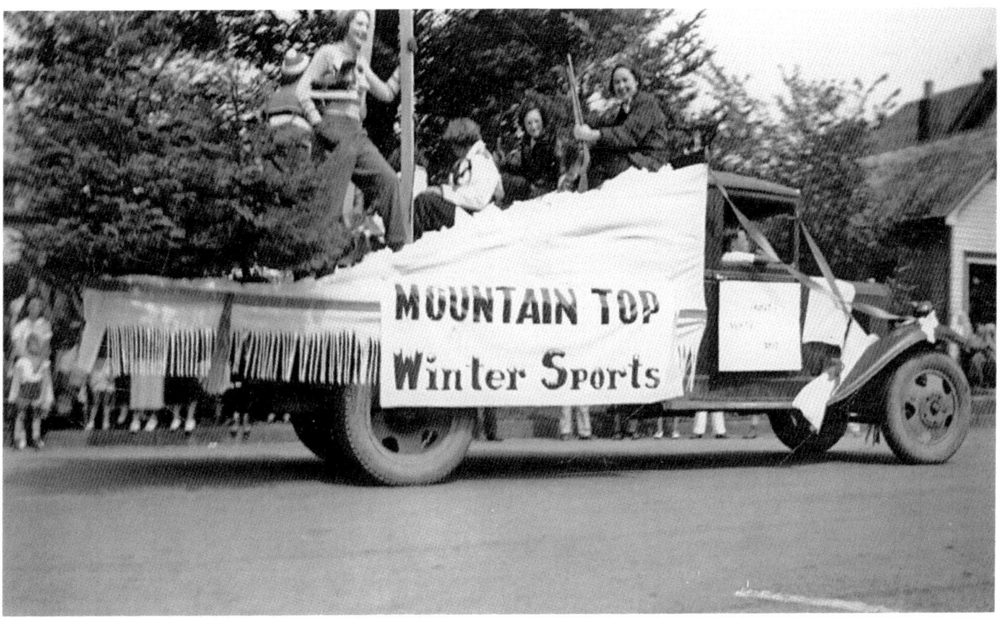

In the summertime parade of 1938, the townspeople of Hunter are showing their enthusiasm and longing for winter sports. It was not until the late 1950s and the construction of Hunter Mountain Ski Bowl that things perked up in the town and changed the local character. The "Mountain Top" in the truck's sign refers to the Hunter-Tannersville region. (Courtesy of John M. Ham.)

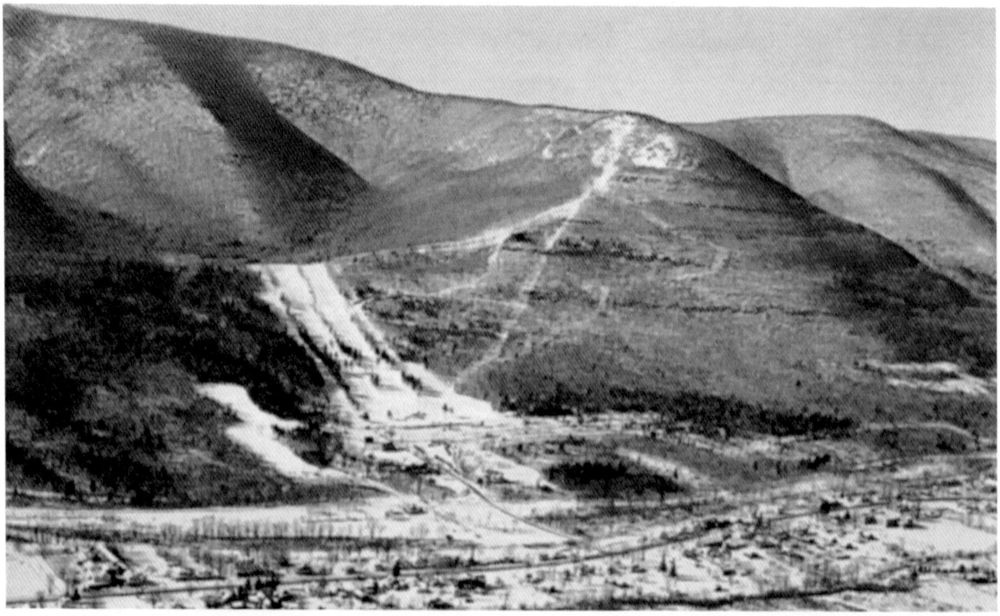

Hunter Mountain Ski Bowl is shown in the early stage of development in 1962. Although now considered a mammoth ski area for the region, the area only occupies a small portion of the vast Hunter Mountain, rising to 4,020 feet in elevation, where a fire tower is located. Efforts over the years to develop this land for ski use have been thwarted as the area has been designated "forever wild" by New York State.

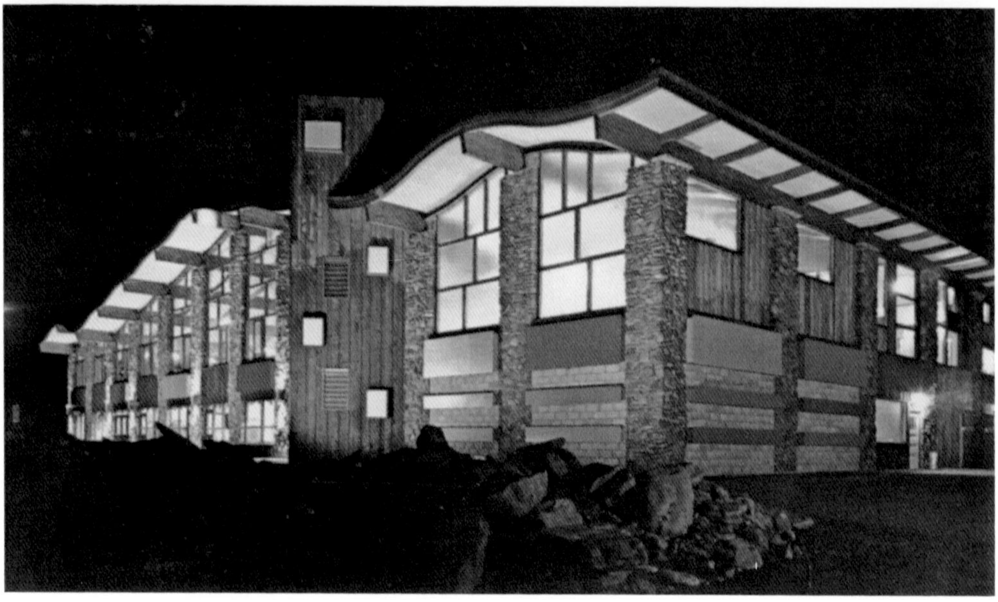

When opened in 1965, the new Hunter Base Lodge was viewed as an architectural gem and became a tourist attraction in itself. It also featured an indoor pool, sauna, and health club. By this period, Hunter had three double chairlifts, a Poma lift, and three tows. It was a period of exponential growth for the area and the Catskills.

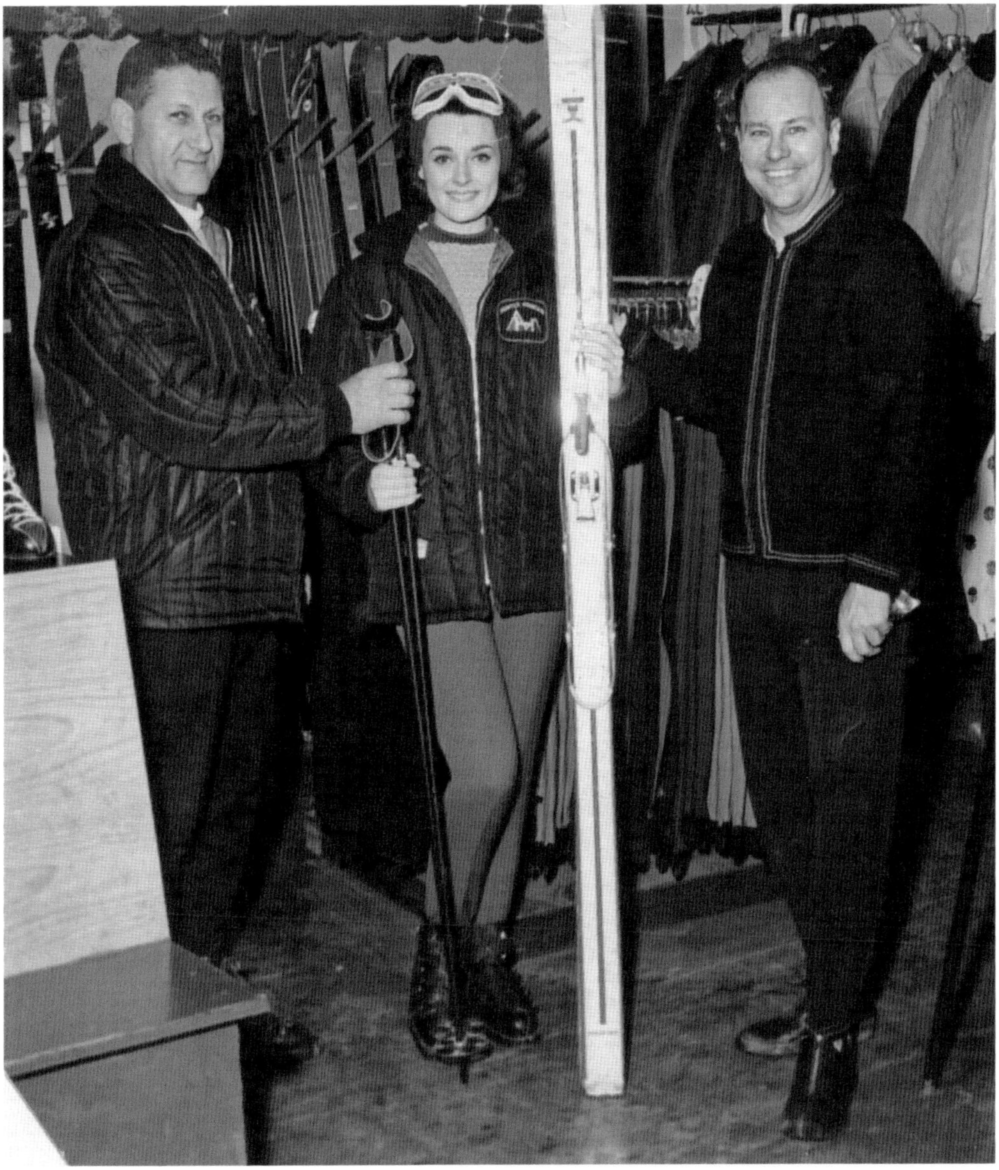

When Miss Rheingold came to Hunter Mountain in early 1963, it was a good opportunity for a photography session. Here, she is pictured with Orville Slutzky (left), who along with his brother Izzy built Hunter into the largest ski area in the region. Native to the Hunter area, they had their own construction company building many local projects, such as schools and bridges, in the region before the creation of Hunter Mountain. Orville still came to work at the lodge every day at 90 years of age. To the right of Miss Rheingold is Vincent Quinn, proprietor of the Hunter Ski Shop.

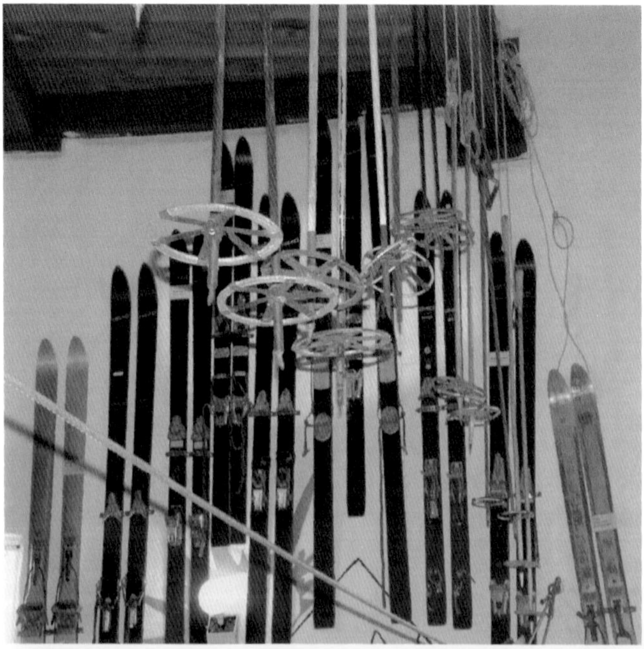

Inside the Summit Castle of Hunter Mountain, a large collection of vintage skis, poles, and other paraphernalia is on display. Hunter is one of the few places in the region that has a museum-exhibition space completely dedicated to ski history.

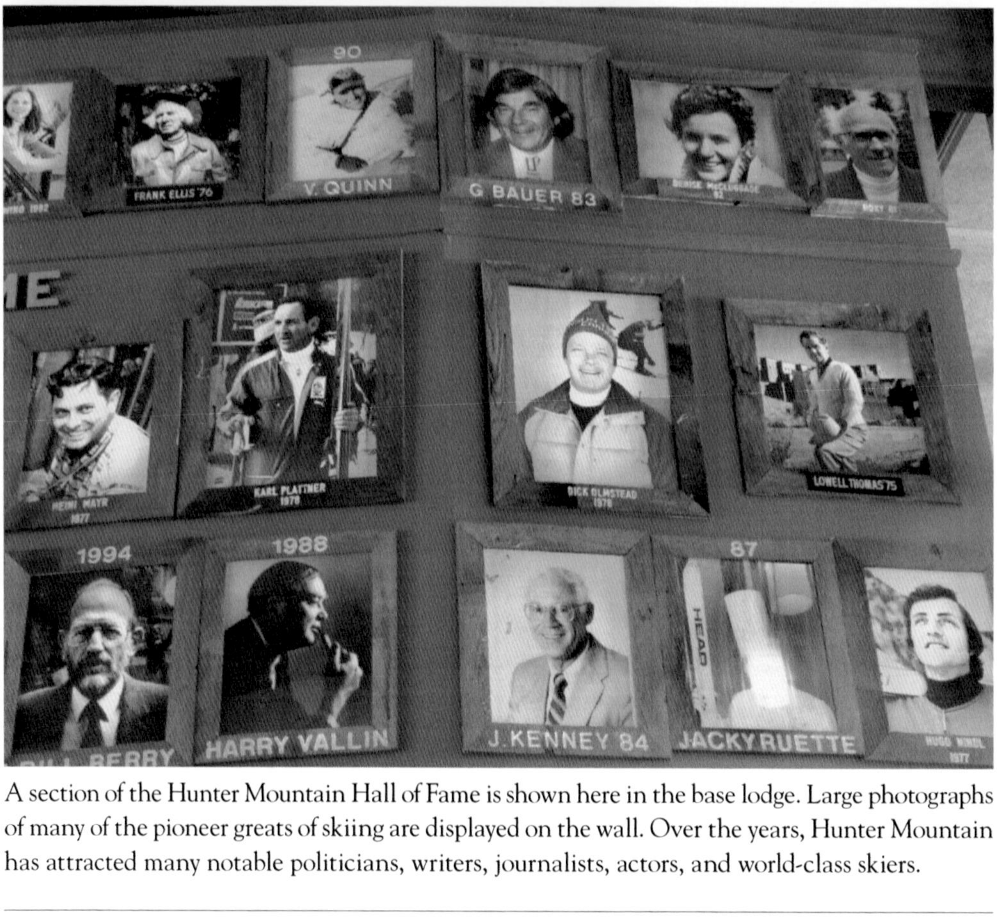

A section of the Hunter Mountain Hall of Fame is shown here in the base lodge. Large photographs of many of the pioneer greats of skiing are displayed on the wall. Over the years, Hunter Mountain has attracted many notable politicians, writers, journalists, actors, and world-class skiers.

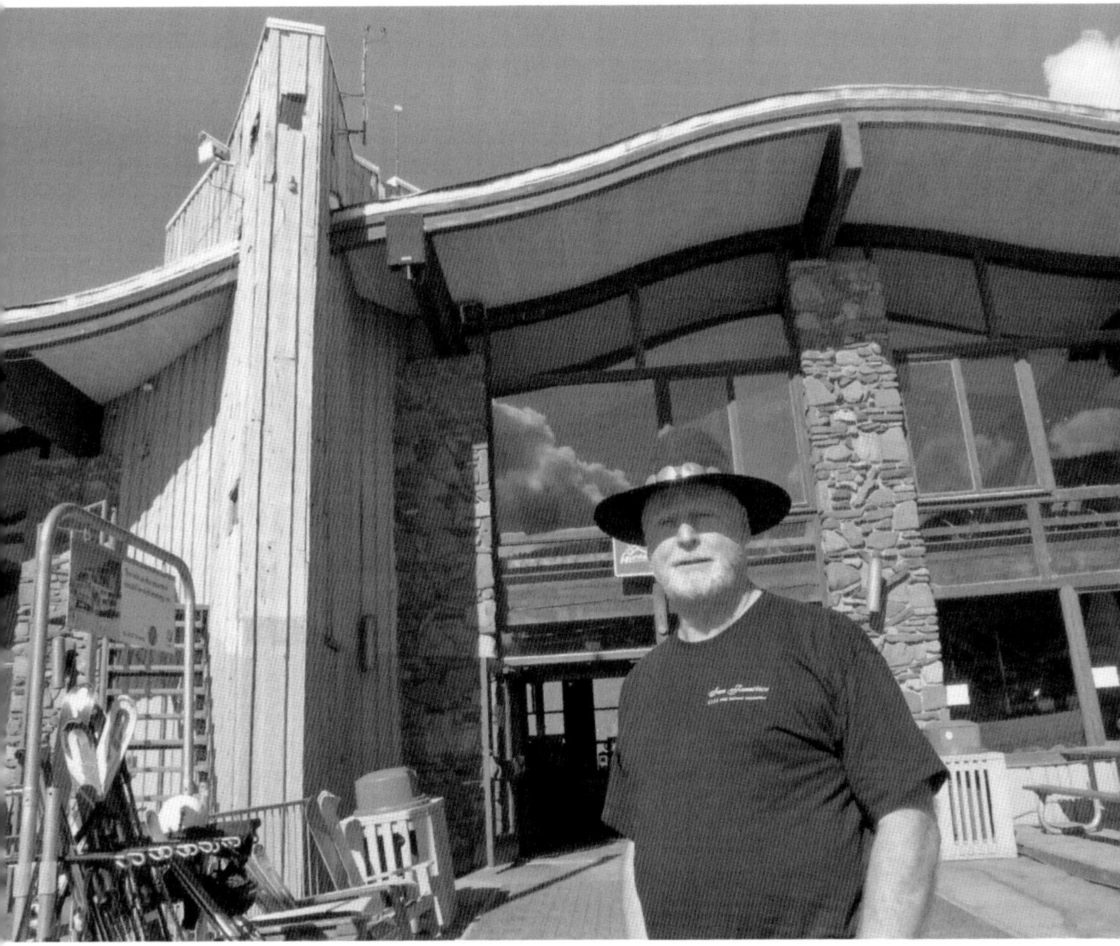

David Slutzky, photographer, artist, and master snowmaker, is standing in front of the slopeside entrance to the Hunter base lodge in his trademark black hat on a 70-degree day in March 2012. Son of Izzy, one of the founding brothers, David took over snowmaking operations at Hunter in 1971 and built it into the "snowmaking capital of the world." His photographs of snowmaking and interpretations of light and snow crystals are featured in his book *Sunrises and Snowmaking.* He has brought his snowmaking talents to other regions of the world, including the high Andes of South America, where the seasons are the reverse of those here.

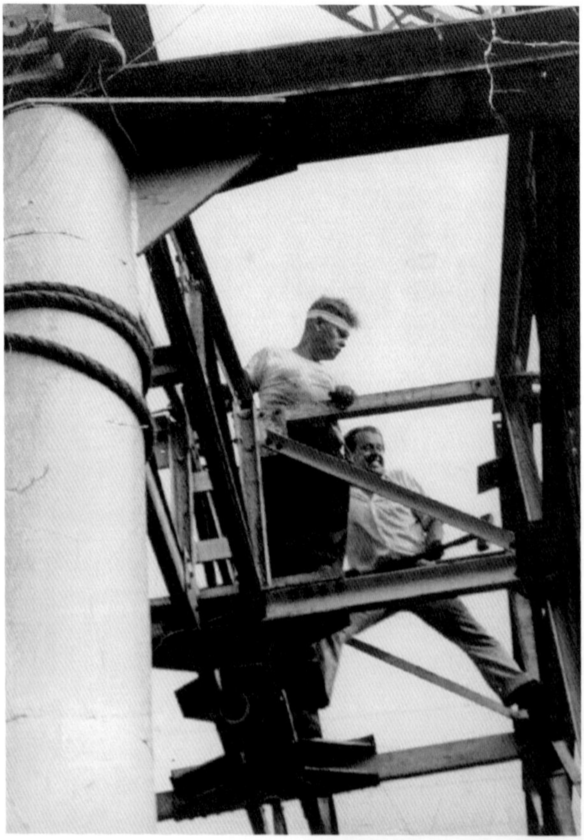

Construction workers stand precariously while banging metal on the original lift towers in the early 1960s. Heini Mayr, the photographer who took this photograph (and many others for the mountain), is pictured on the wall in the Hunter Mountain Hall of Fame in the base lodge. (Photograph by Heini Mayr.)

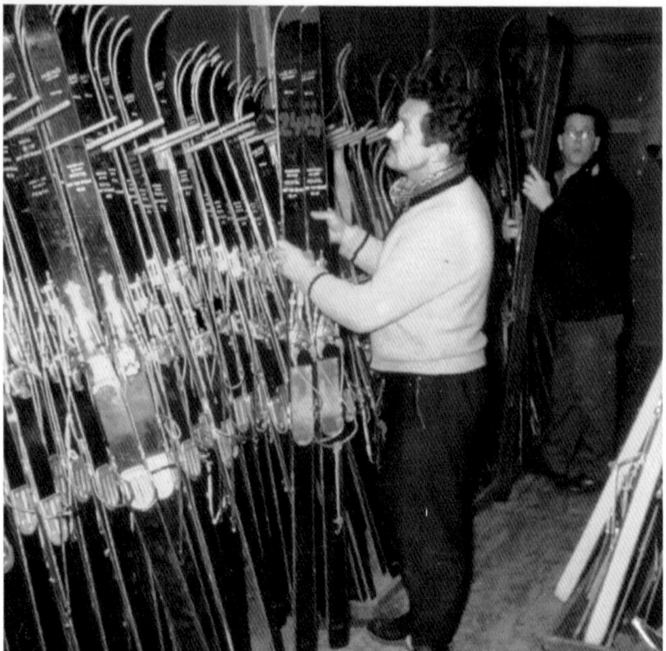

Pictured in 1961, Leo Kodyme (foreground) and a fellow worker look at the fleet of tall Head rental skis in the original Hunter Ski Shop. This was located in an old rooming house that was part of the original lodge complex. The length of the metal skis would range from 190 to 230 centimeters.

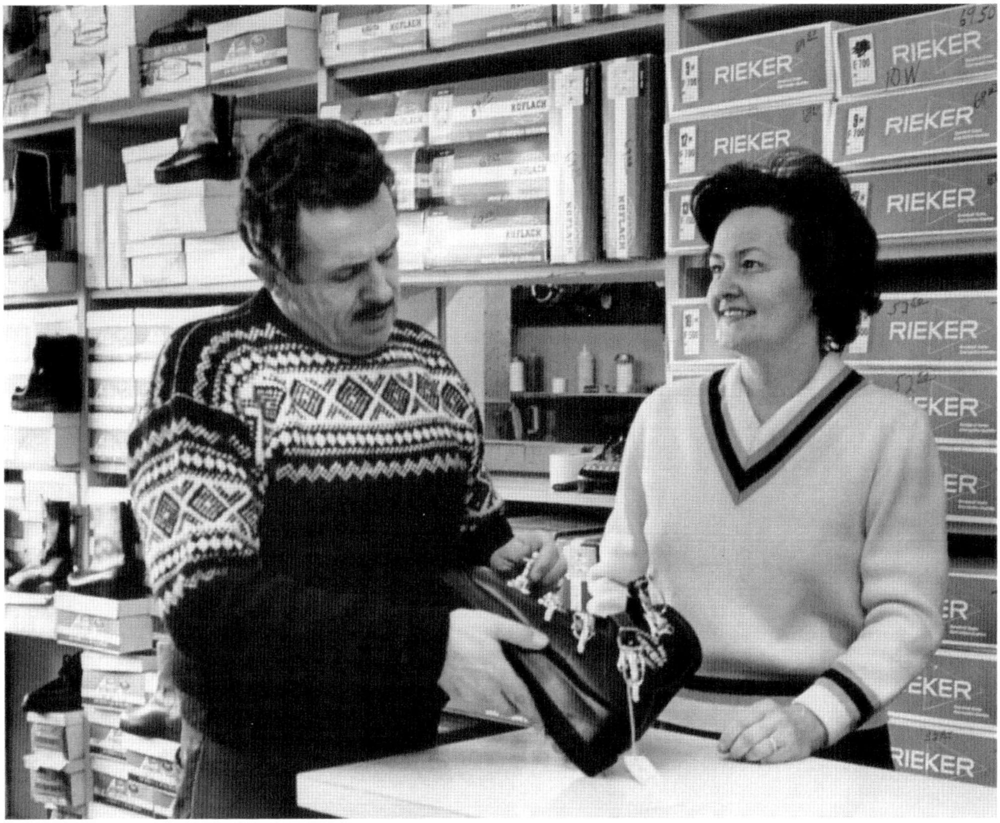

Leo Kodyme and Hilde Quinn examine new premium Reiker ski boots, which retailed at $69.50 in 1965. It does not sound like a high a price today; however, the minimum wage at the time was only $1.25 an hour. This photograph is from the ski shop located in the new base lodge. To the left of Leo is a large selection of sealskin après-ski boots, soon to become nonexistent as a commodity after the federal government enacted a ban on the trading of the skins in 1972.

Karl Plattner (left), head of the ski school, stands with an unidentified friend in front of the slopes of Hunter Mountain in the early stages of development. His jacket has a small emblem indicating he is the "Director." The background shows the clearing of land for the soon-to-be-constructed Lift A, which was not completed until the summer of 1962. Lift B, which was once to the left, in front of the base lodge, was built right away. (Courtesy of Karl Plattner.)

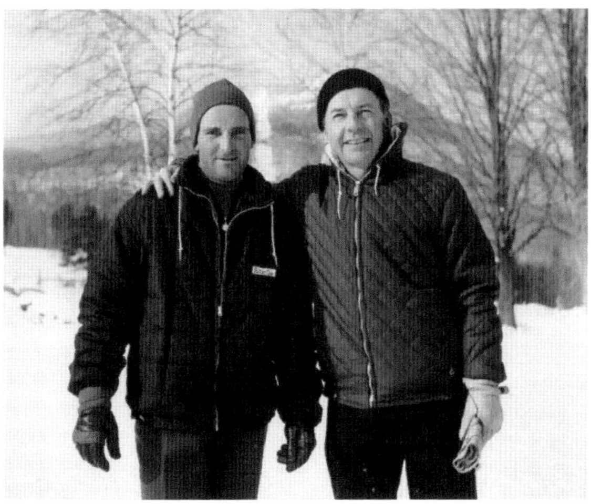

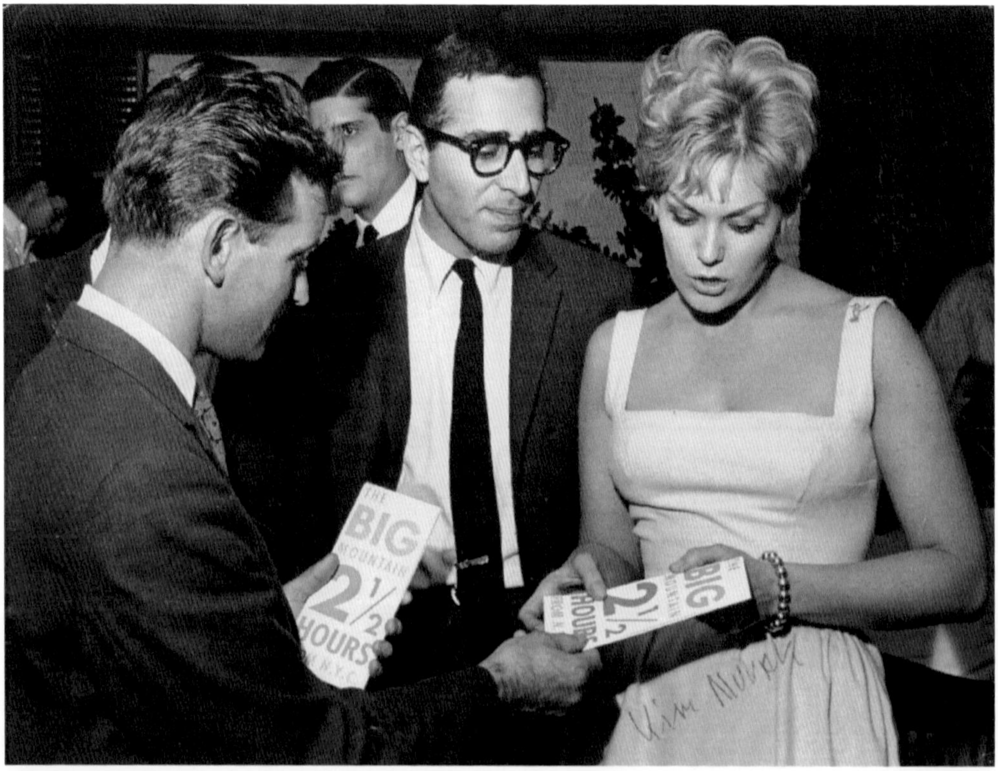

Actress Kim Novak receives the very first Hunter Mountain brochure from Karl Plattner at a New York City trade show as her manager looks on in 1959. The front of the brochure simply refers to Hunter as "the Big Mountain." Novak, an avid skier and early investor at Hunter Mountain, could often be seen sliding down Catskill-region slopes. (Courtesy of Karl Plattner.)

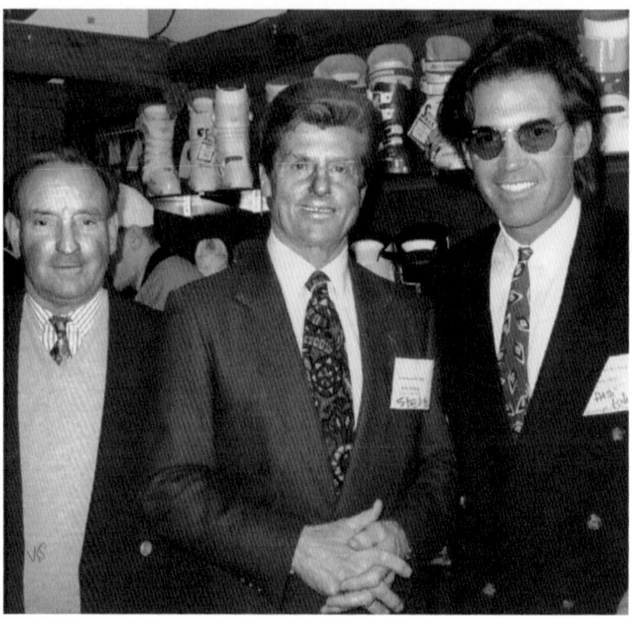

Three top skiers convene at a ski promotion at the Scandinavian Ski Shop on Fifty-seventh Street in Manhattan. They are, from left to right, Karl Plattner, the head of the Hunter Mountain Ski School; Stein Eriksen, a Norwegian gold medalist at the 1952 Olympics; and Andy Mill, the top American Olympic skier in 1976. The shop sent bus tours to Hunter Mountain for many years and had a lodge complex and ski shop near Phoenicia until the mid-1970s. (Courtesy of Karl Plattner.)

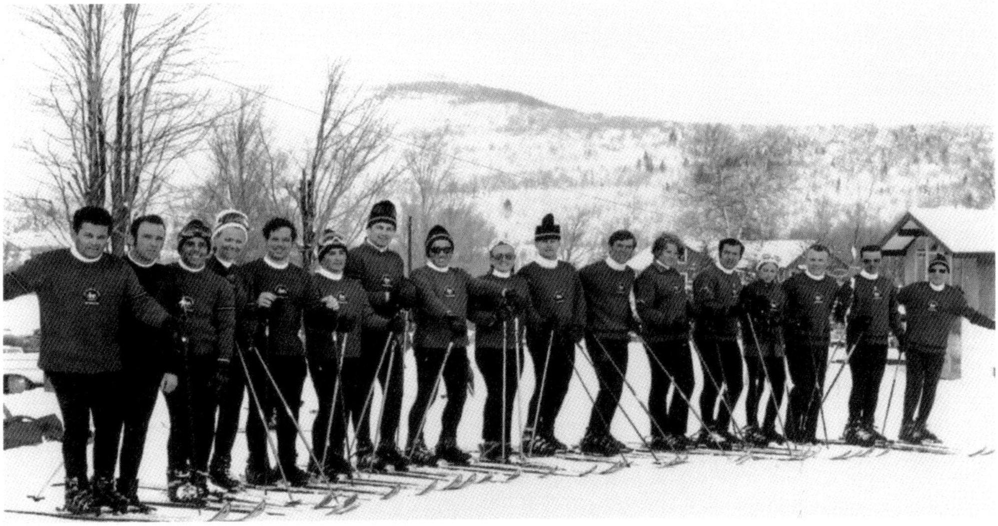

The Karl Plattner Ski School staff is standing in a wide row in the early 1960s. They are situated on the site of what is now the base lodge. With his wife, Margo, Karl built the school into one of the most successful and longest-serving in the country. Second from the left is Heinz Plattner, Karl's brother. The original lodge, formerly the Starr Hotel, is in the background to the right. (Courtesy of Karl Plattner.)

Ken Corrock (left) of Sun Valley, Idaho, competes with Norwegian Lasse Hamre at Hunter Mountain. As they soar over the second of two jumps, Hamre's goggles go flying. Corrock would go on to win the Miller Cup in 1969.

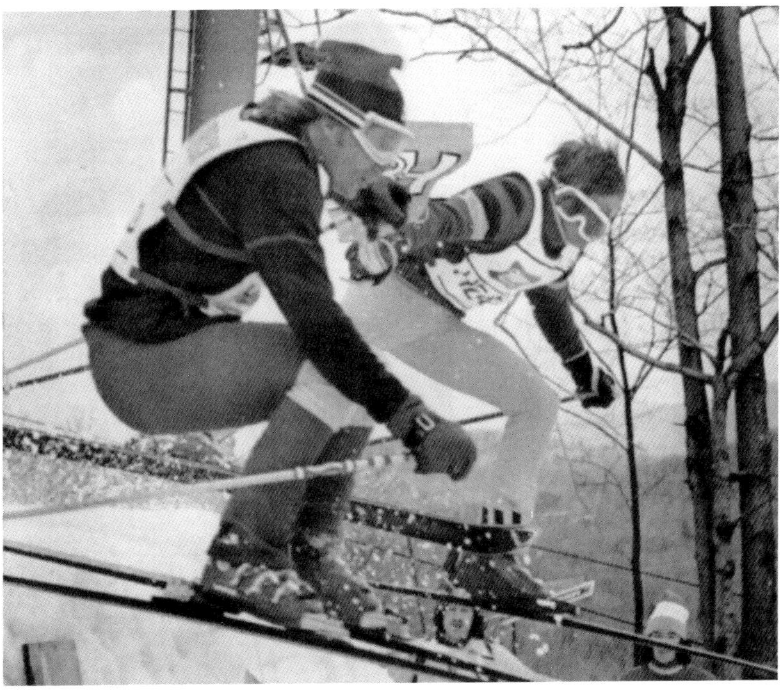

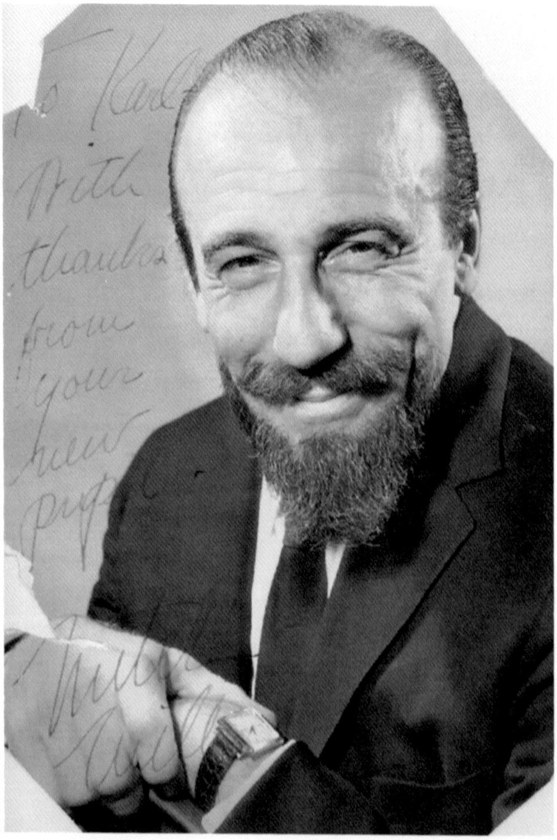

Bandleader, music producer, and television personality Mitch Miller, an early proponent and investor at Hunter Mountain, shows thanks to the ski school in this autographed picture to Karl Plattner. (Courtesy of Karl Plattner.)

Pictured here is the Starr Hotel at the base of Hunter Mountain in the early 20th century. When Hunter Mountain Ski Bowl was developed in 1959, the building was painted a bright red and converted into the base lodge. With a cafeteria and bar inside, the lodge was a lively place after skiing and featured rock bands and dancing. Farther up the hill, in a drafty, old rooming house, was the first ski shop on the mountain.

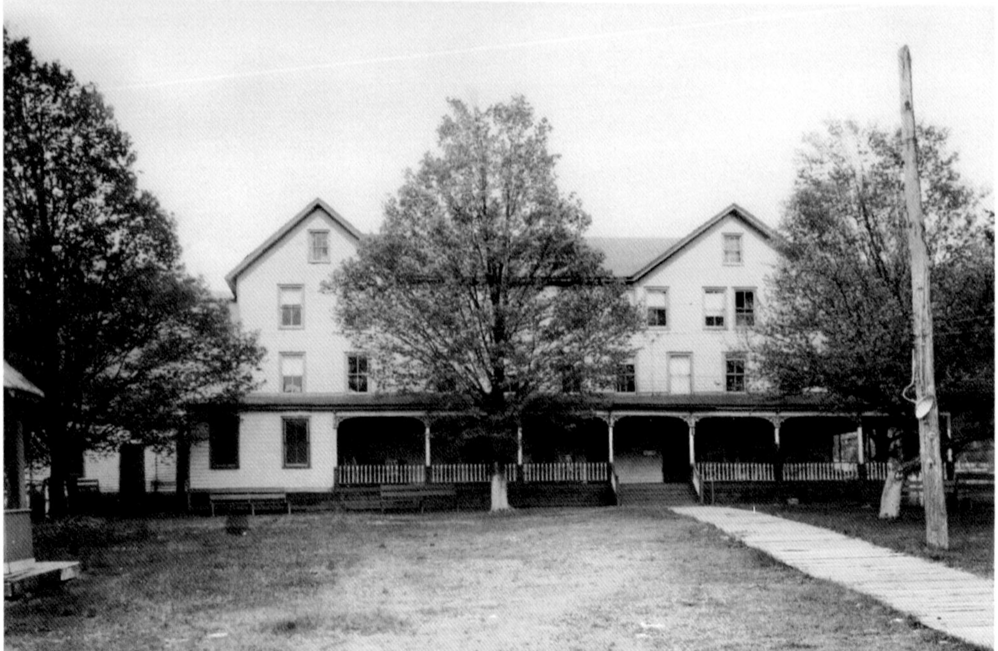

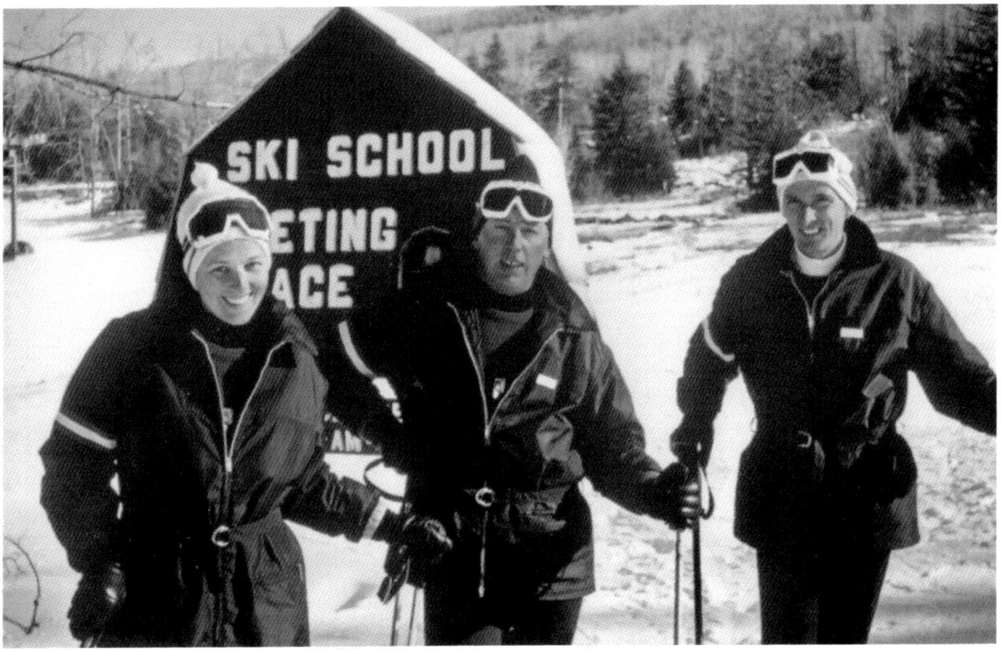

Pictured here are, from left to right, Edith (Shrems) Brody, Martin Jereb, and Ray Melz. They were early instructors of the ski school at Windham. (Courtesy of Edith Brody.)

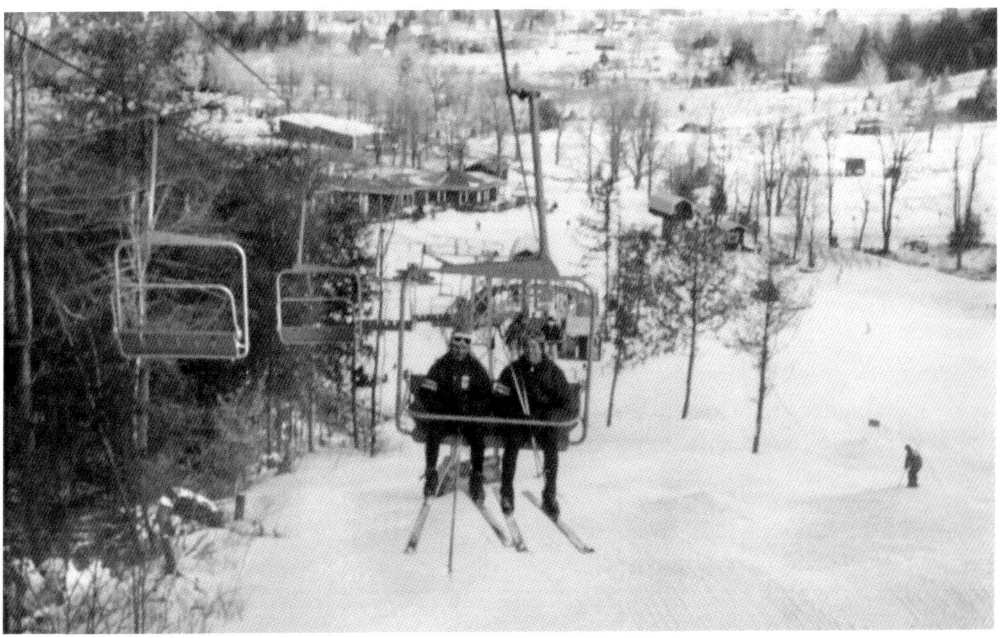

Windham Mountain opened in 1960 as the Cave Mountain ski area. This view from the chairlift shows the original lodge and base area in the mid-1960s. At this time, Windham also had an enclosed-cabin chairlift to the summit. (Courtesy of Edith Brody.)

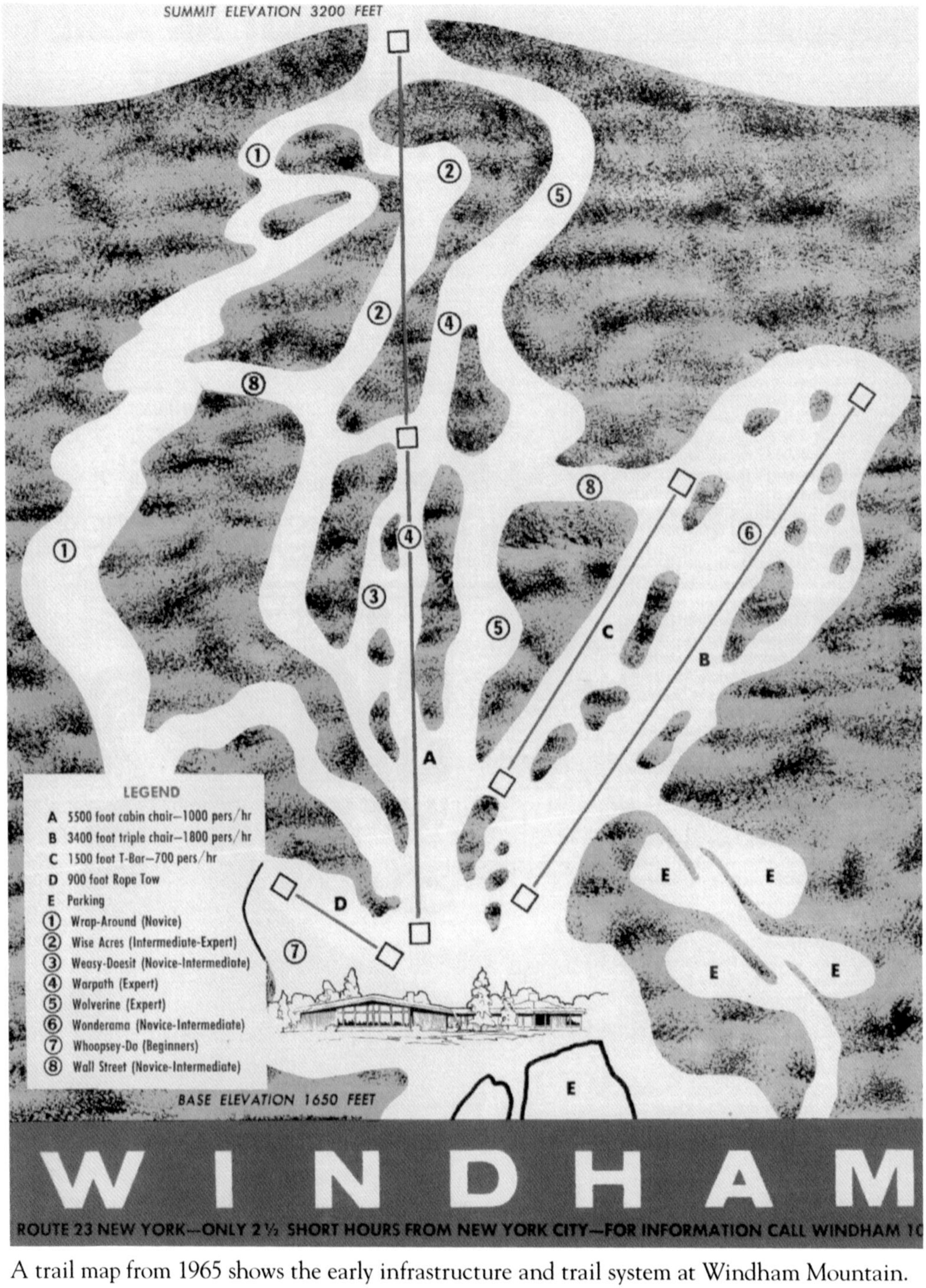

A trail map from 1965 shows the early infrastructure and trail system at Windham Mountain.

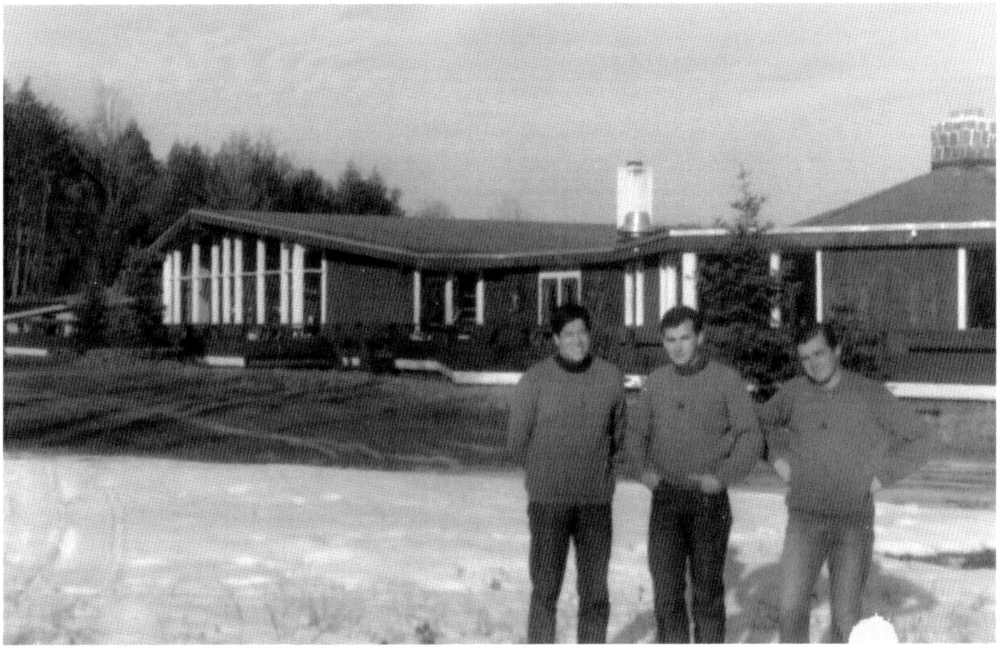

Three ski instructors from Argentina—Fito (left), Pedro (center), and Oswaldo—stand in front of the original base lodge, also known as the Sky Lodge, at Windham Mountain in the mid-1960s. This lodge burned late in the night in 1970. It was soon rebuilt only to replaced by yet another base lodge as the area grew. (Courtesy of Edith Brody.)

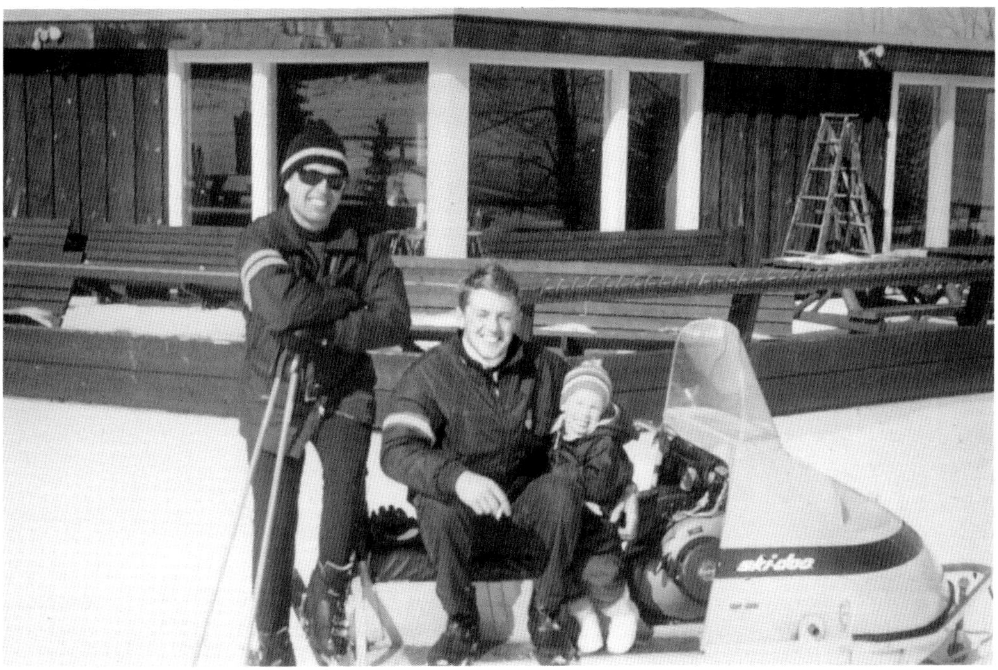

Dinko Bertonceli (left), a ski instructor from Argentina, poses with Jens Sirset and son Tor on a new Skidoo snowmobile in front of the original lodge at Windham. (Courtesy of Edith Brody.)

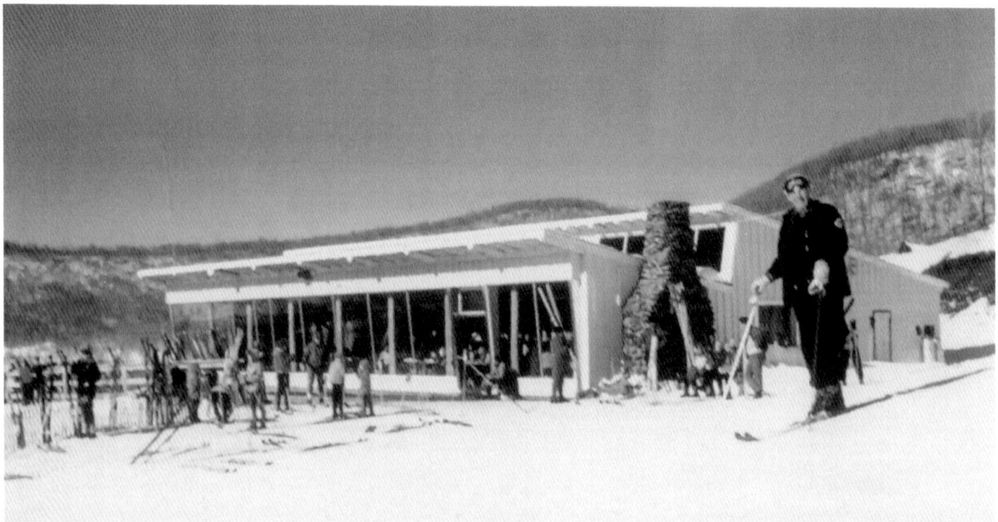

This close-up of this base lodge at the Roxbury ski area shows a solar design, unusual for the time. Painted a bright yellow, the lodge survived the area's closing in the early 1970s and is still in use today as a private hunting club amid the reforested ski trails. (Courtesy of Howard C. Lindemann.)

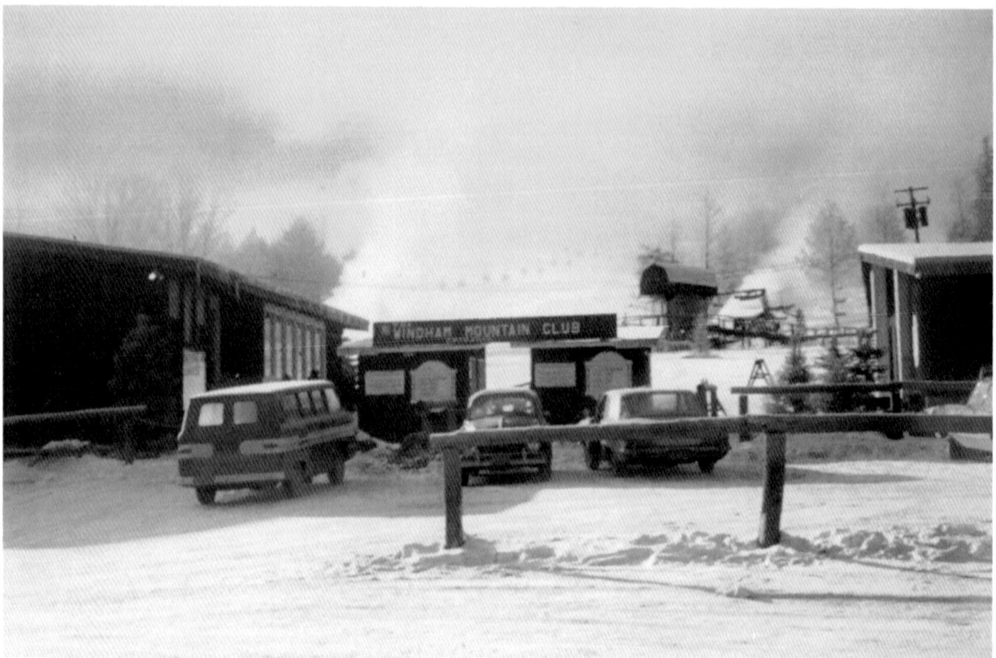

In 1965, Windham Mountain became the private Windham Mountain Club. Ski celebrities Stein Eriksen and Suzy Chafee, among others, made regular visits. In this image of the entrance to the ski area, a ground-based, artificial snowstorm can be seen in the background. Like nearby Hunter Mountain, snowmaking was well established here by the mid-1960s. (Courtesy of Edith Brody.)

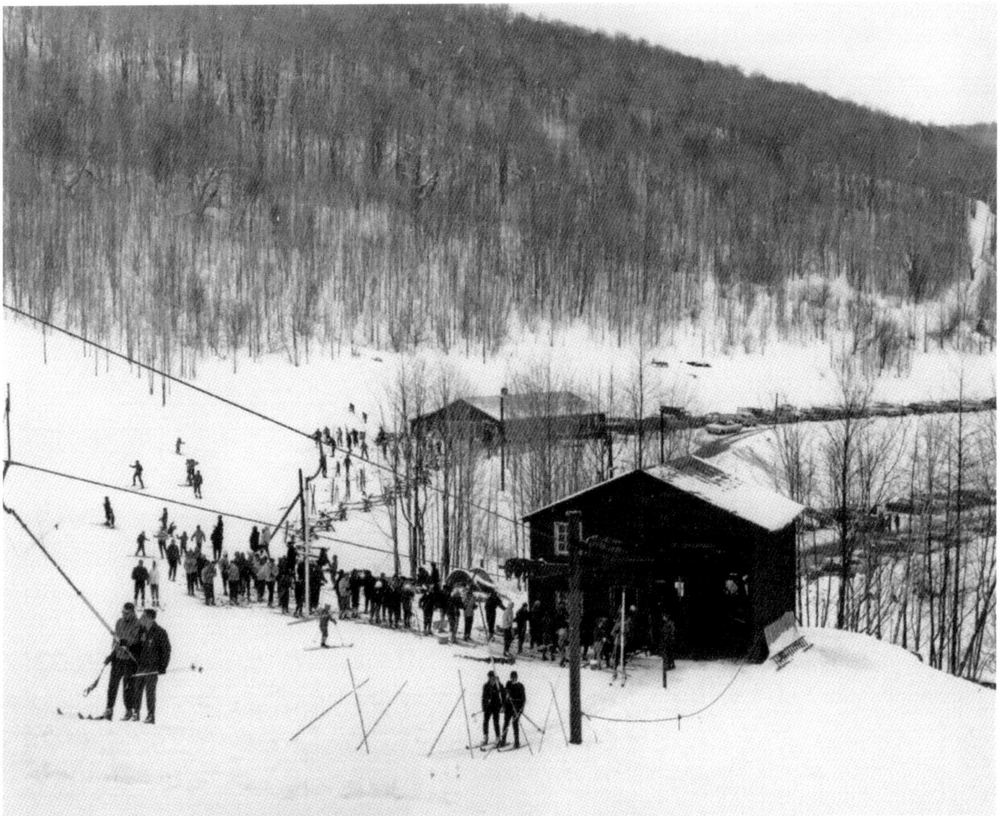

The north-side T-bar lift at Plattekill Mountain lasted over 40 years before being replaced by a used double chairlift from Belleayre Mountain. A high base elevation of over 2,300 feet and frequent lake-effect squalls ensured Plattekill long seasons. The building in the foreground is still standing. (Courtesy of Bea Hinkley.)

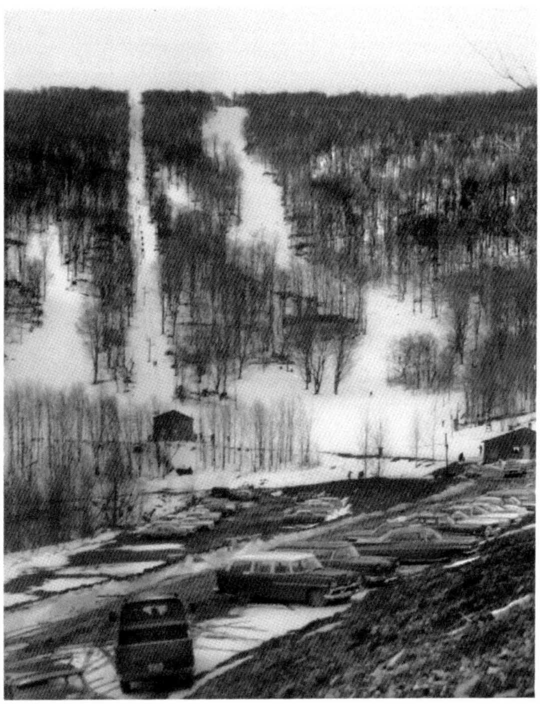

The view from the parking lot shows early north-side trail development at Plattekill Mountain. Brothers Gary and Sanford Hinkley joined together to build the trails on this side of the mountain and opened the area in 1959. (Courtesy of Bea Hinkley.)

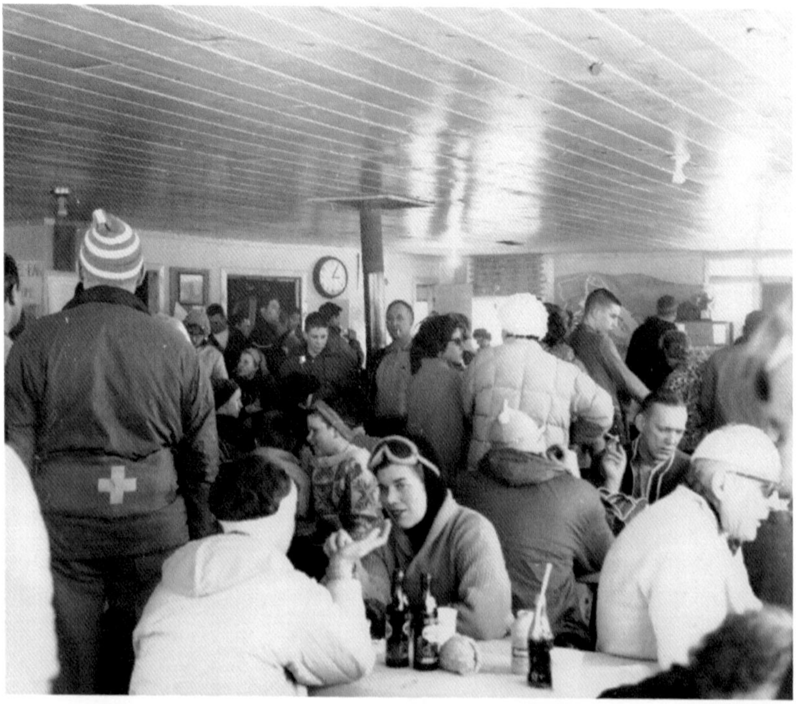

Here is a typical ski lodge scene in 1962: smoky, crowded, and the soda sipped by a straw. Posted in the background, the lift ticket prices for Plattekill are $3.50 for a full day on the T-bar. As lodges began to grow in size, a little of the small-town ambience was lost. (Courtesy of Bea Hinkley.)

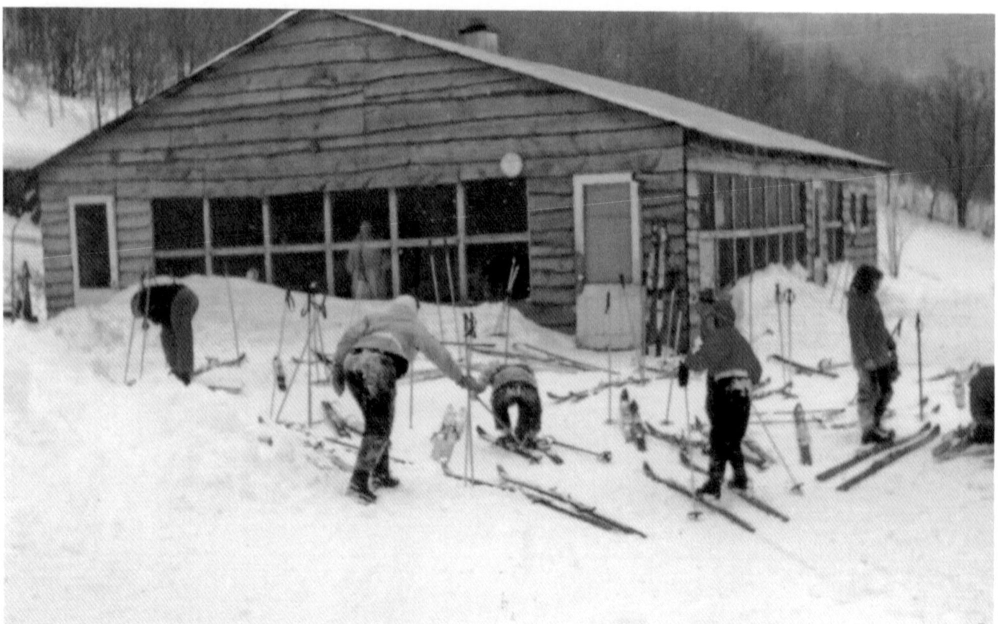

These skiers are parking their skis around the first base lodge at Plattekill Mountain, built in the early 1960s. (Courtesy of Bea Hinkley.)

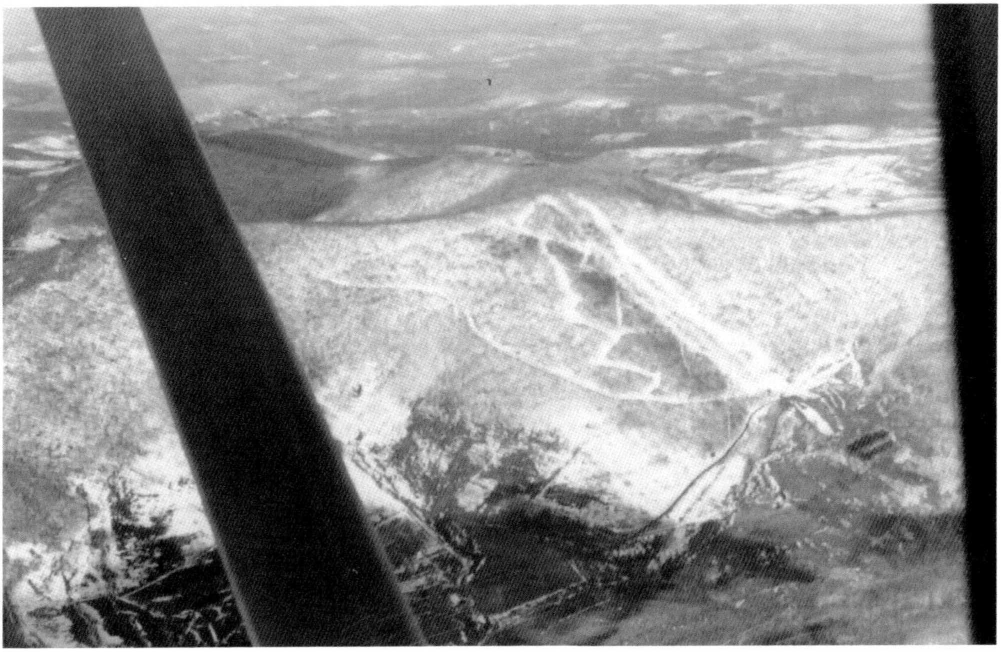

The early development of Plattekill Mountain is shown in this aerial view. The triple-chair side is yet to be developed. Behind the mountain, smaller hills in the background thin out to western New York State. (Courtesy of Bea Hinkley.)

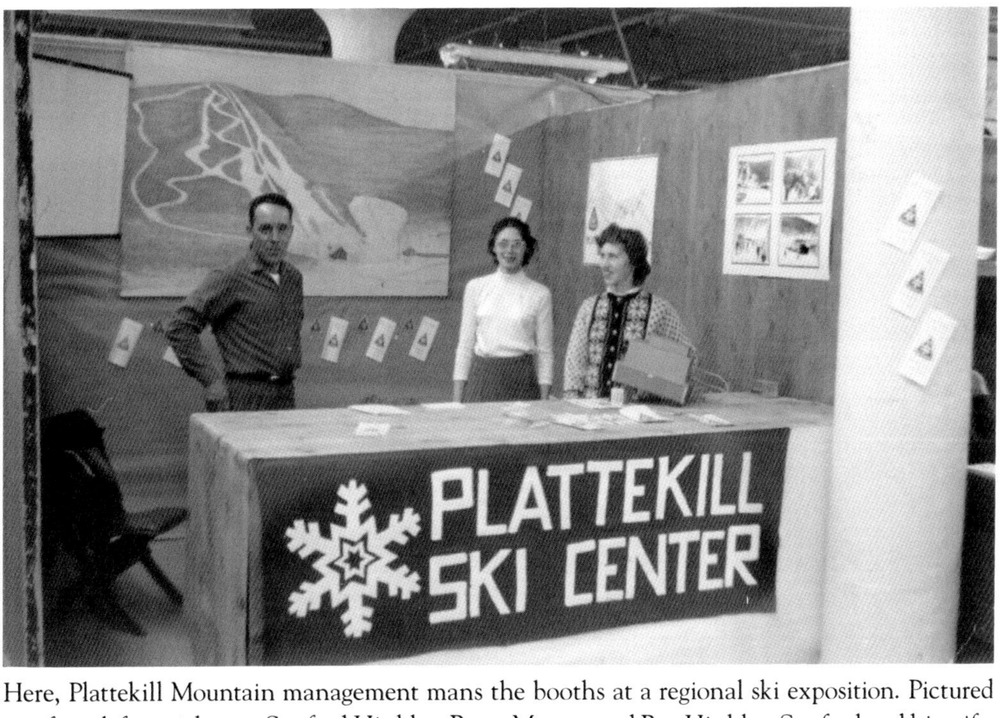

Here, Plattekill Mountain management mans the booths at a regional ski exposition. Pictured are, from left to right are, Sanford Hinkley, Betty Munro, and Bea Hinkley. Sanford and his wife, Bea, founded Plattekill Mountain. (Courtesy of Bea Hinkley.)

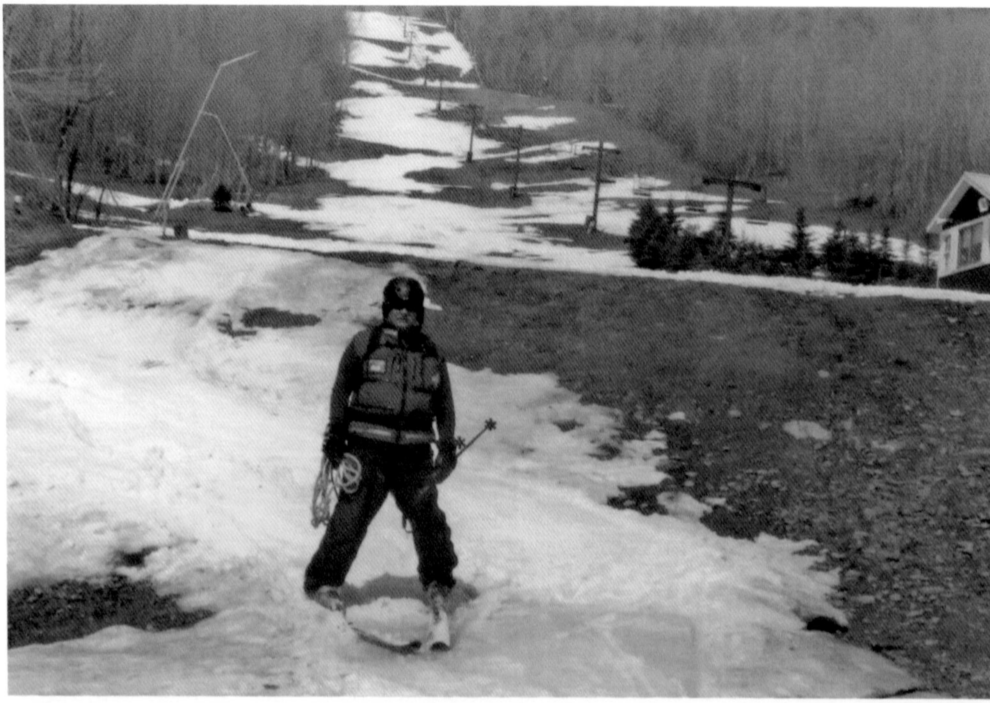

Bob Leonard, in full ski patrol regalia on a 78-degree day in early April, is getting ready to close the mountain for the season. This angle is looking up at the sun-drenched Face ski trail. Bob and his wife, Sue, ran the ski school for many years and then went on to join the ski patrol.

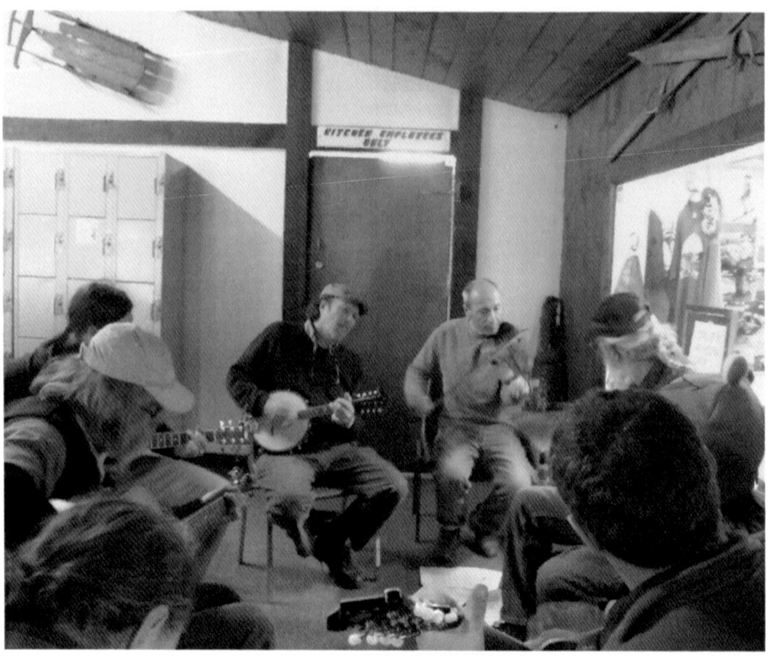

Members of the Plattekill Mountain ski patrol, the staff of the ski shop, and visiting skiers join in for an acoustic jam after the trail sweep at the end of the day. The scene here is just outside the kitchen and ski shop in the mid-level area and characterizes the informal nature of the ski area.

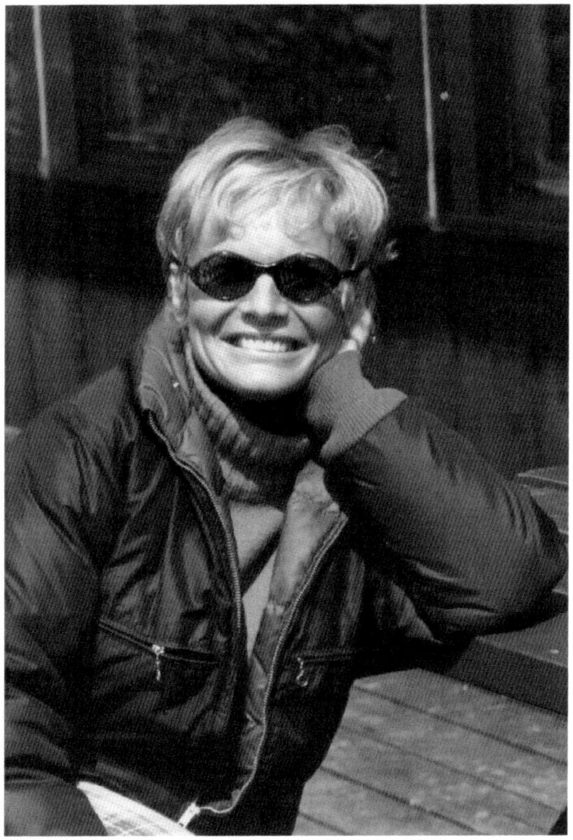

Bonnie Hinkley, pictured here, along with her husband, Gary, took over the operation of Plattekill Mountain in 1971 and ran it until the early 1990s. Allen, the son of Gary, took over mountain operations during the latter 1970s, while Bonnie, an avid skier herself, managed most of the office work in addition to handling public relations. (Courtesy of Gary Hinkley.)

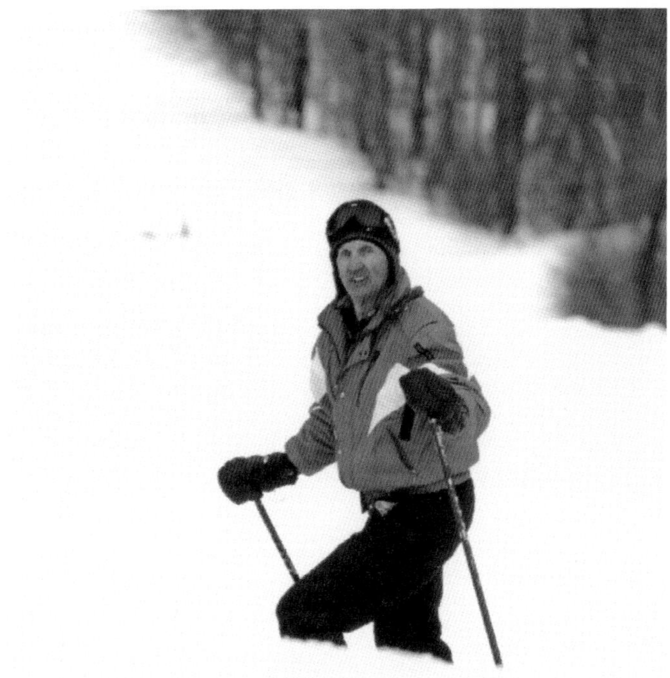

Sylvester Van Ort, simply known as "Van," could still bomb Plattekill's double-diamond Blockbuster trail at 80 years of age, leaving much-younger people in his wake. An ordained minister, Van would also preach the appreciation of the different qualities of snow and heavy weather to an enthralled audience around the fireplace in the base lodge. His recommendation for a long, healthy ski life: drink lots of orange juice.

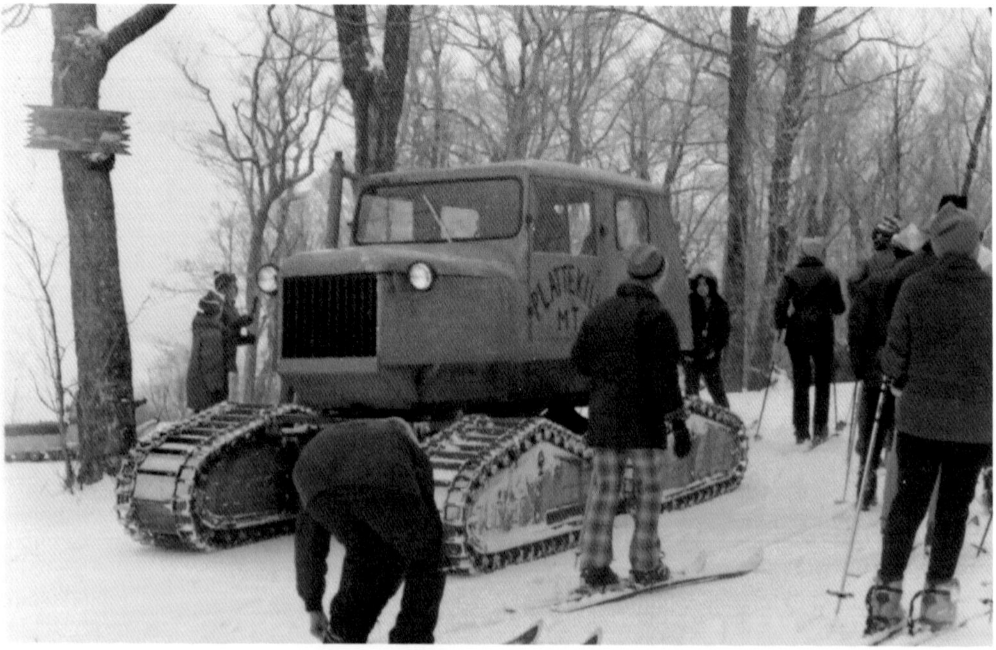

The Tucker packing machine is a magnet for skiers on the top of Plattekill Mountain in the mid-1960s. (Courtesy of Gary Hinkley.)

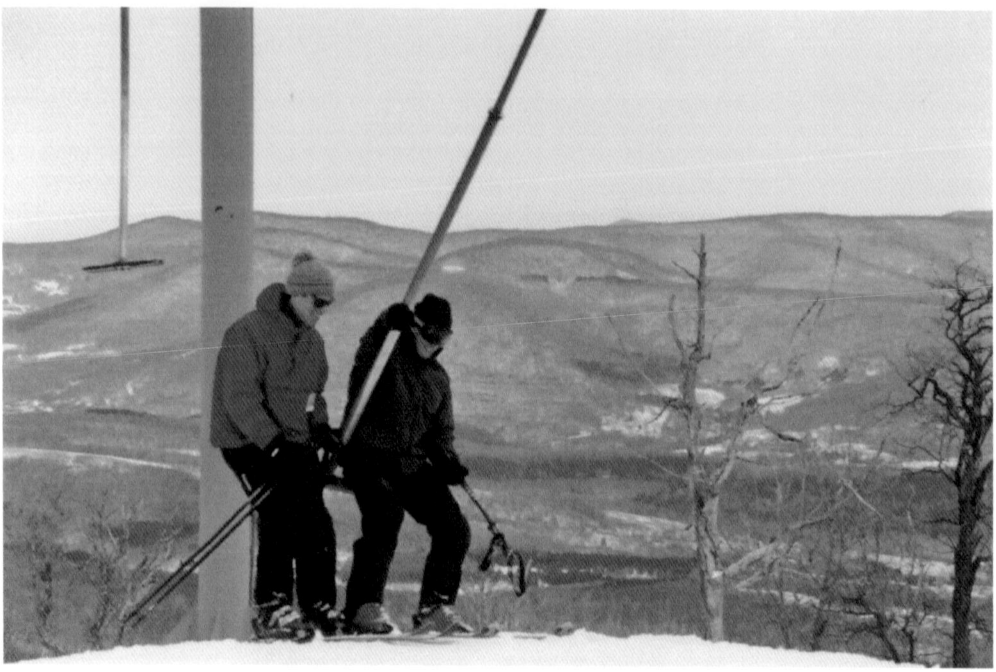

These skiers are getting ready to unload at the summit of Plattekill Mountain on one of the last days of the long, steep north-side T-bar. Snowboarders had more trouble staying on the lift than did skiers. Shovels were placed along thin-snow spots during thaws to keep snow on the track. It was "shovel as you go."

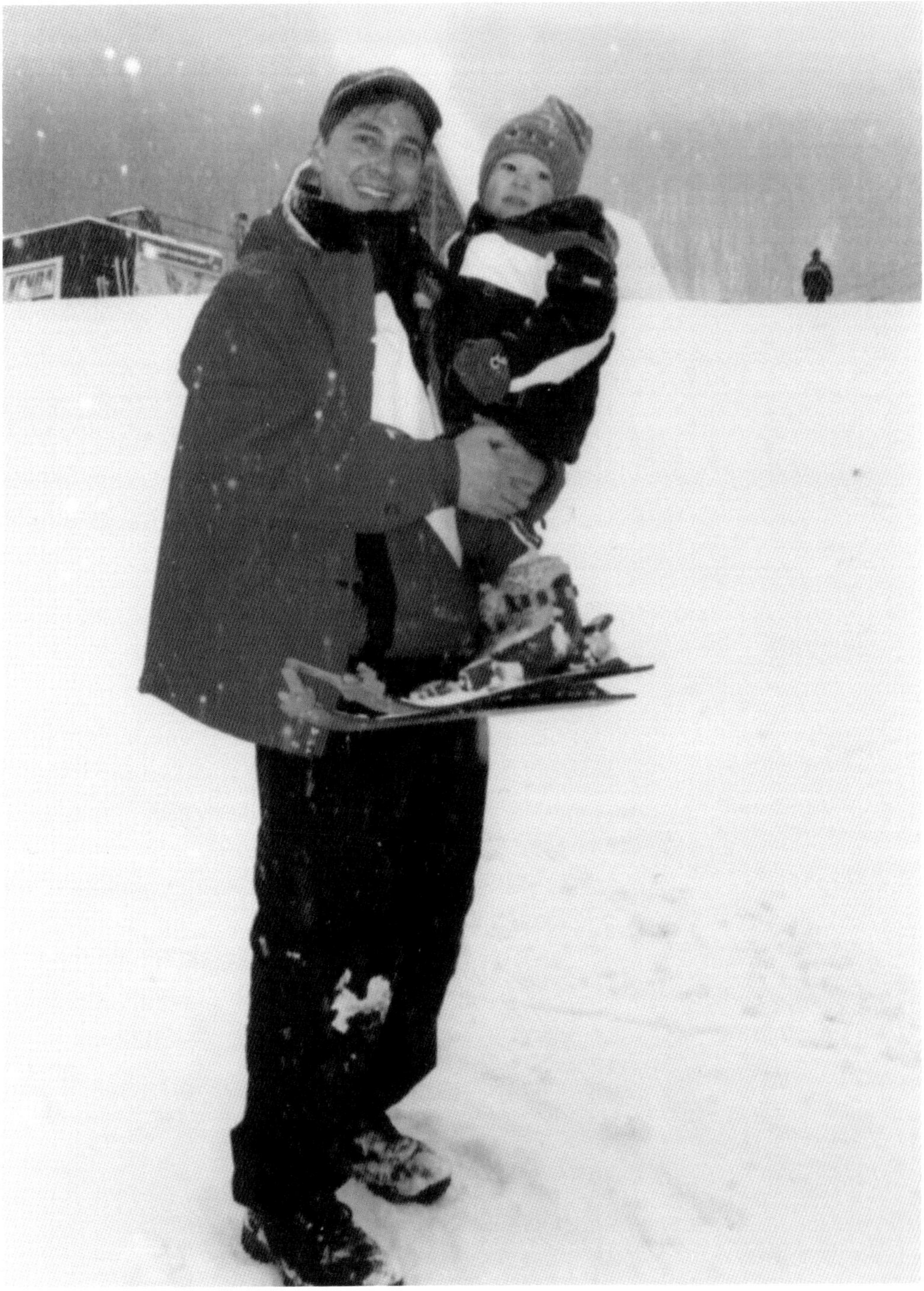

Laszlo Vajtay stands with son Nicholas in front of the base lodge at Plattekill Mountain in 2003. Along with his wife, Danielle, Laszlo purchased the old ski area in the early 1990s and, through hard work and dedication, made it a viable business. This is one of the last family-operated ski areas in New York State.

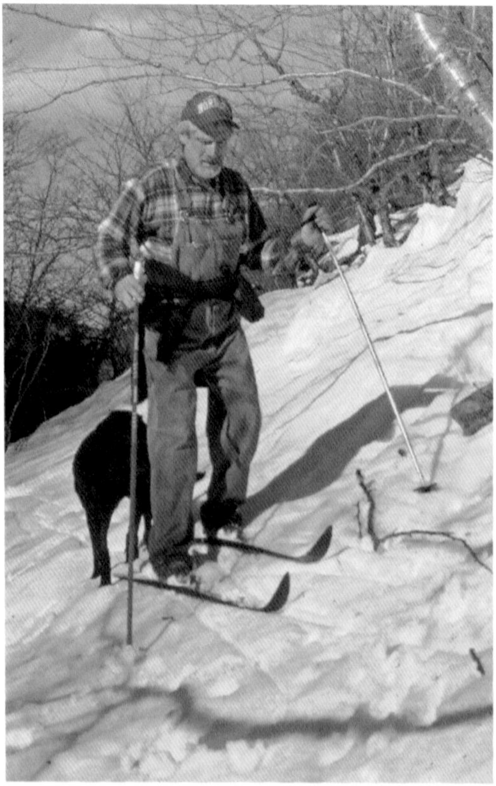

Local artist Farmer Artie, with his faithful dog trailing behind him, navigates the high point in elevation on the snow-packed Diamond Notch trail near Lanesville. This was another of the Department of Environmental Conservation (DEC)–designated backcountry ski trails listed by New York State in brochures in the 1950s. Many of these trails were either too narrow or steep for the average skier of the time.

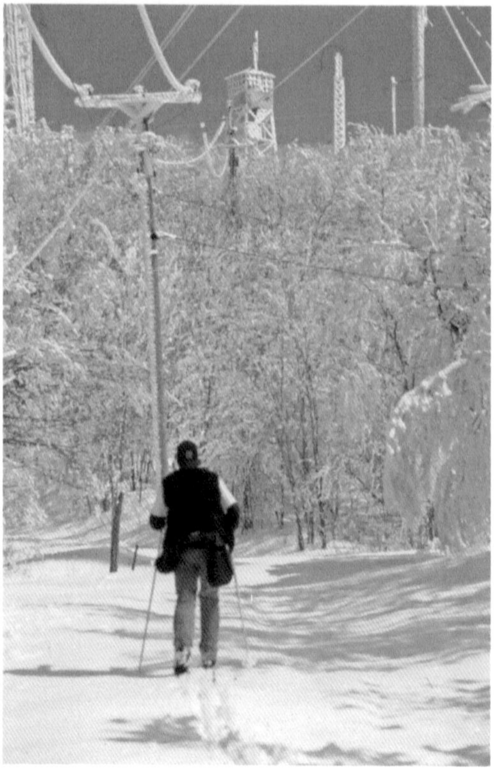

A cross-country skier nears the frosted towers of Mount Utsayantha on the edge of the northwest Catskills above Stamford. As ski technology improved through the years and gear became lighter, access to the backcountry snow became easier.

7

Belleayre Mountain and Points South

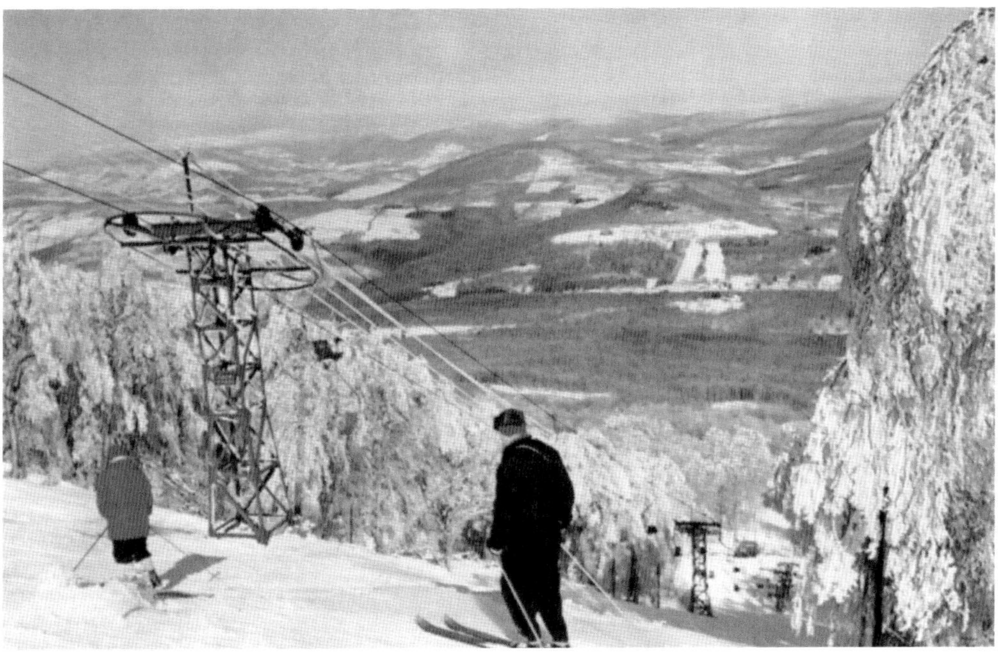

This view is looking in a northerly direction near the top of Belleayre Mountain. The far slopes in the center right were part of a golf course for the huge Grand Hotel. A small ski area was also located there.

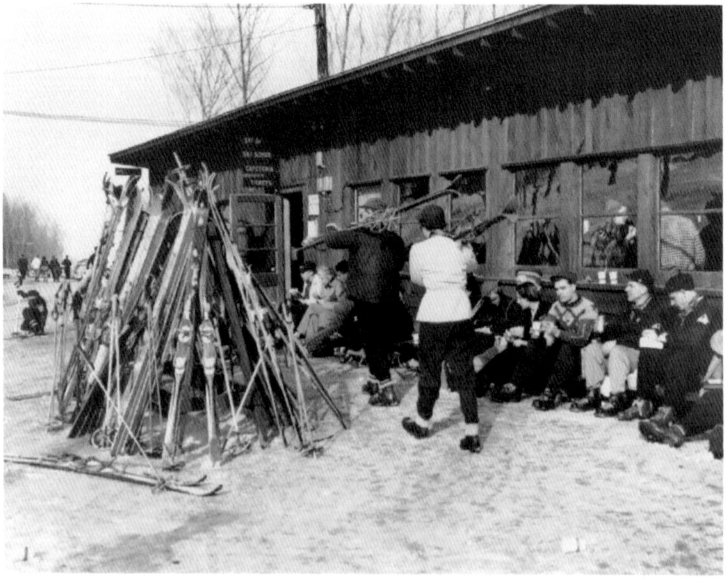

Here, skiers lounge in front of the original base lodge at Belleayre Mountain. The structure featured a gravel floor and outhouse. When the new lodge was built in 1950, this building was dismantled and moved farther down the mountain to be used as a maintenance shed. (Courtesy of Belleayre Mountain.)

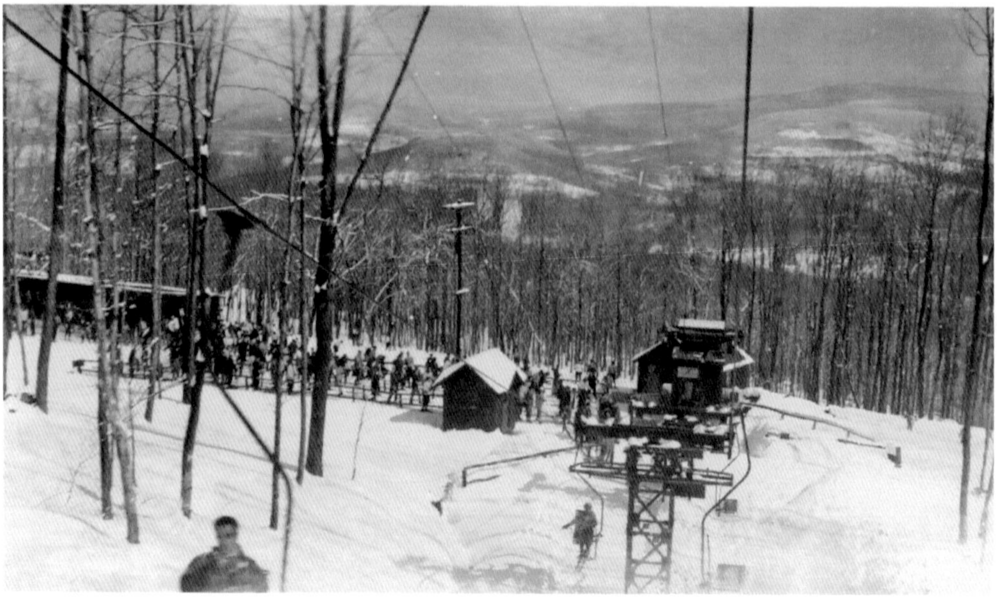

This very early photograph of the single chairlift at Belleayre Mountain was taken in 1949. A long lift line would quickly form on this low-capacity lift. To the left is the original base lodge with the gravel floor. With the highest base elevation in the Northeast at 2,584 feet, Belleayre was the leader in natural snow for the Catskills, with seasons often extending into April.

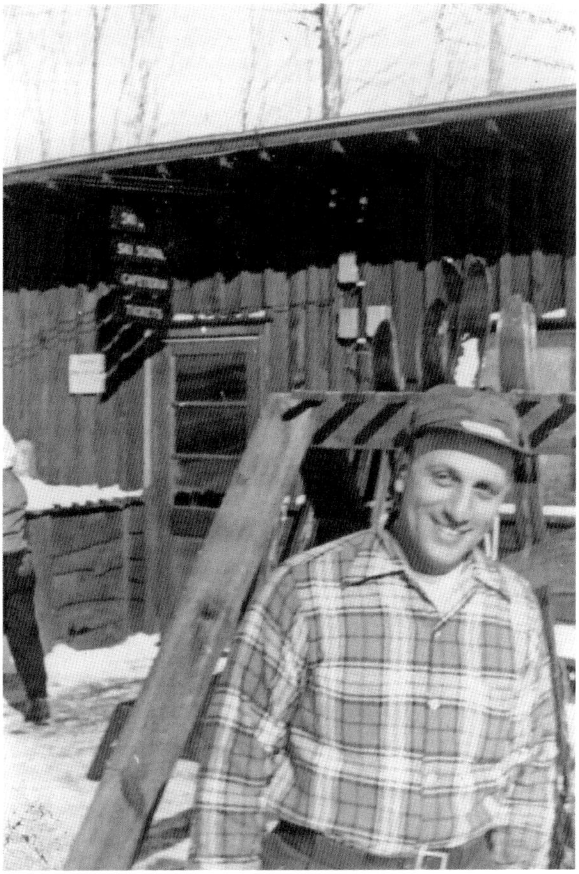

Mario Geofredi stands outside the entrance to the original base lodge at Belleayre Mountain. With his warm personality, he helped popularize the sport locally while working in ski-related businesses. (Courtesy of Belleayre Mountain.)

The second base lodge at Belleayre Mountain is shown in the early 1950s. The New York State ski area has expanded many times over the years and includes a whole separate novice area below this lodge.

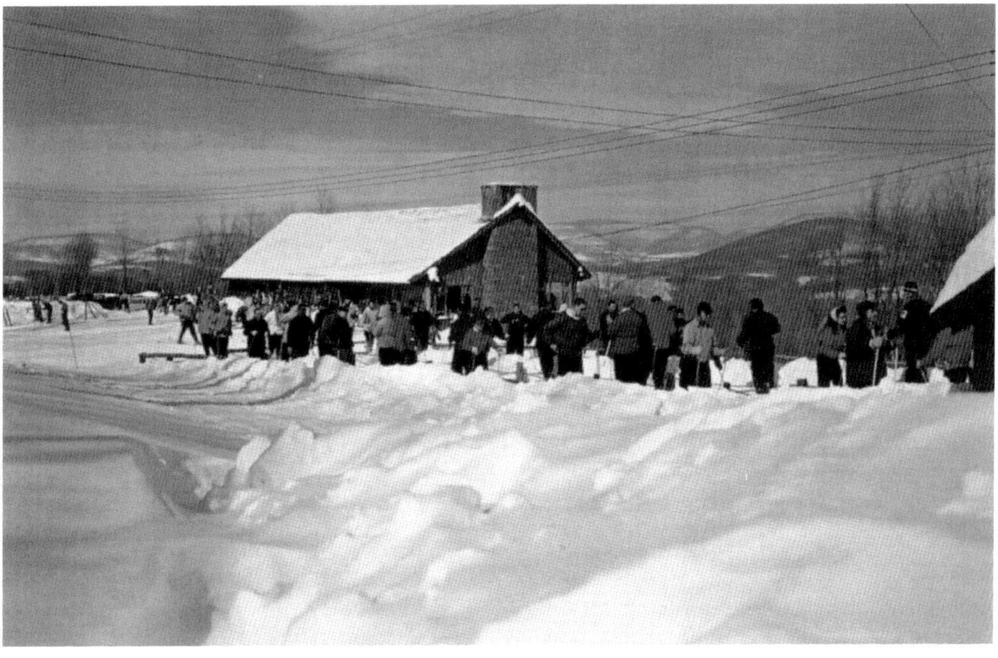

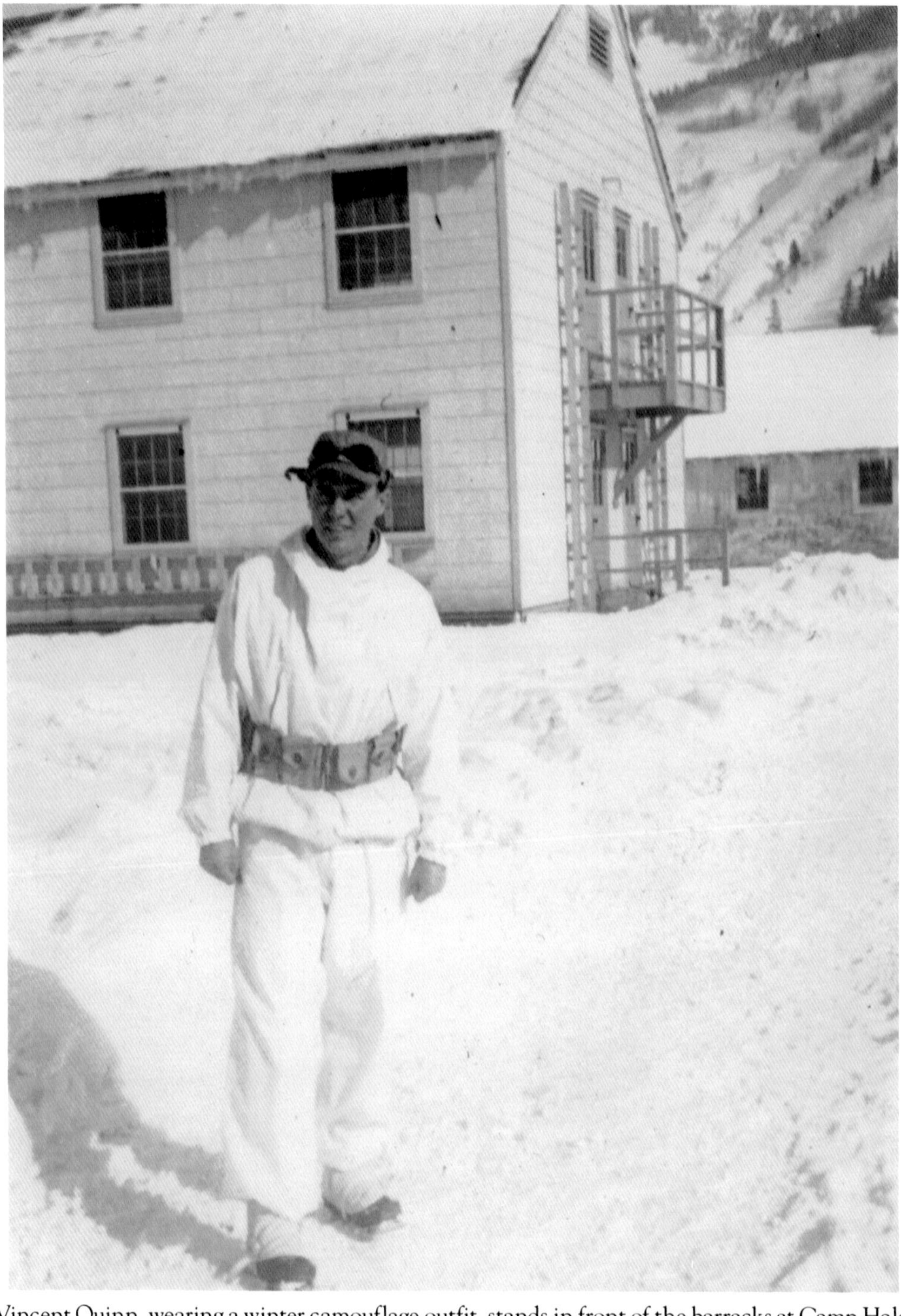

Vincent Quinn, wearing a winter camouflage outfit, stands in front of the barracks at Camp Hale, Colorado, in 1943. Like many of the 10th Mountain Division members who became pioneers in the ski industry, Vincent went on to start ski shops in the Catskill region and as far south as Newark, New Jersey.

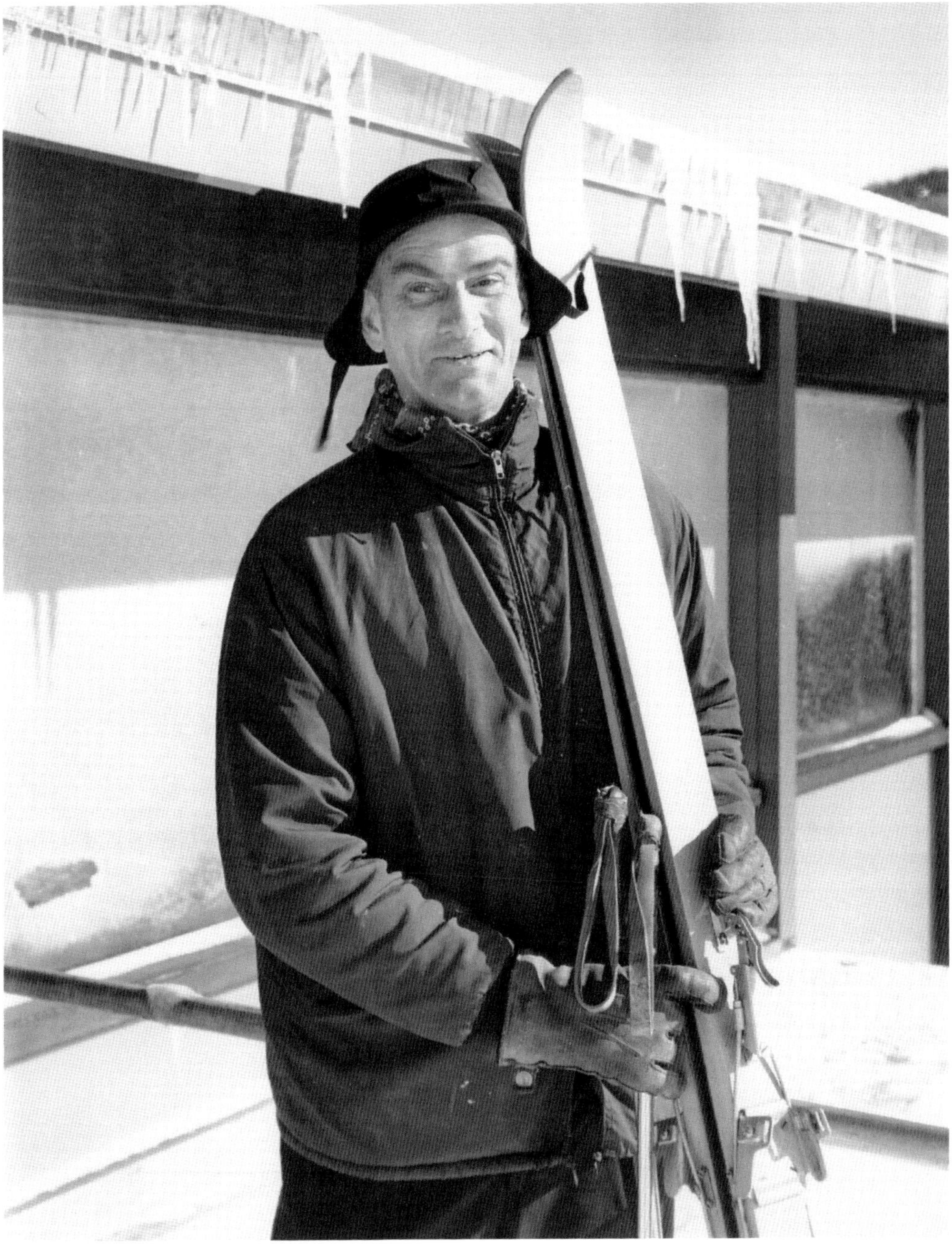

Art Draper became the first superintendent at Belleayre Mountain in 1949. As a member of the 10th Mountain Division and a returning World War II veteran, he had helped design the first three slopes at the mountain. Belleayre would go on to become the first ski area in New York State to have a chairlift. (Courtesy of Belleayre Mountain.)

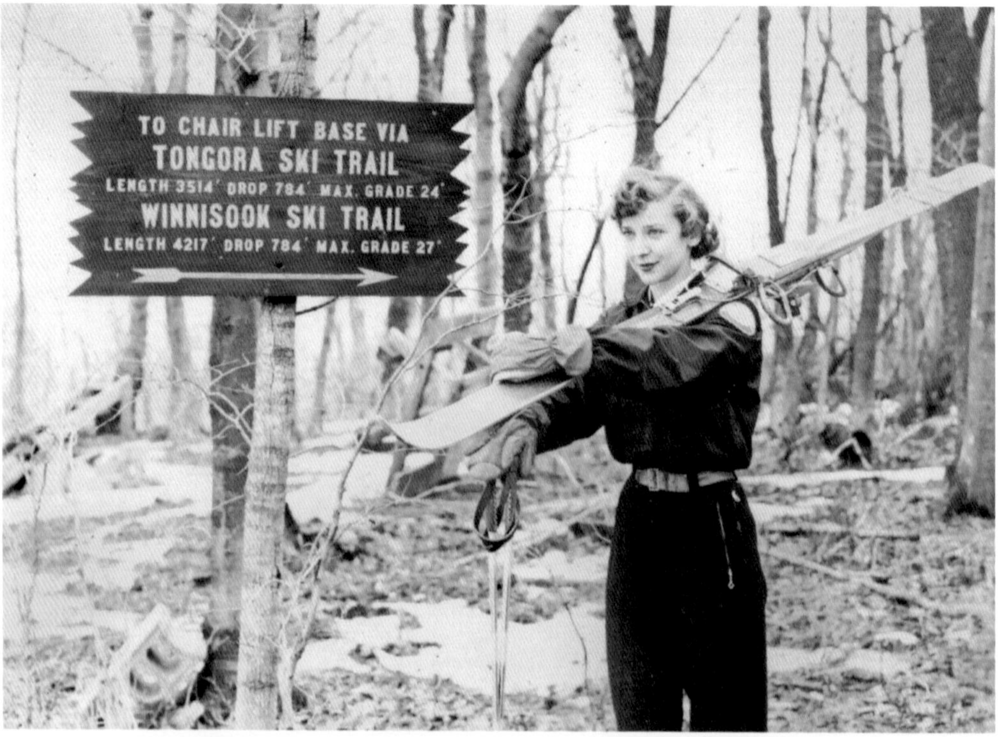

Joan Ballard stands in front of a detailed wooden sign that indicates the length of trail (4,217 feet), vertical drop (784 feet), and maximum grade (270 feet) at the top of Belleayre Mountain in 1957. (Courtesy of Trailsweepers Club.)

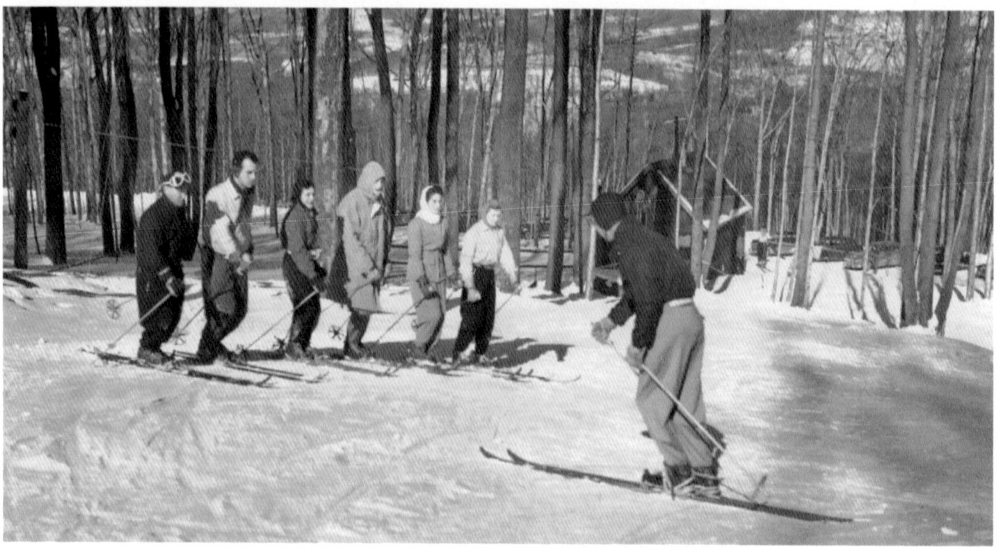

These skiers are getting a lesson in turning from a Belleayre Ski School instructor in the 1950s. The rope-tow building behind the skiers was eventually converted into a summit T-bar and then later replaced with a double chairlift on what is now named the Yahoo trail. (Courtesy of Belleayre Ski School.)

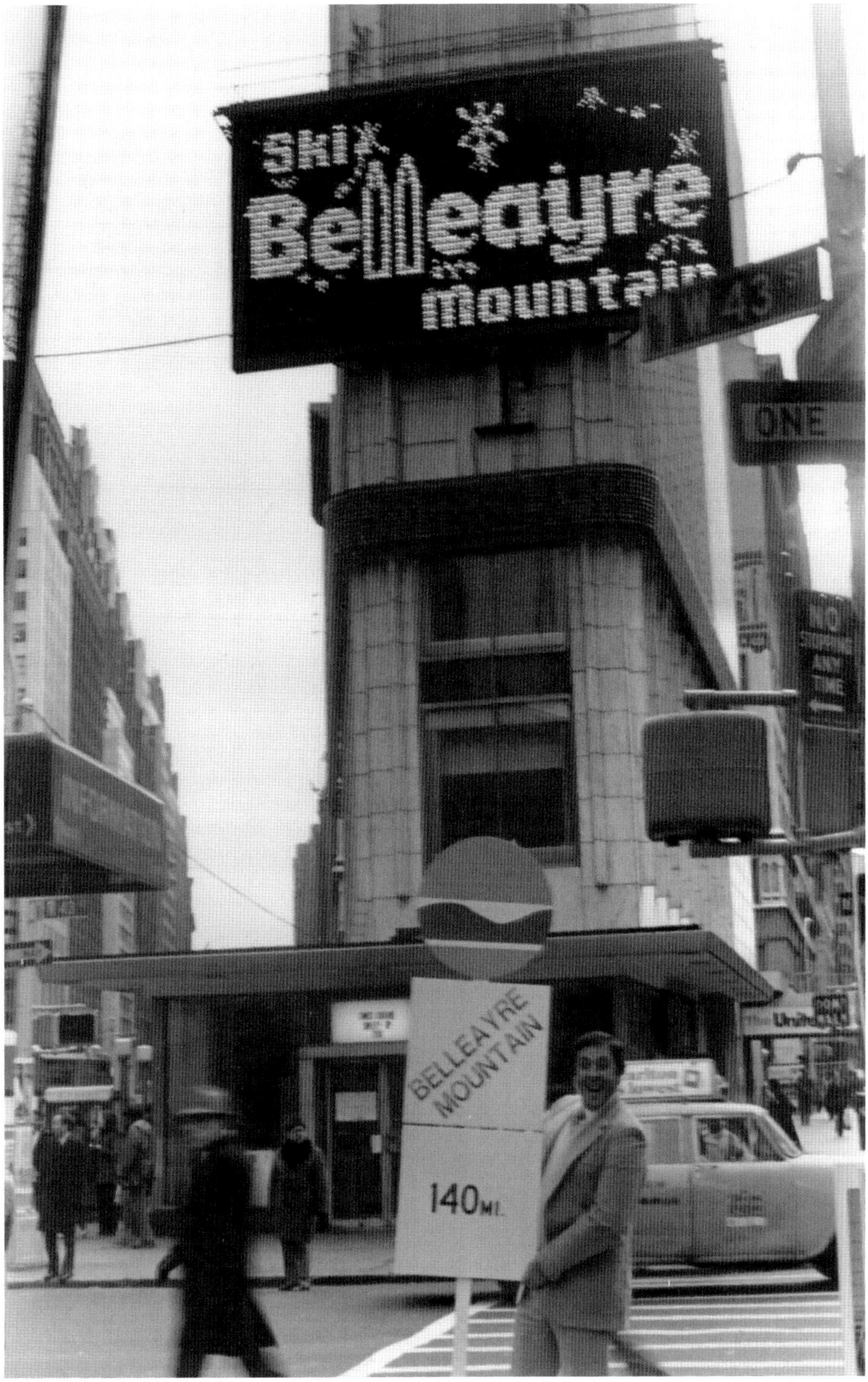

Pictured here in the middle of Times Square, Belleayre superintendent John Johnson is extolling the benefits of skiing at Belleayre Mountain. (Courtesy of Belleayre Mountain.)

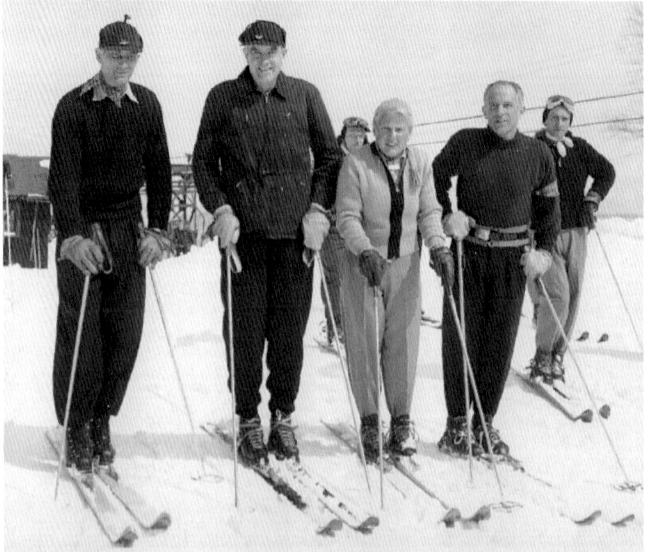

Pictured in front are, from left to right, Art Draper, William Averell Harriman, Dot Nebel, and her husband, Charlie, who helped coach Olympic skier Andrea Mead. Dot helped design the area, including the layout of the trails. She qualified for the 1940 Winter Olympics, but the games were never held because of World War II. Belleayre honored Dot by naming a wide racing trail after her. (Courtesy of Belleayre Mountain.)

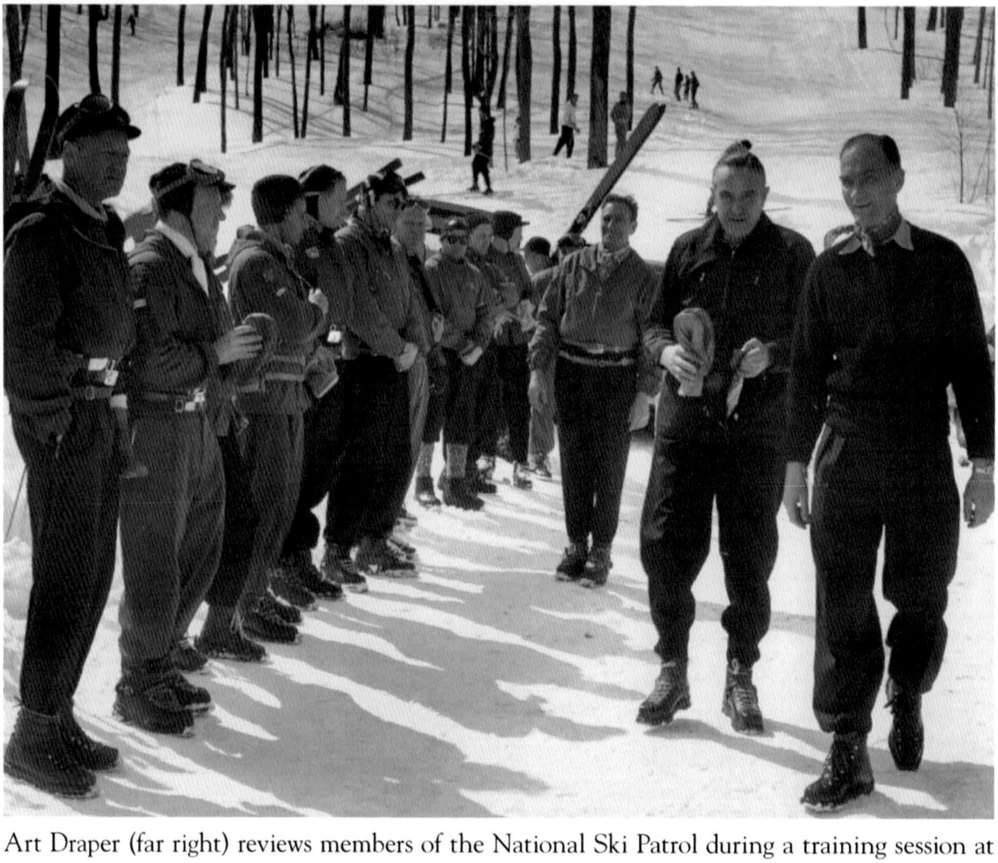

Art Draper (far right) reviews members of the National Ski Patrol during a training session at Belleayre Mountain. To his left is William Averell Harriman, an avid skier and governor of New York State from 1954 to 1958. Harriman created the Sun Valley ski area in Idaho and was a big promoter of New York State skiing. (Courtesy of Belleayre Mountain.)

Posing in front of the base lodge at Belleayre are, from left to right, Cliff Bellows, Vic Glider, and Vincent Quinn. Bellows, a former superintendent of Belleayre Mountain, went on to run the food concessions there in addition to operating the Base Station restaurant and ski shop at the Highmount Post Office location. The building in the upper background was later removed to make room for a slope under the high-speed quad chairlift.

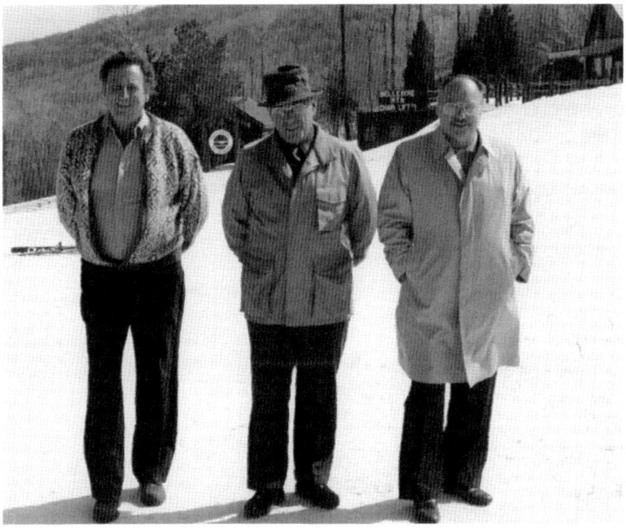

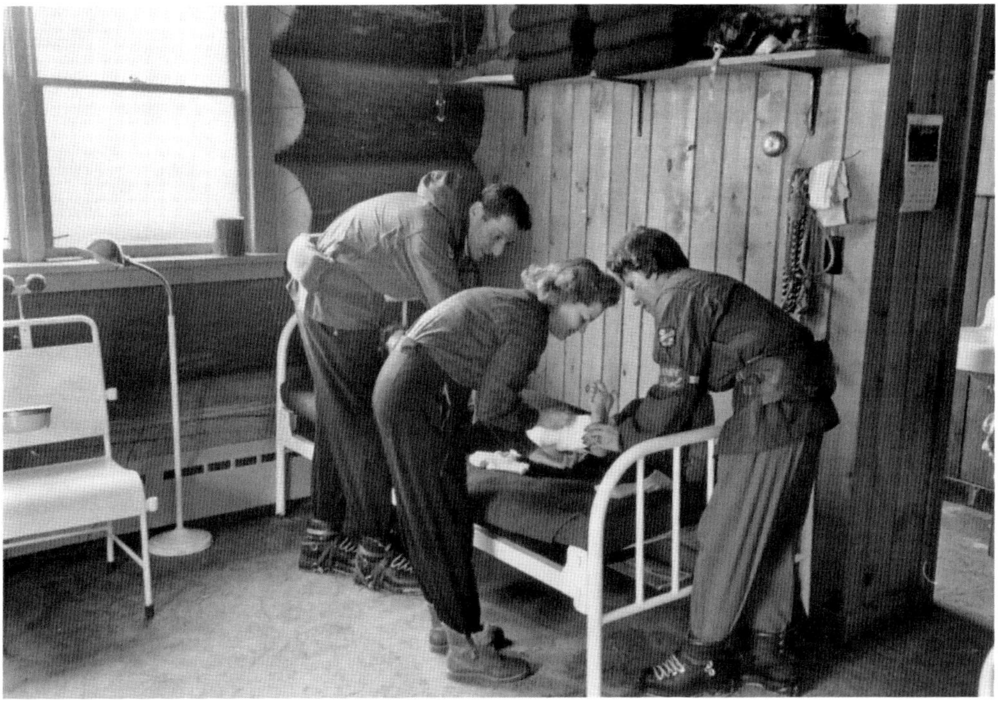

Pictured here from left to right, Jay Reichback, Elsie A. Kent, and an unidentified ski patroller tend to an injured skier in the same area of the lodge that is used today. The National Ski Patrol began in 1938 in Stowe, Vermont, under the direction of Charles Minot "Minnie" Dole. The firm membership requirements have expanded to include all levels of emergency training. (Courtesy of Belleayre Mountain.)

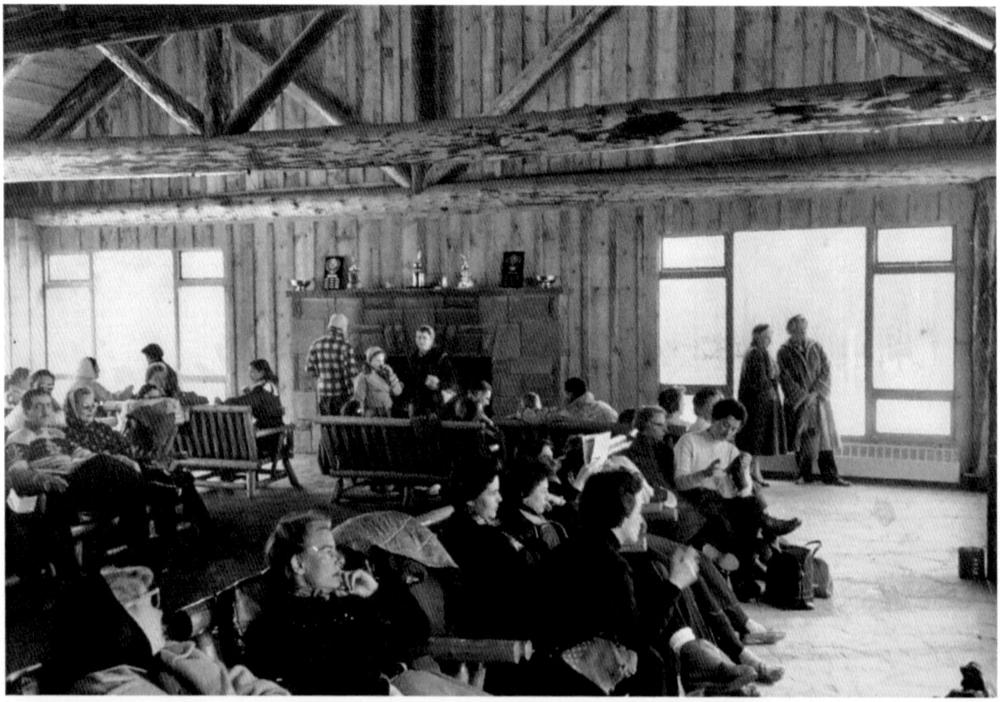

It was a relaxed atmosphere with padded Adirondack-chair seating in the newly built Belleayre Mountain lodge in the early 1950s. The building's large logs were salvaged from a massive blowdown during a fierce windstorm in the Adirondack Mountains in the early 1950s. (Courtesy of Belleayre Mountain.)

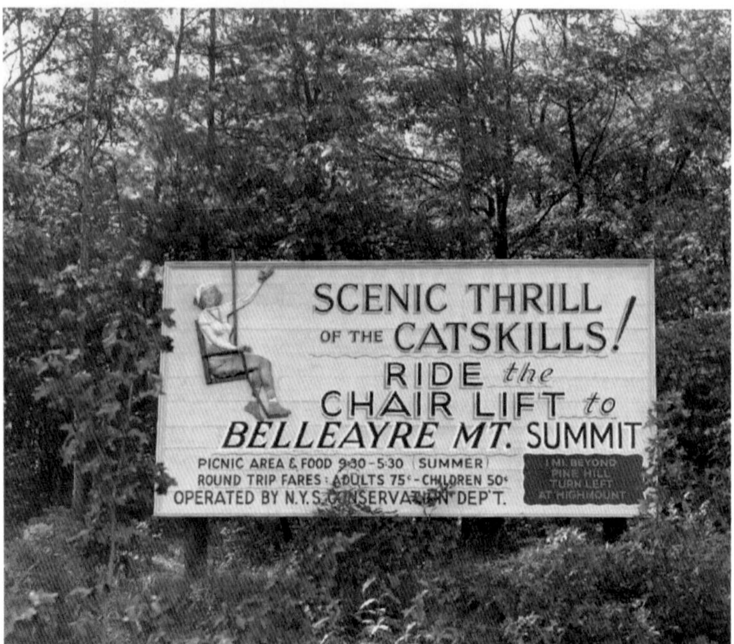

A large, handcrafted billboard on old New York Route 28 extols the thrills of riding to the top of Belleayre Mountain in the summer. The chairlift was a big tourist attraction for many years, and it helped employ many of the local residents. (Courtesy of Belleayre Mountain.)

A young woman is going solo up the single chairlift for a promotional picture at Belleayre Mountain. The lower background shows the patchwork of open fields of Fleischmanns and Halcott Valley villages leading up to Bearpen and Vly Mountains. The chairlift, ready for the 1949 ski season, was the first one in New York State.

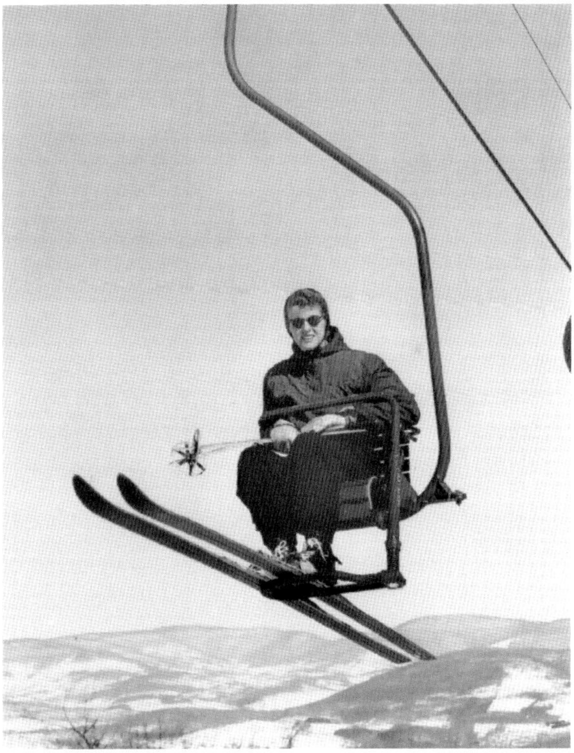

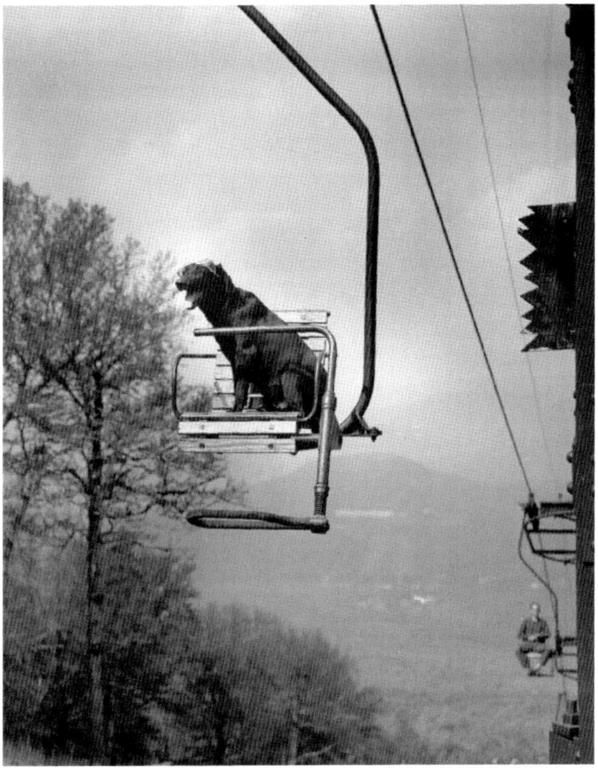

This dog must have met all the special requirements to get on a single chairlift at Belleayre Mountain. Art Draper brought his dog to many lifts in the Northeast and used him for promotions. Before the installation of the lift, skiers would hike or sidestep up the mountain to ski down on the woody trails. (Courtesy of Belleayre Mountain.)

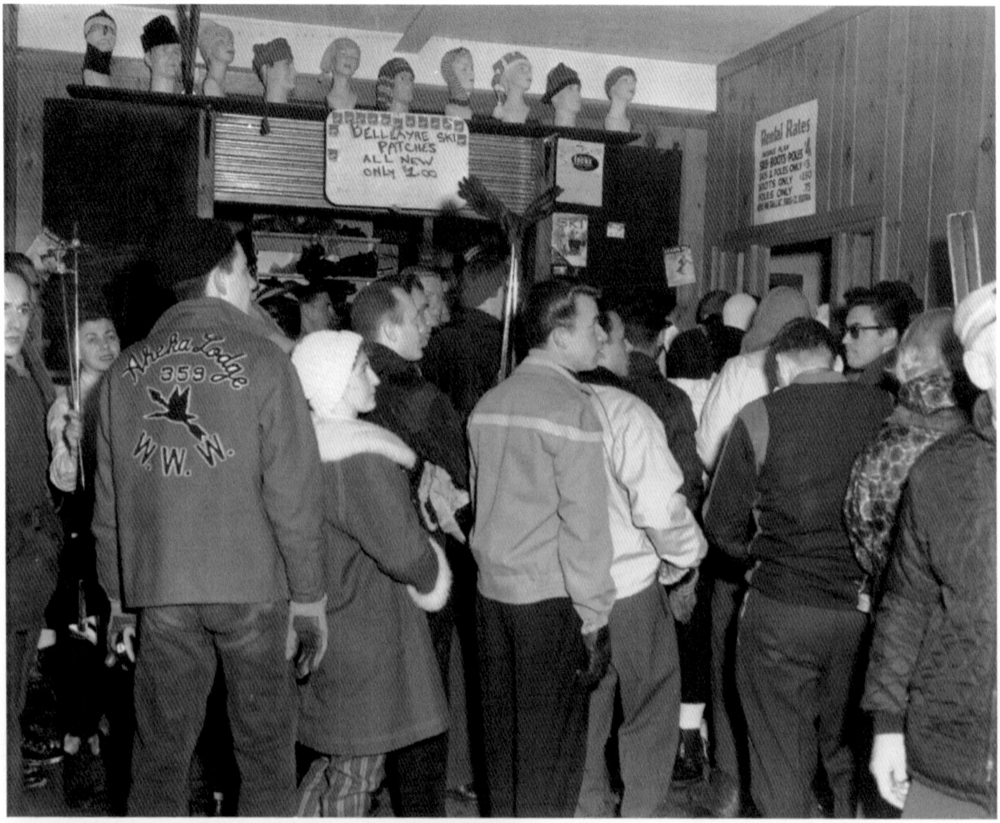

Skiers funneling into the rental area in the Belleayre Ski Shop are shown in 1956. The wonderful handwritten sign near the mannequin heads advertises new ski patches, which many people collected at the time, for $1. Ski, boot, and pole rentals were $4.

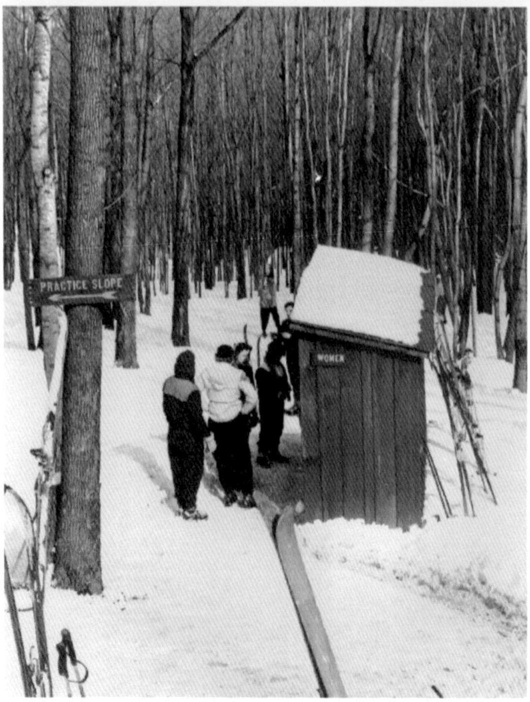

As evidenced in this image of an outhouse located near the main lodge at Belleayre Mountain, amenities were hard to come by at many of the first lodges in the Catskills. The facilities had gravel floors and no electricity, and it would be a slow process for some ski areas to modernize.

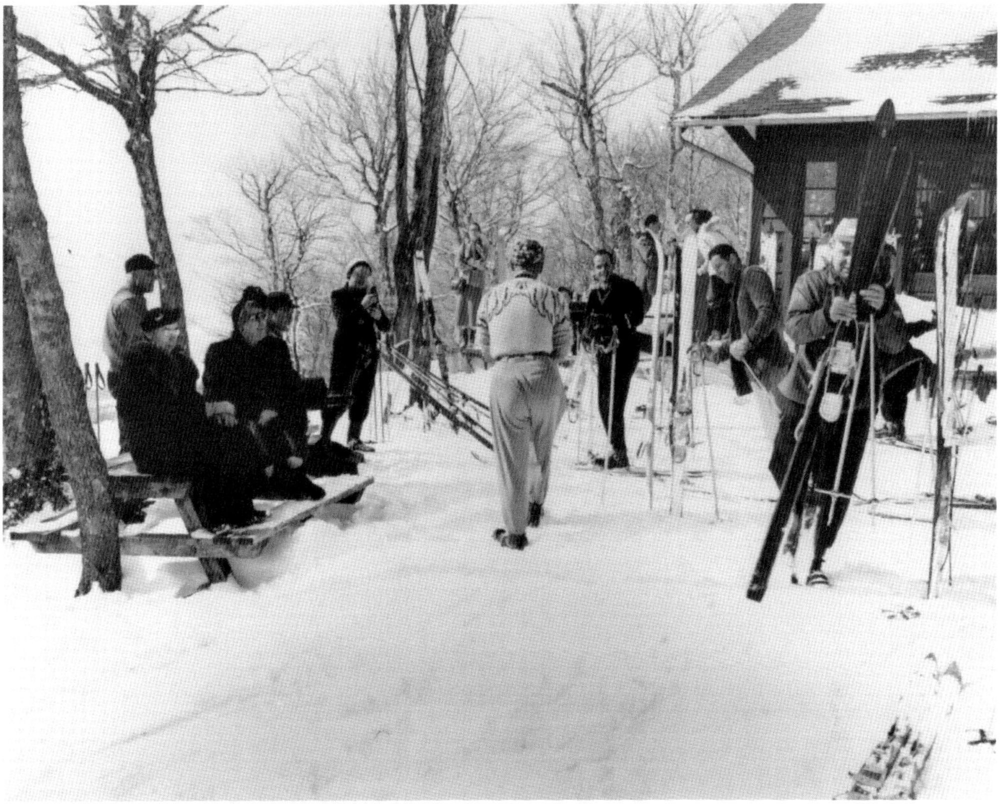

Skiers and sightseers mingle together in the mid-1950s at the summit lodge at Belleayre Mountain, located at 3,429 feet. The ladies donning full-length fur coats, seen sitting on the benches at left, probably bought a single ride for 50¢. By the 1960s, single-ride tickets had been discontinued. (Courtesy of Belleayre Mountain.)

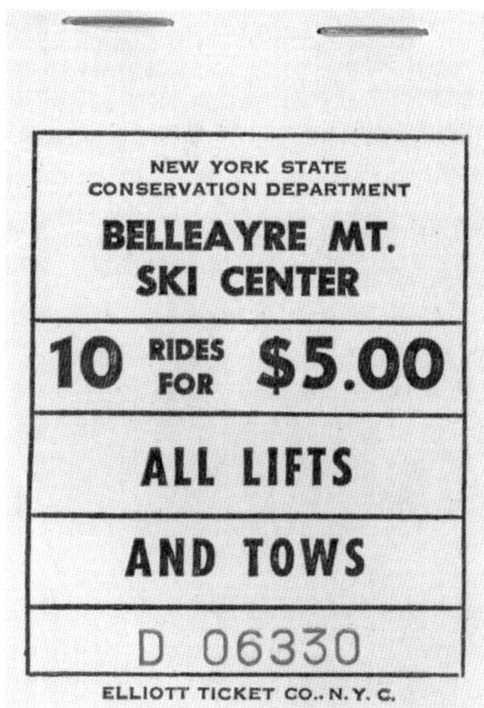

These are the early lift-ticket packages for Belleayre Mountain. Spectators would also buy single-ride tickets to see the view from the summit lodge. (Courtesy of Belleayre Mountain.)

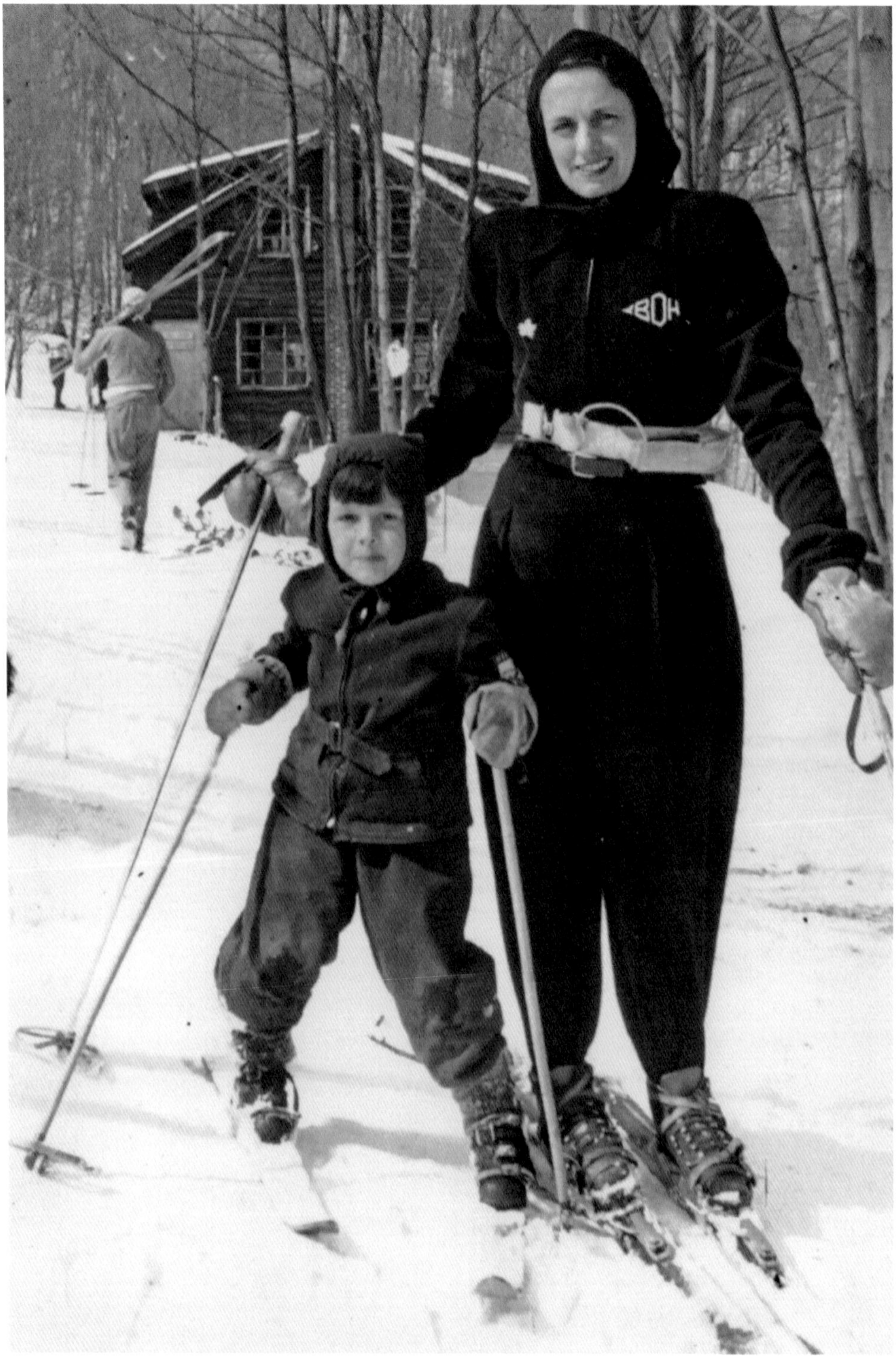

A young Phil Davenport tries to keep his footing standing next to his mother, Blanche. (Courtesy of Phil Davenport.)

Posing here are, from left to right, Dan Morehouse, Judy Dewey, and John Clake. Dan was the head of the ski patrol at Highmount from the mid-1950s to the 1980s. (Courtesy of Trailsweepers.)

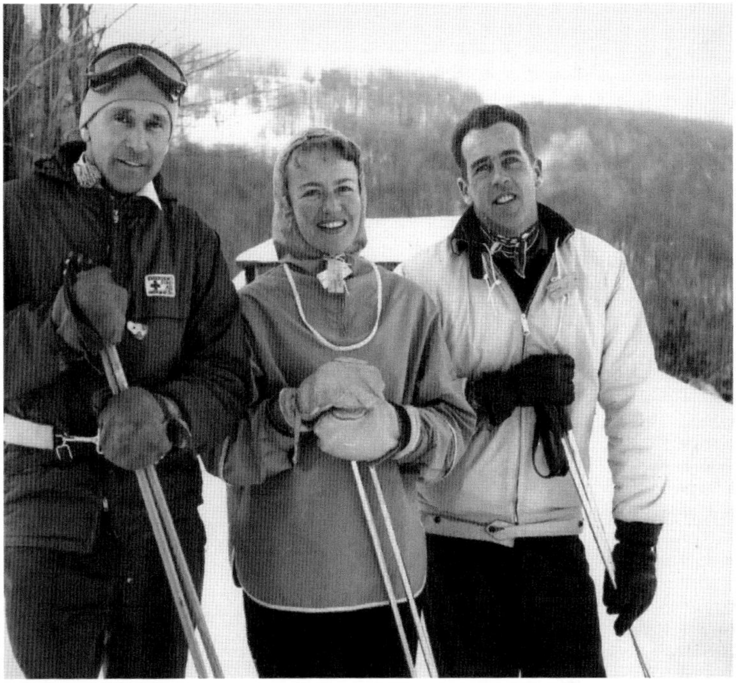

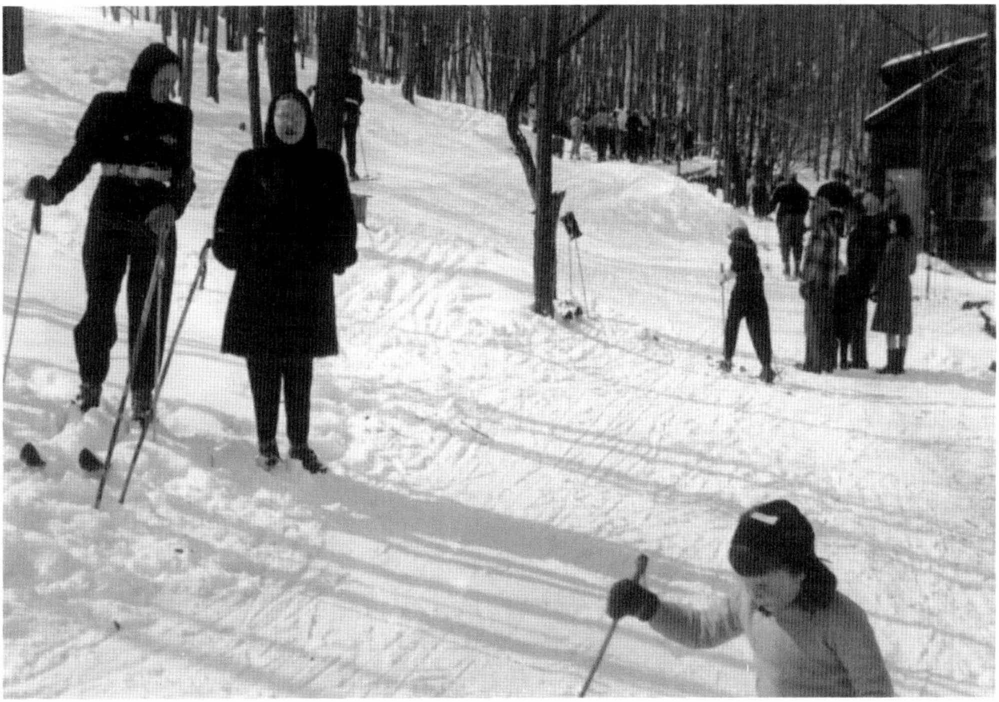

The first trails at Highmount were woody in nature. Some gradually became wide slopes. Skiers in the far background are queuing up by the lodge to take the first of three rope tows in tandem to reach the summit. Standing to the left are Blanche (far left) and Witte Davenport. (Courtesy of Phil Davenport.)

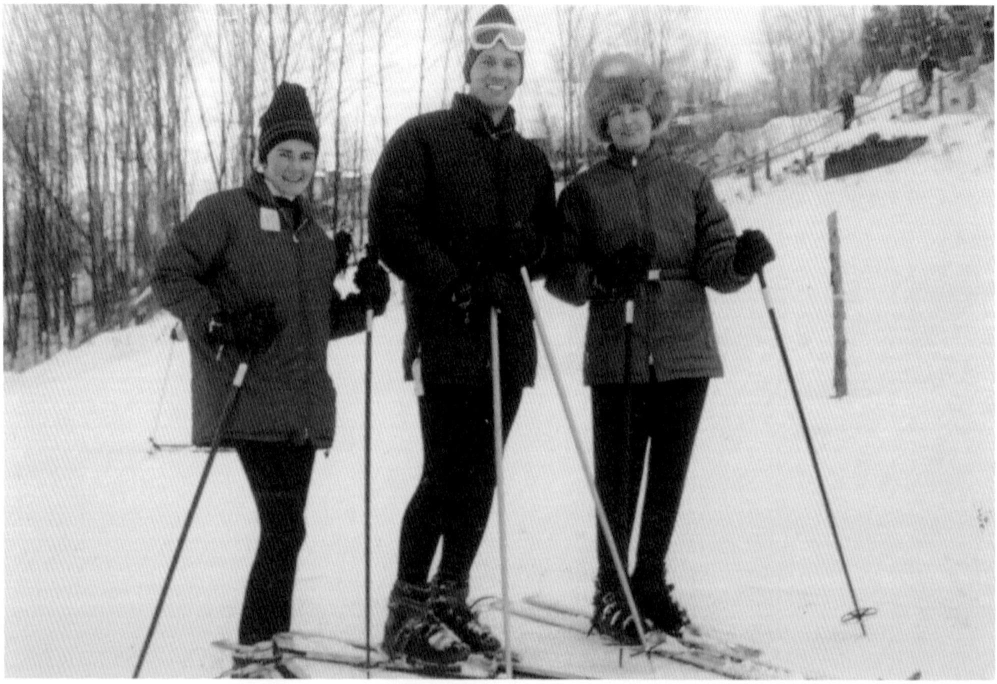

Posing slopeside in 1969 are, from left to right, Anne, Phil, and Blanche Davenport. The family ran the area from the beginning of 1947 until well into the 1980s. After Highmount closed under different management in the mid-1990s, there has been constant chatter about Belleayre Mountain ski area annexing the old slopes. (Courtesy of Phil Davenport.)

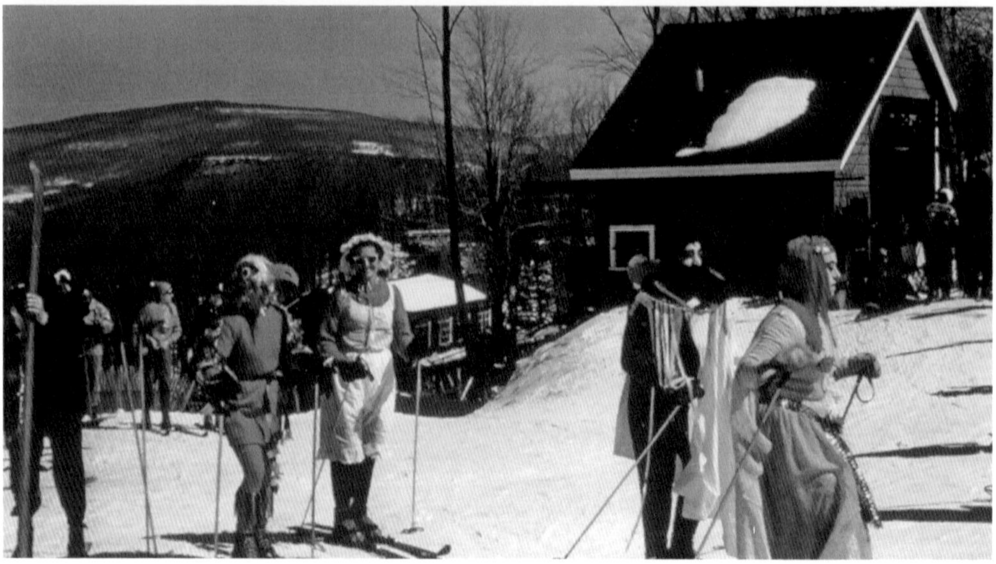

Skiers participating in Springfest in 1960 are making their way in costume up to the T-bar at Highmount. This event was held on Easter. It was not until the 1980s that Highmount first installed a chairlift, which came from another mountain. The seats on the chairlift were separated by a partition with their own safety bars. (Courtesy of Howard C. Lindemann.)

Elinor Lindemann is standing against her car, which is mounted with an early-model ski rack, at Highmount. Elinor met her husband, Howard, while on a ski-club trip to the area. Both skied for nine decades. (Courtesy of Howard C. Lindeman.)

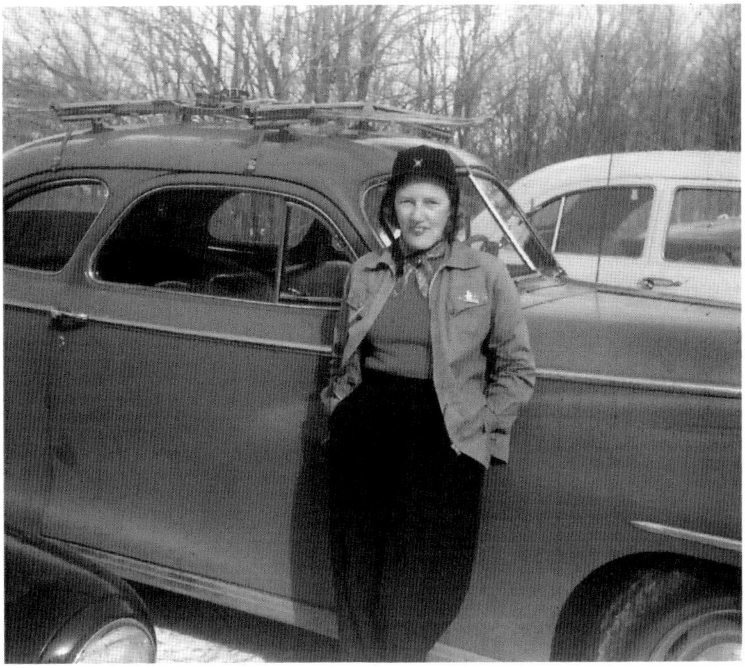

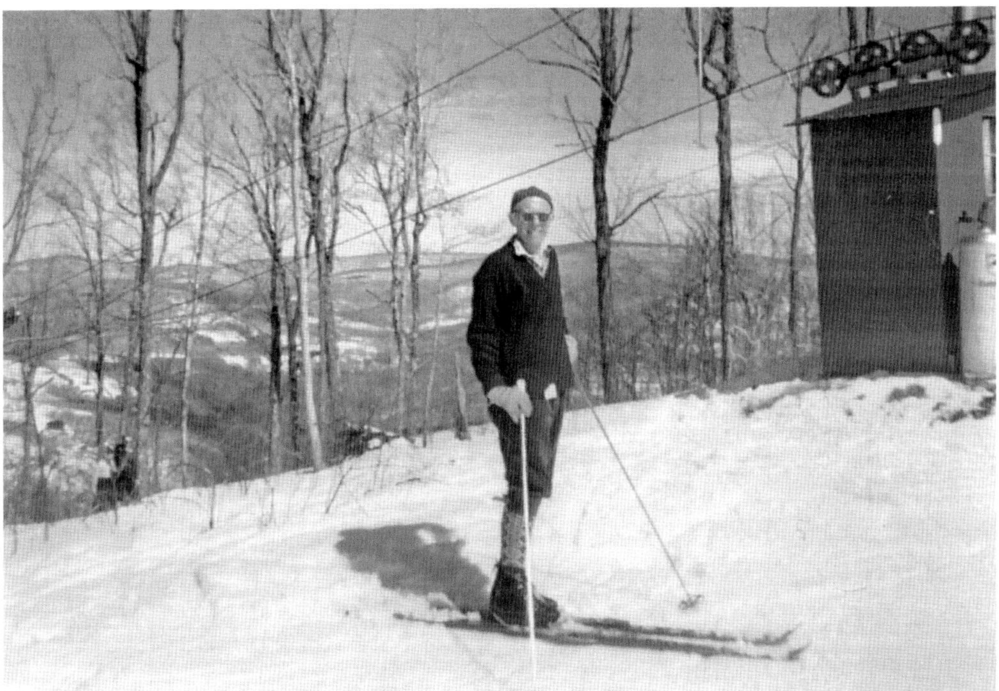

Howard Lindeman, donning knicker socks, is standing near the Highmount T-bar located at the summit in the early 1960s. (Courtesy of Howard C. Lindemann.)

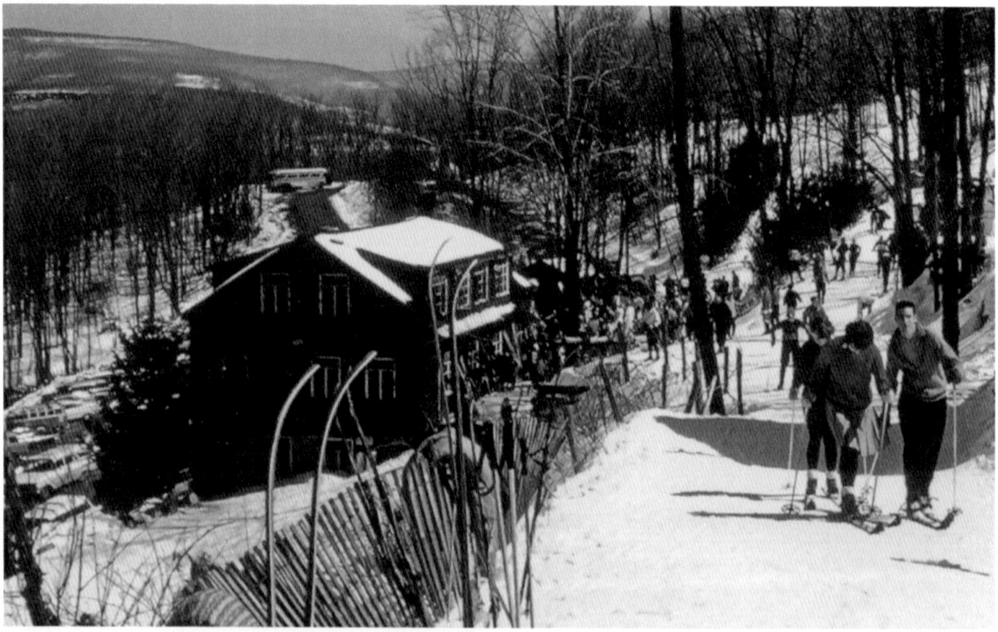

In this view looking northeast around 1960, the Highmount Lodge is to the left. The ski area was separated by a county road, which also doubled as parking lot. To the left of the road, novice slopes were developed going farther down the mountain. There was little room to expand the mountain past the original borders. The first chairlift, installed near the location in the photograph, was bought from another area in the 1980s. The area closed in 1993 under different owners. (Courtesy of Howard C. Lindemann.)

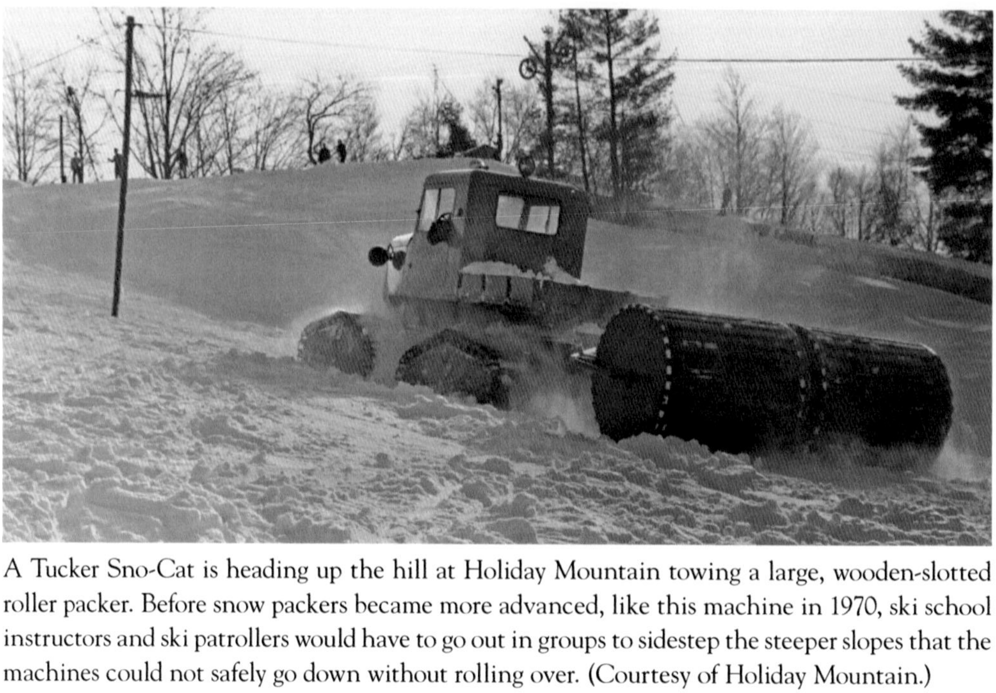

A Tucker Sno-Cat is heading up the hill at Holiday Mountain towing a large, wooden-slotted roller packer. Before snow packers became more advanced, like this machine in 1970, ski school instructors and ski patrollers would have to go out in groups to sidestep the steeper slopes that the machines could not safely go down without rolling over. (Courtesy of Holiday Mountain.)

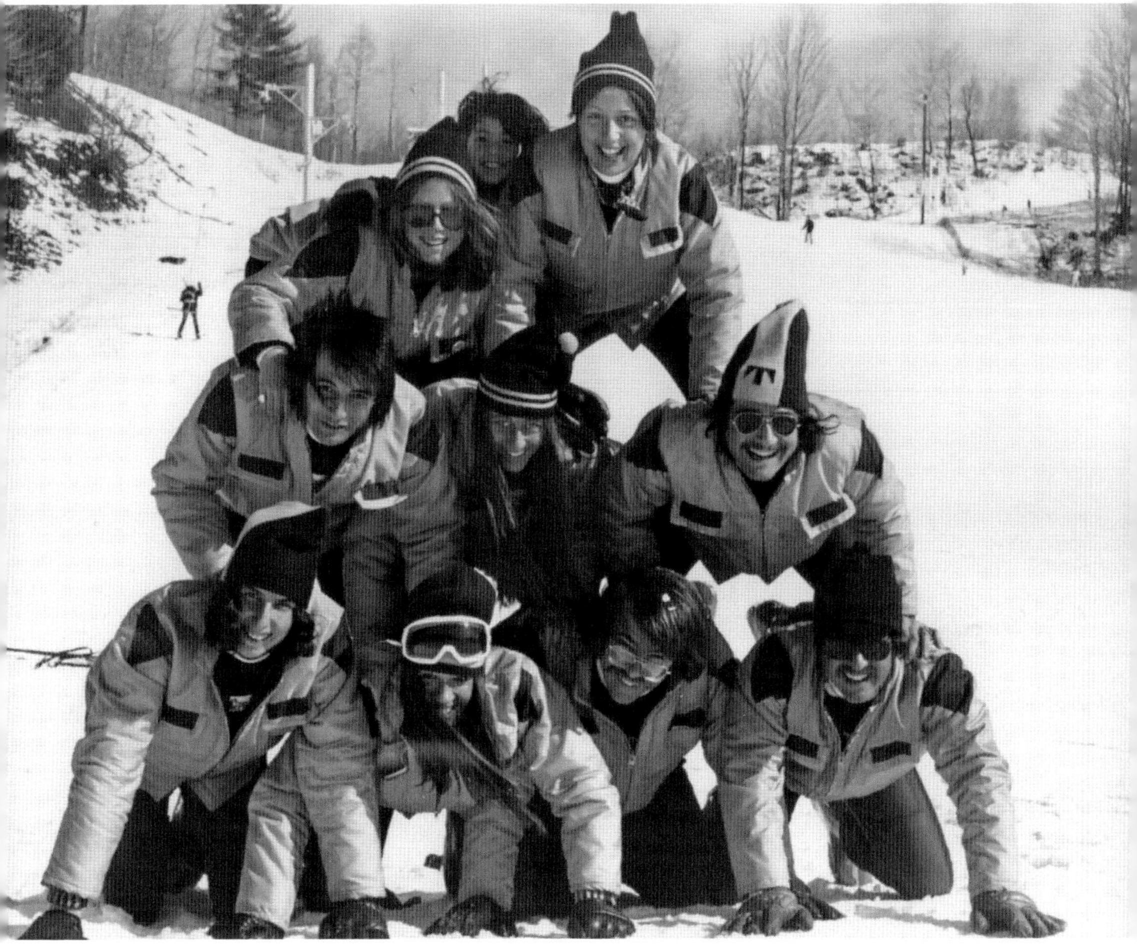

The instructors of the Holiday Mountain Ski School show what they are made of in this pyramid in 1974. (Courtesy of Holiday Mountain.)

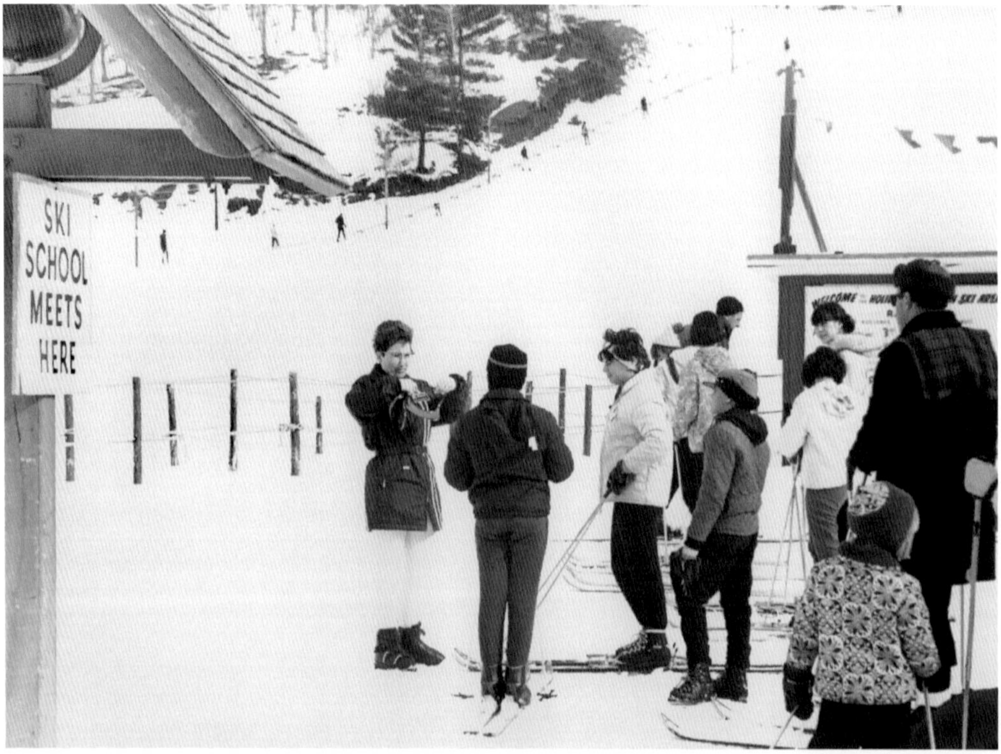

Head ski director Caroline Norris Kreuger means business while demonstrating the use of goggles at the Holiday Mountain Ski School meeting place. (Courtesy of Holiday Mountain.)

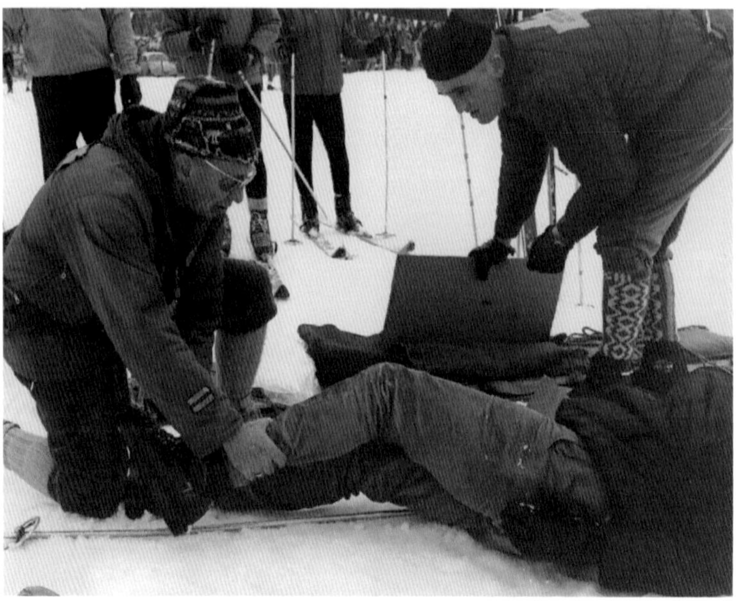

Clint Wilcox (left) and R. Bruce Burr (right) are pictured treating an injury near the Holiday Mountain base lodge. (Courtesy of Holiday Mountain.)

Skiers wait their turns at the J-bar in 1965. By the 1970s, the J-bar was fading from memory in the Catskills as it lacked sufficient uphill capacity. (Courtesy of R. Bruce Burr.)

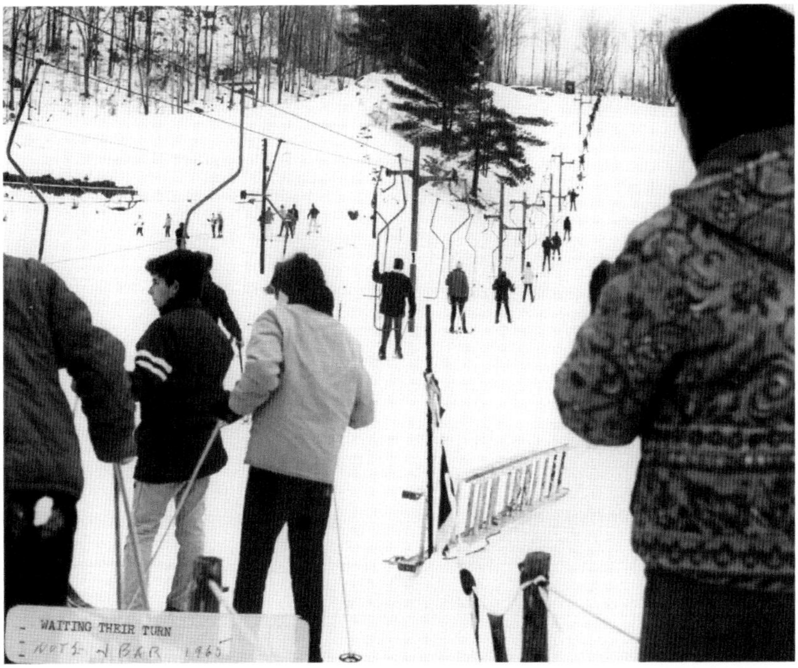

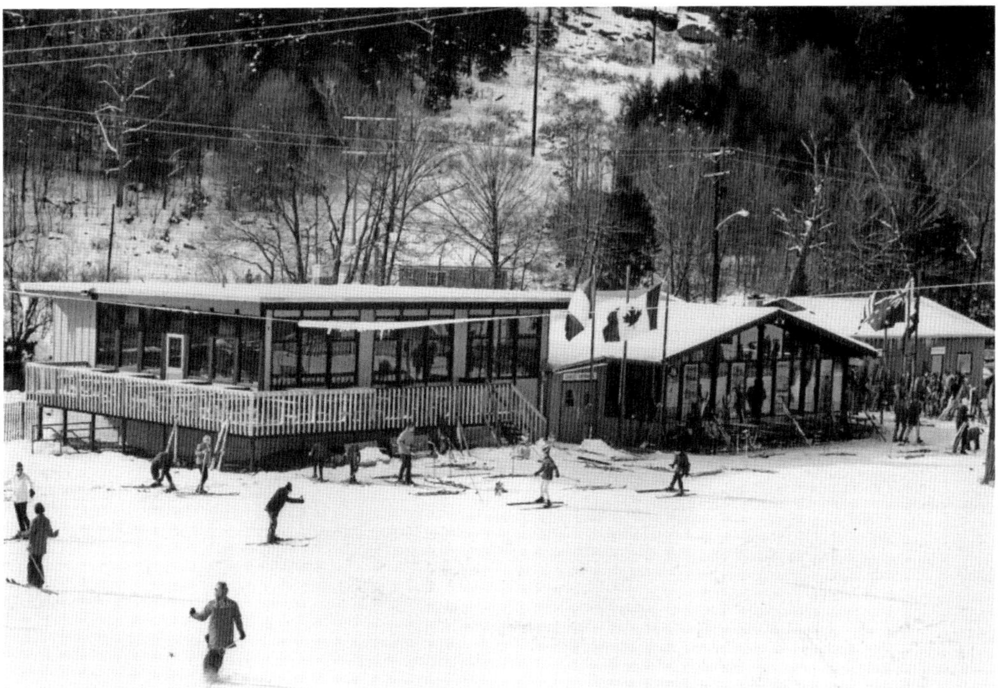

The new chalet addition to the Holiday Mountain base lodge was built on in the mid-1960s. This small ski area's location near a four-lane, major highway—New York Route 17—and the town of Monticello has enabled it to survive with just a handful of other areas into the 21st century.

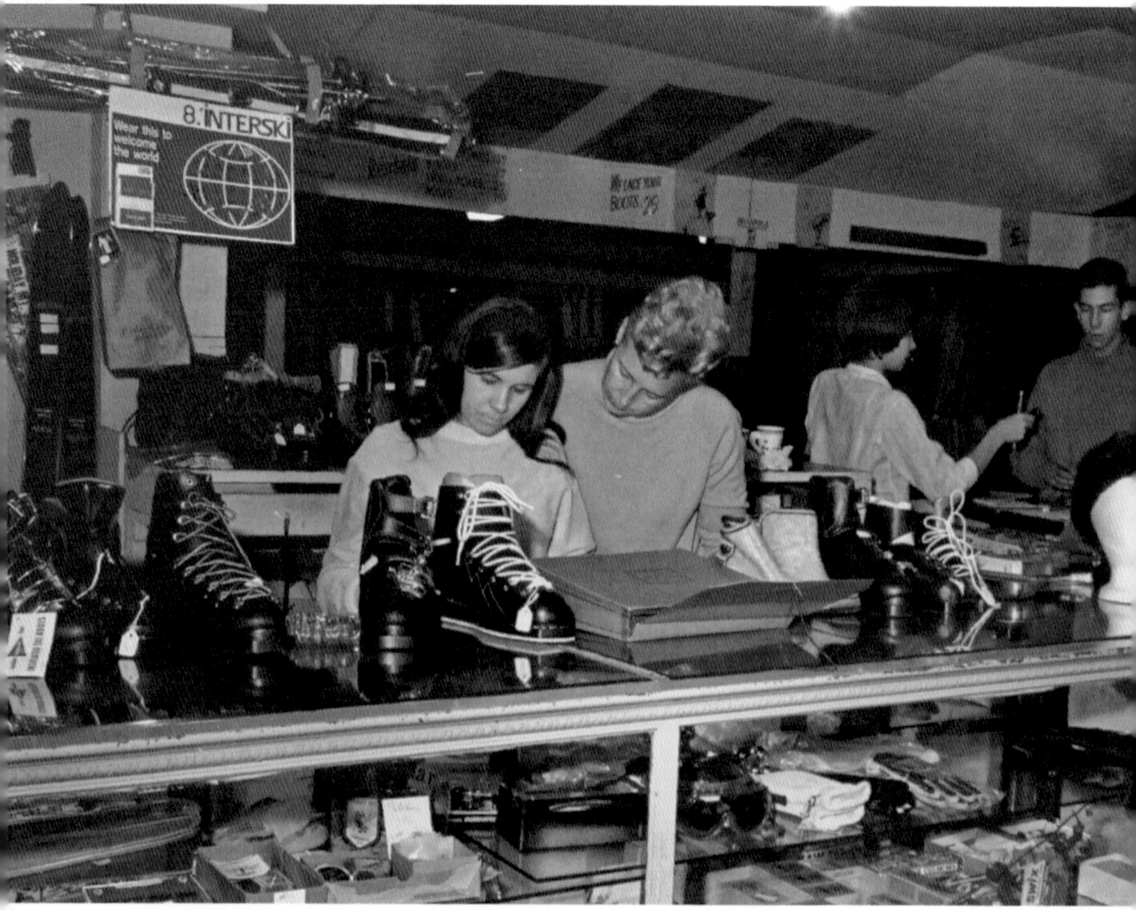

Emma Baily's ski shop is pictured here in 1966. As represented by the ski boots on the counter, the transition from laces to buckles has commenced. The sign above the salespeople reads, "We lace your boots . . 25¢." (Courtesy of Holiday Mountain.)

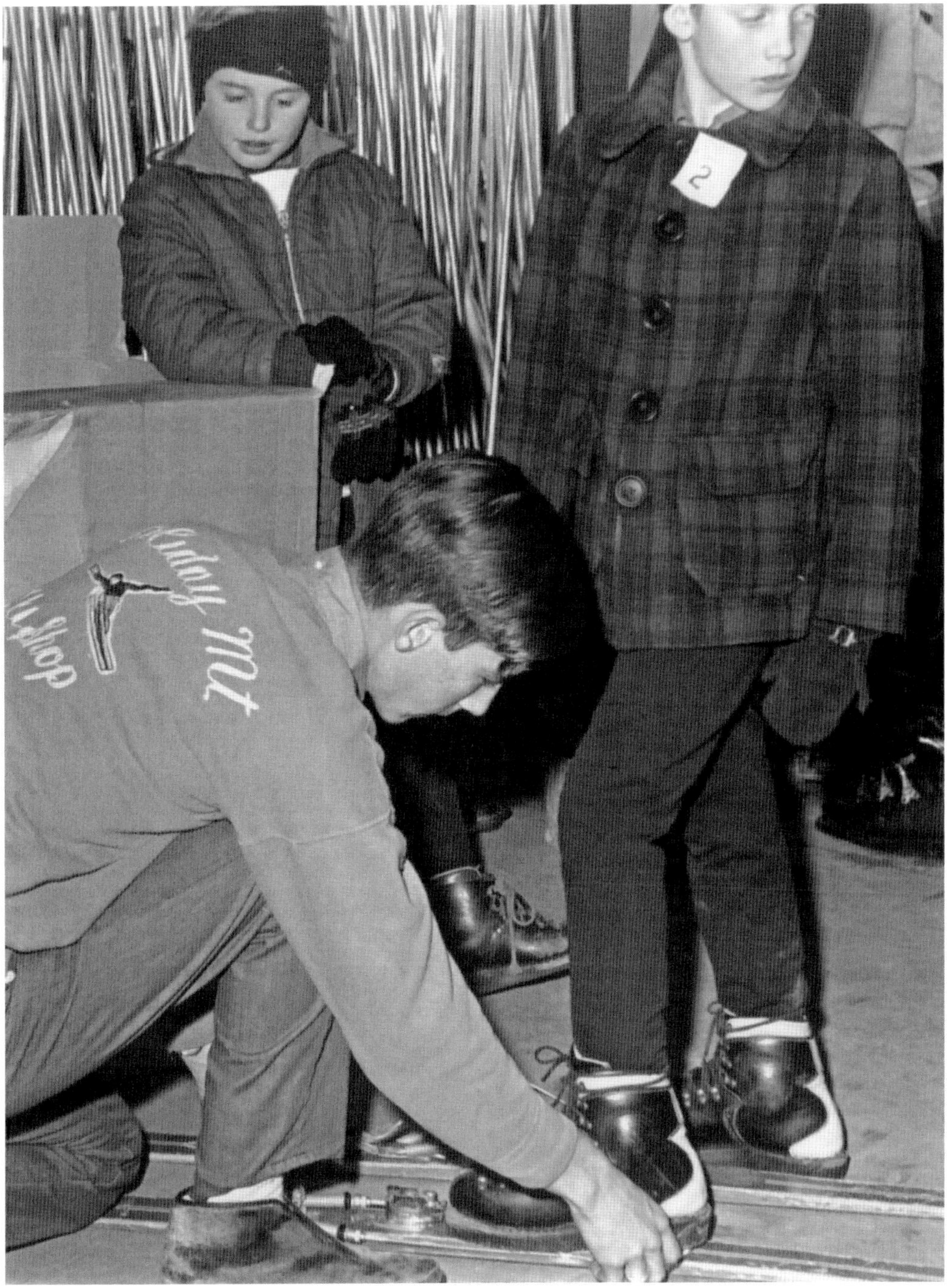

The life of a ski adjuster was not an easy one in the mid-1960s. Adjusting the cable bindings was a very tedious process and involved having to ask repeatedly for the customer to step in and out. Expletives were frequently hurled by the ski adjuster as the inattentive customers crunched their fingers. If that were not enough, a backache was assured by the end of the day from working off the floor. (Courtesy of Holiday Mountain.)

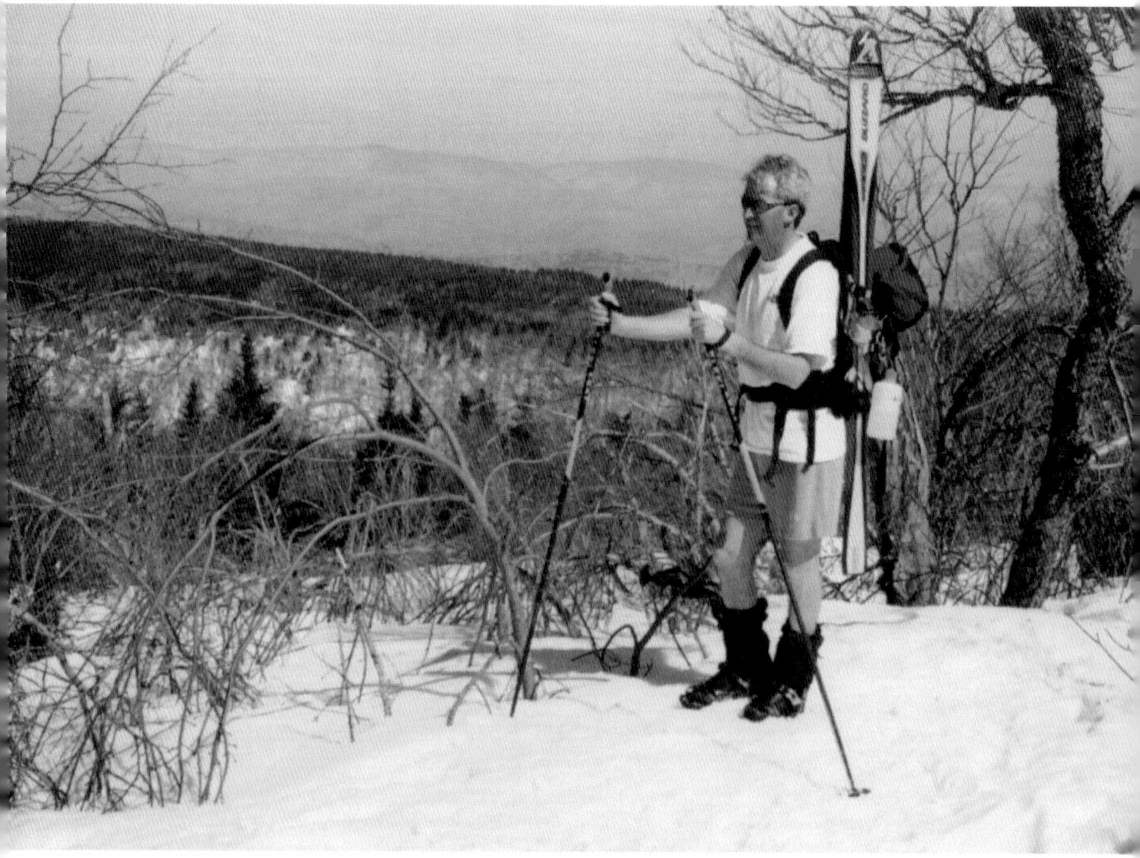

Sean Reilly, also known as "the Pied Piper of Meeker Hollow," stands on the high, western ridge of Slide Mountain searching for the perfect glade. New York State tried to promote skiing here along with other wilderness trails with mixed success. Backcountry and glade skiing became more popular going into the 21st century.

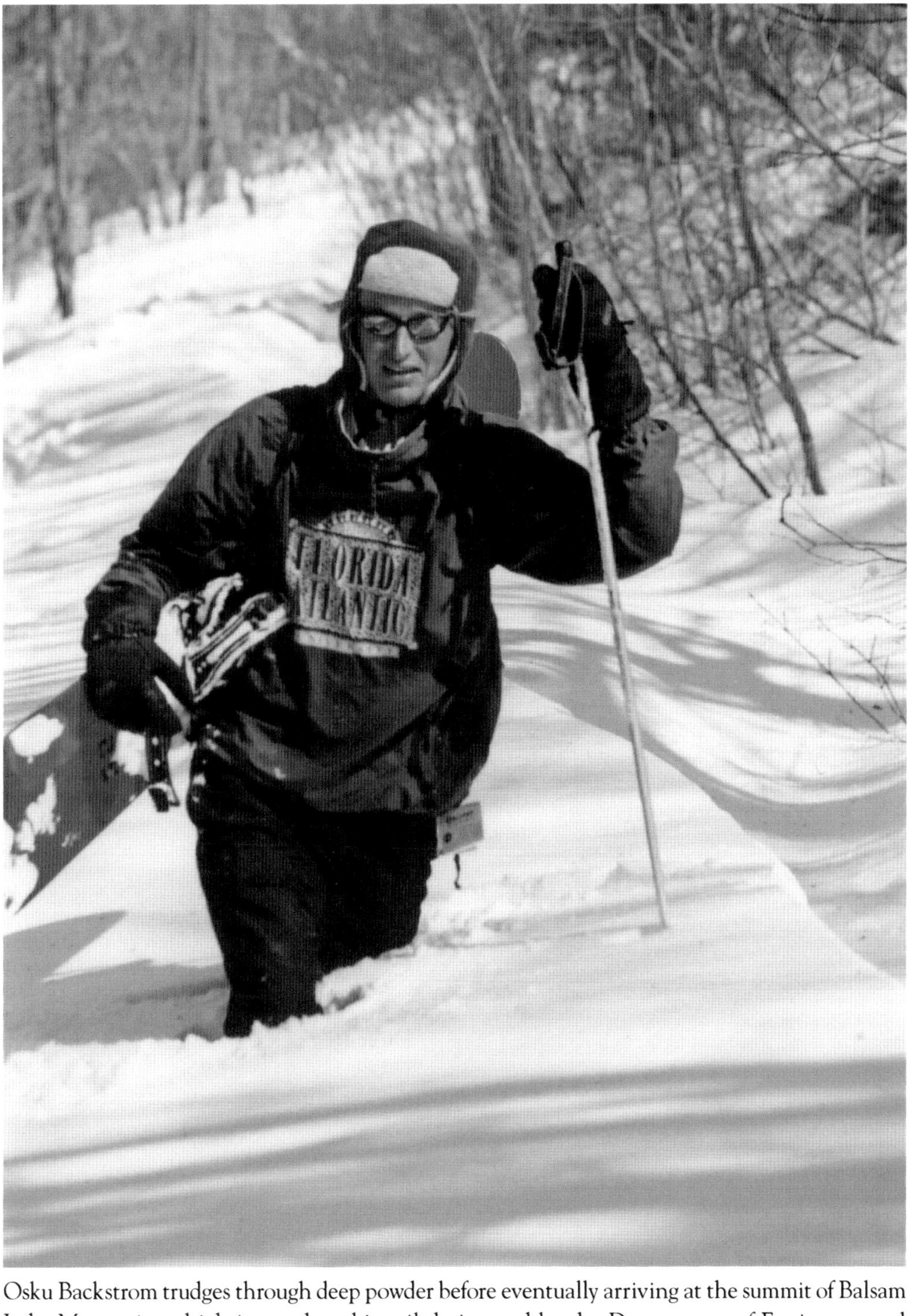

Osku Backstrom trudges through deep powder before eventually arriving at the summit of Balsam Lake Mountain, which is another ski trail designated by the Department of Environmental Conservation (DEC) in the 1950s. The ski pole he uses is to push himself on the flat areas of the trail while snowboarding down.

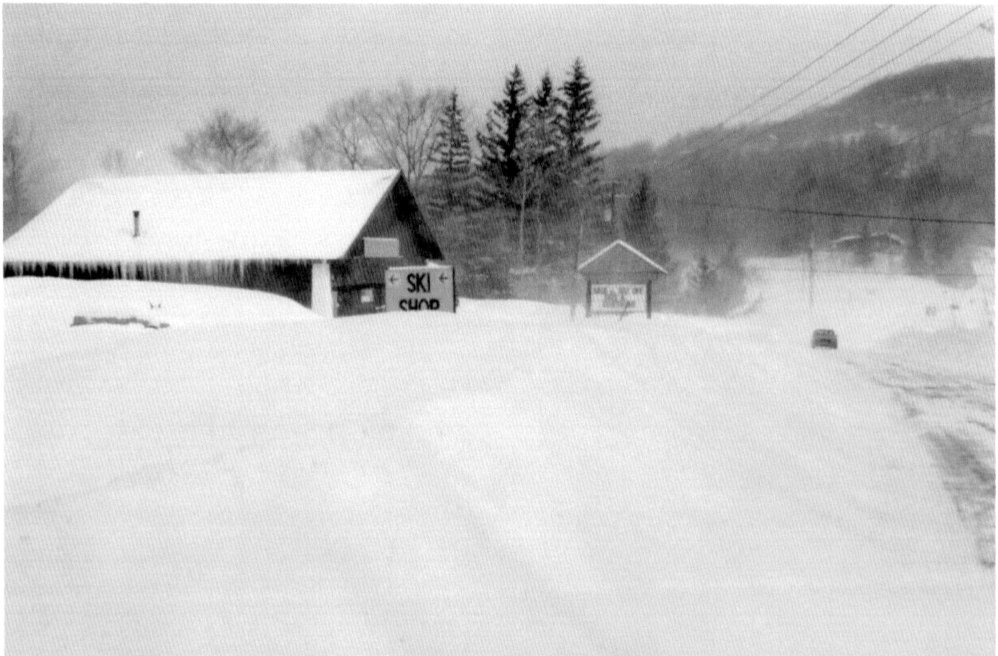

Billed as the storm of the century, the blizzard of March 12 and 13, 1993, hit the high Catskills with over three feet of champagne powder. The problem was that very few skiers could get there as state roads were officially closed for days. Here, a lone car scrambles up the road past the closed and snowbound Belleayre Ski Shop.

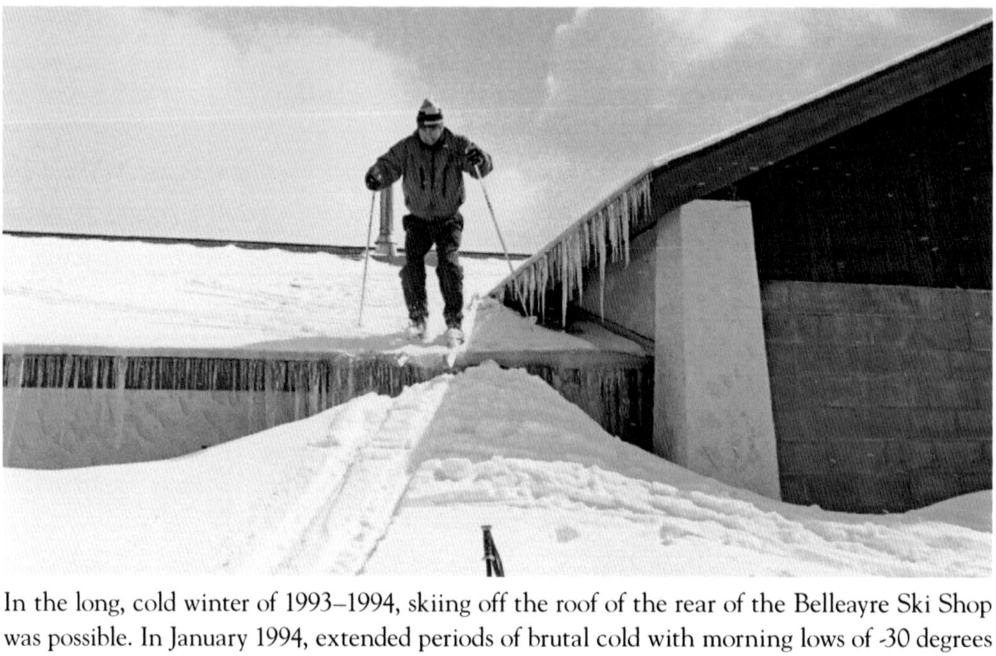

In the long, cold winter of 1993–1994, skiing off the roof of the rear of the Belleayre Ski Shop was possible. In January 1994, extended periods of brutal cold with morning lows of -30 degrees kept most skiers away, despite the fantastic snow. The deep snowpack lasted well into mid-April, even in the valleys.

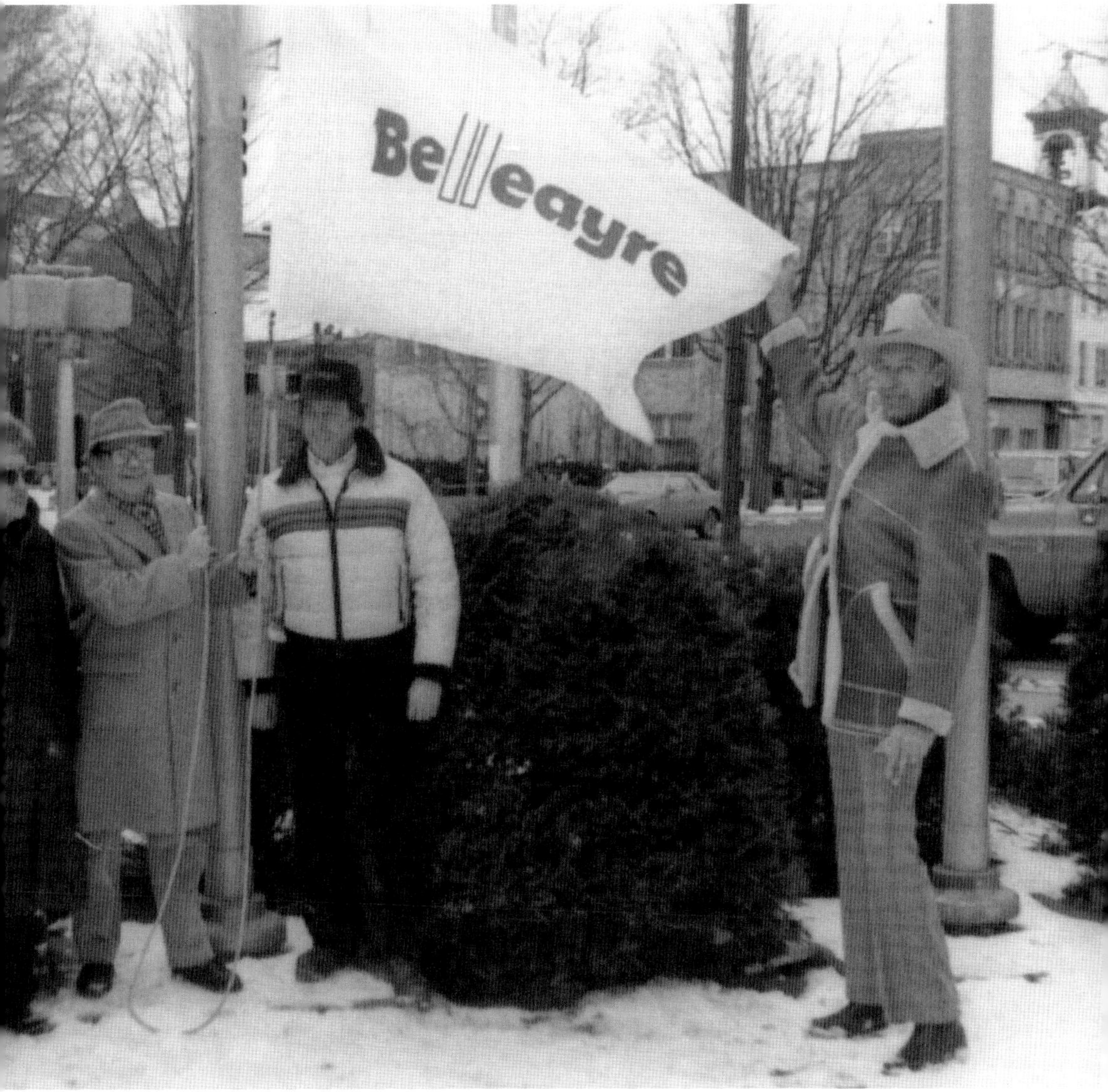

Here, a group of Belleayre supporters celebrates Belleayre Day in front of the Ulster County Office Building in Uptown Kingston in the early 1980s. Pictured are, from left to right, Ulster County legislators Marian Umhay and Bill West, superintendent of Belleayre Mountain John Johnson, and an unidentified man. There have been several attempts during constant state fiscal crises to close the mountain or privatize it, but they always drawing huge opposition from area supporters. (Courtesy of Sheila U. Parker.)

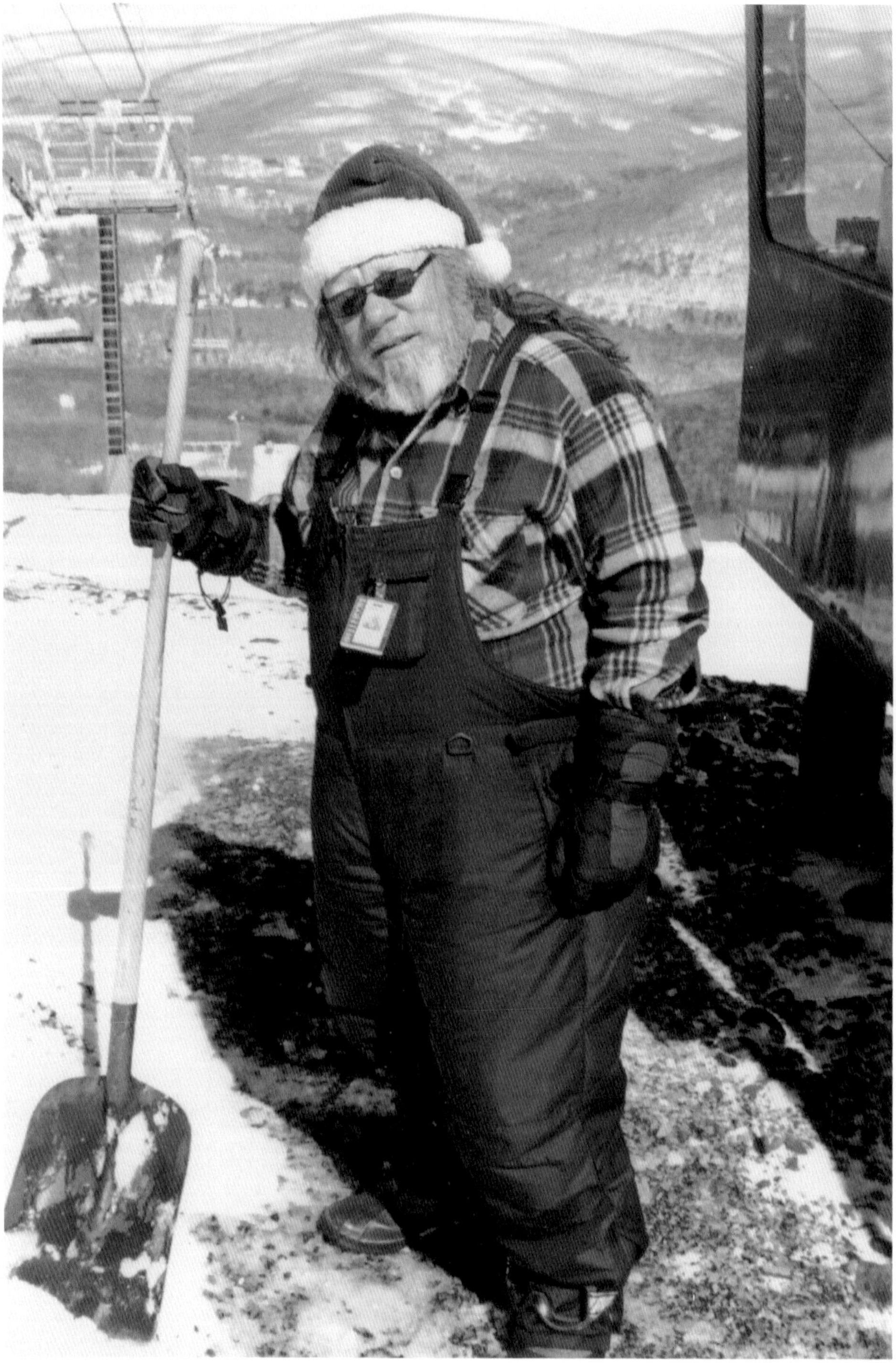

Mike Kelley, also known as "Interstate Mike," displays his Christmas attire on top of Belleayre Mountain. Mike was known for trading verses of song with skiers on the chairlift zooming by at mid-station.

8

GONE HOME

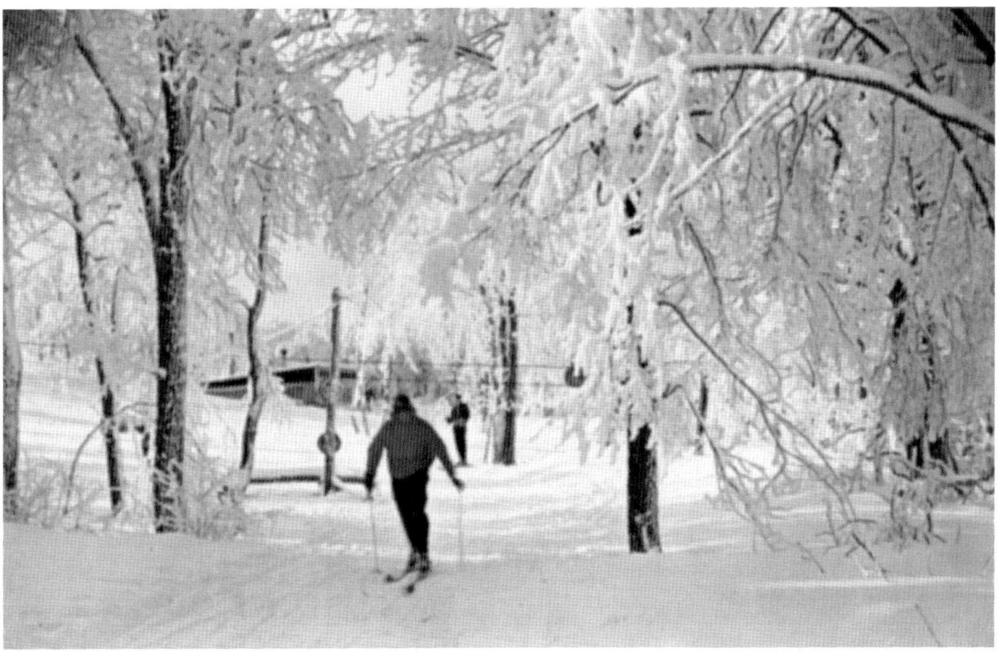

Near the summit of Bearpen Mountain in the late 1950s, there was an unusual base lodge, as shown in the background of this photograph. It could only be reached by a Sno-Jitney shuttle from a parking area well below the summit, on a distant ridge. When heavy snow fell, the shuttle vehicles could not make it up the snowbound roads, further complicating development of the Princeton ski area.

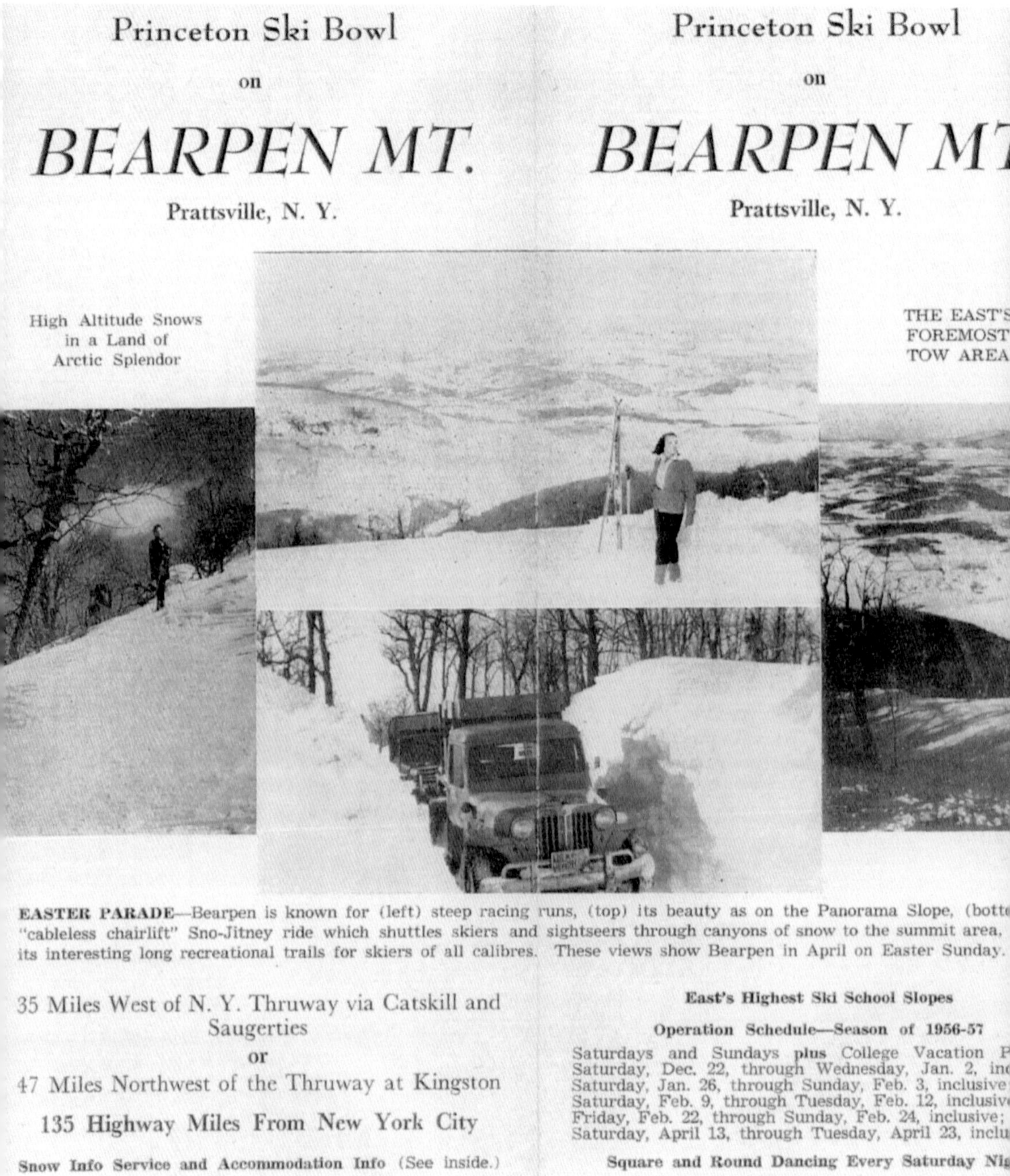

Perhaps no other lost ski area in the Catskills has drawn as much curiosity today as Princeton Ski Bowl, located high in the northwest Catskills in a snowbelt. The area design was very unusual for any period. At the end of day, skiers could descend on the ski-out trail, which, at 1,900 feet to the valley floor, was the largest vertical in Catskill mountain skiing. (Courtesy of Vic Wortman.)

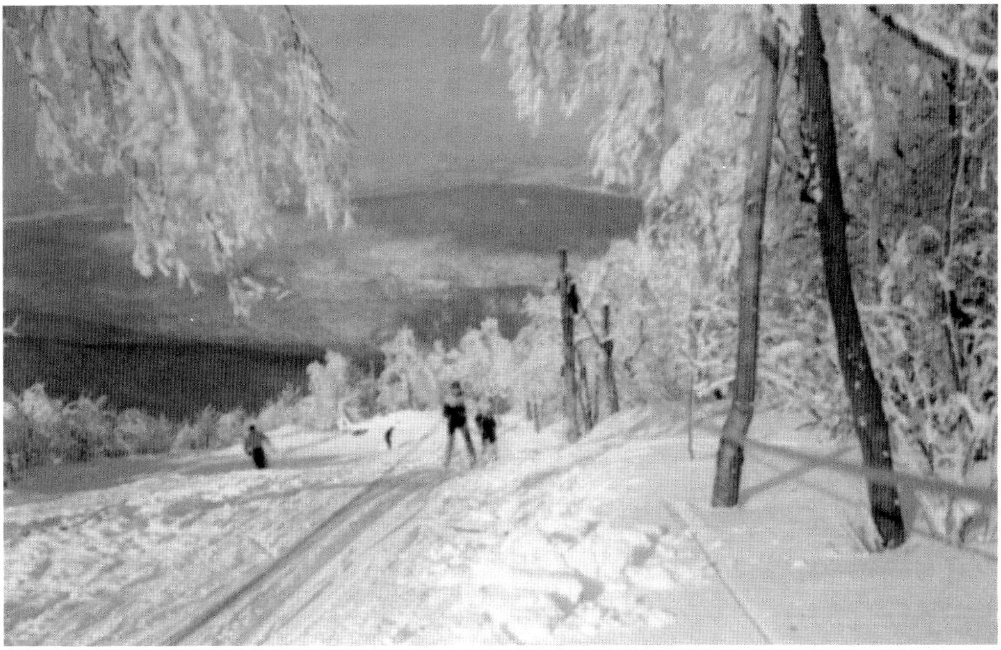

Skiers on one of the rope tows are photographed above 3,000 feet in elevation at Princeton Ski Bowl. The 3,600-foot summit was the highest of all Catskill ski areas. Brochures in 1956 advertised skiing until May 20 on the upper level—on natural snow, of course. Grandiose plans for development were never realized because of land-surveying issues, and by 1960 Princeton had closed down.

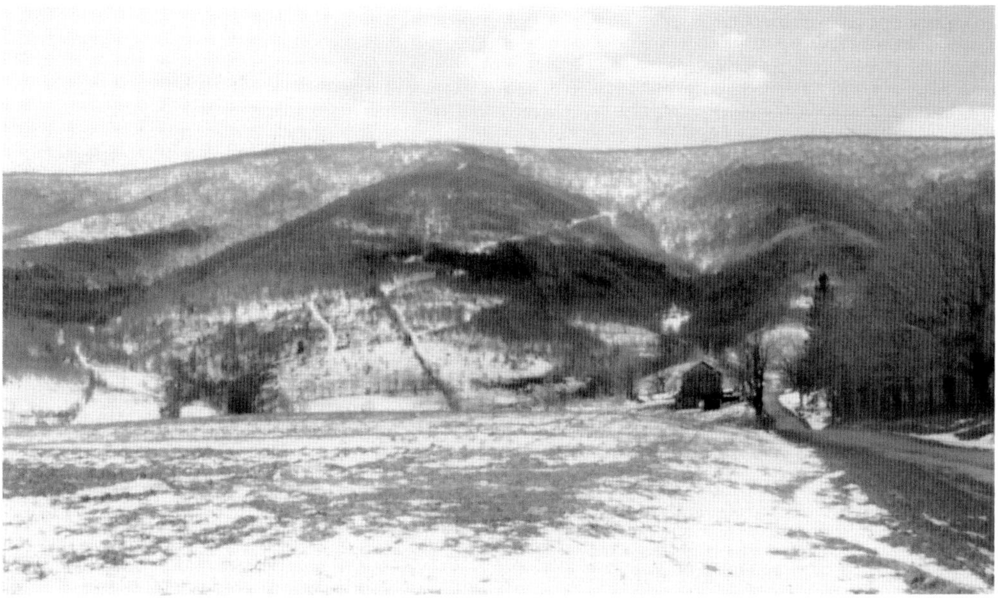

A mid-1990s photograph shows some of the trails and slopes of the Princeton Ski Bowl. The shuttle to the summit began on Ski Run Road, across from the road to the lower right and curved around after four miles to the summit of Bearpen Mountain.

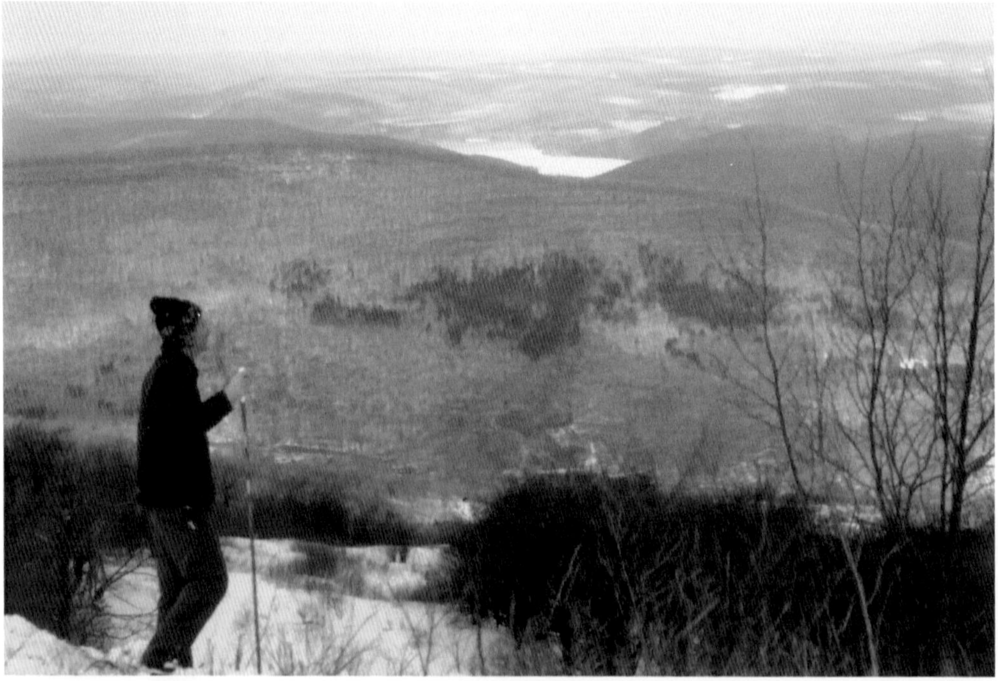

A view from just below the summit of Bearpen Mountain shows the big vertical drop to the valley below. In the background is the Schoharie Reservoir. A state right-of-way lets hikers get to the summit today.

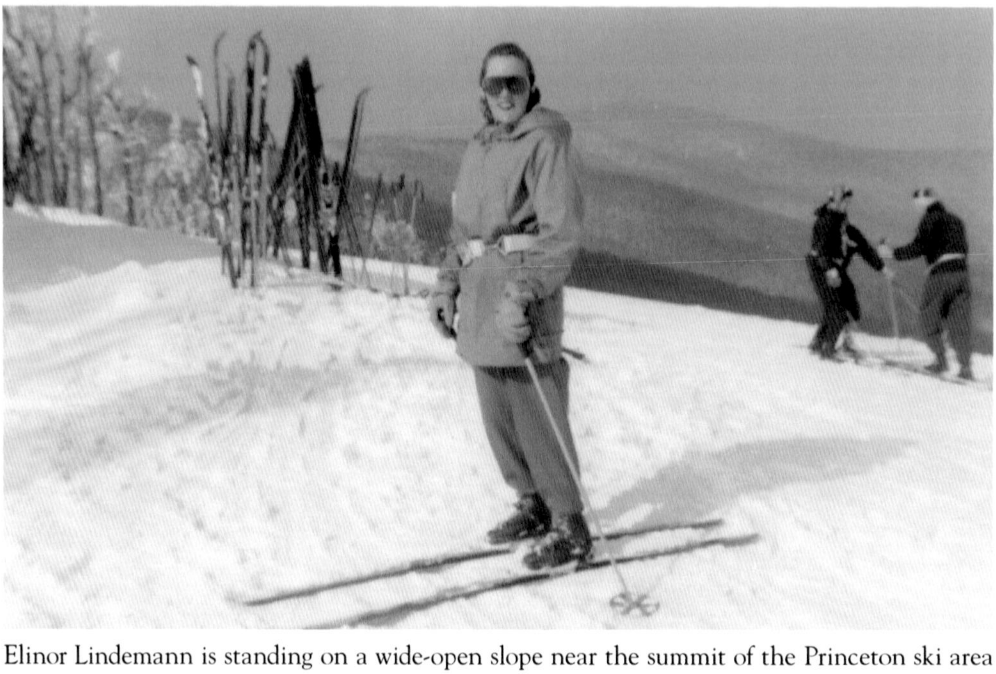

Elinor Lindemann is standing on a wide-open slope near the summit of the Princeton ski area in 1956. "Arctic splendor and superlative high altitude snow as nowhere else" is how this scene is described in a brochure of the time. (Courtesy of Howard C. Lindemann.)

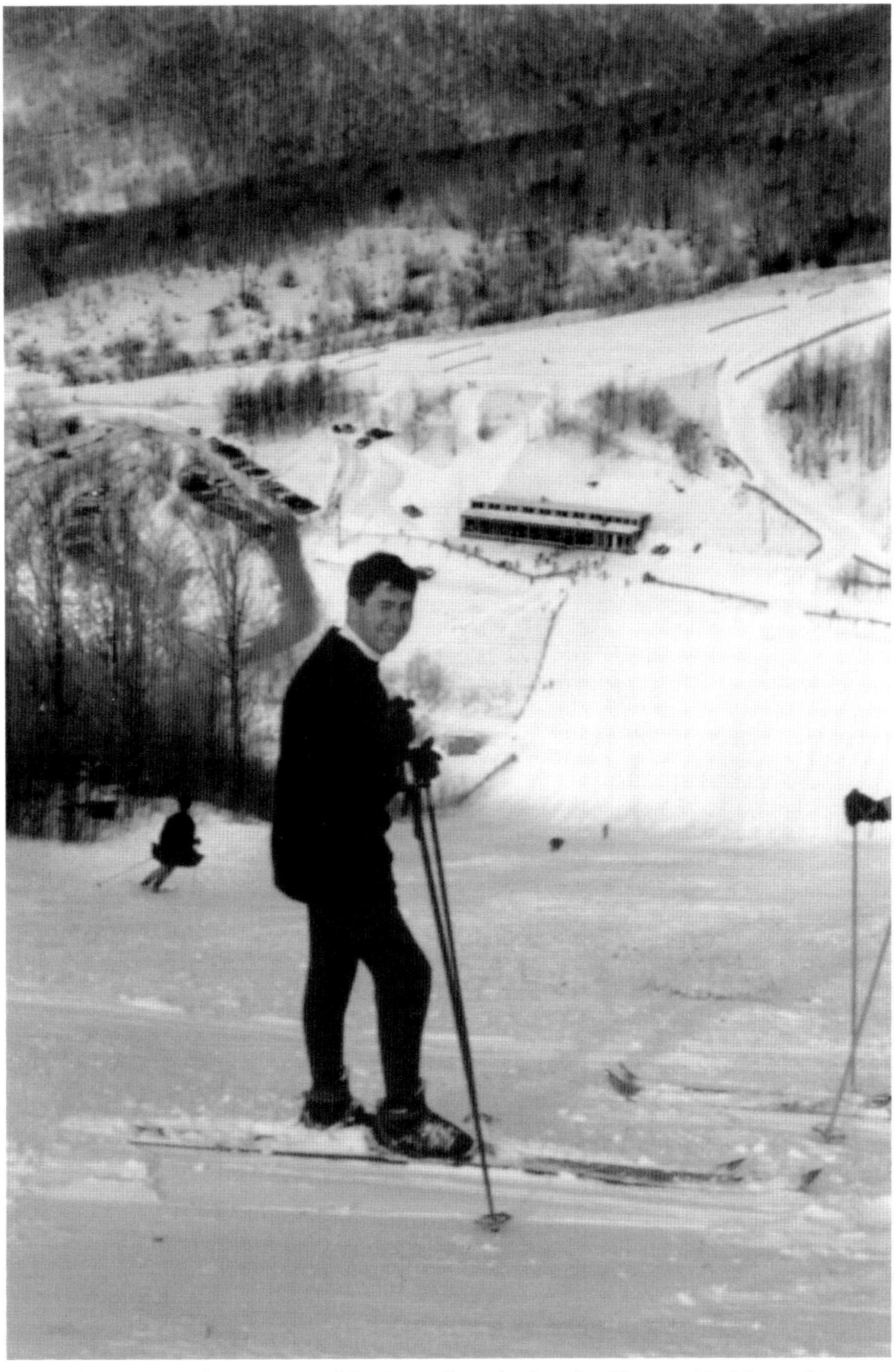

Hermann Amsz is standing on top of the legendary Avalanche Slope at No Name ski area. This was one of Catskill's steepest pitches at the time. The slope would pitch up again at the bottom, and the ski patrol would be waiting for those who fell all the way from the top to the bottom. (Courtesy of Hermann Amsz.)

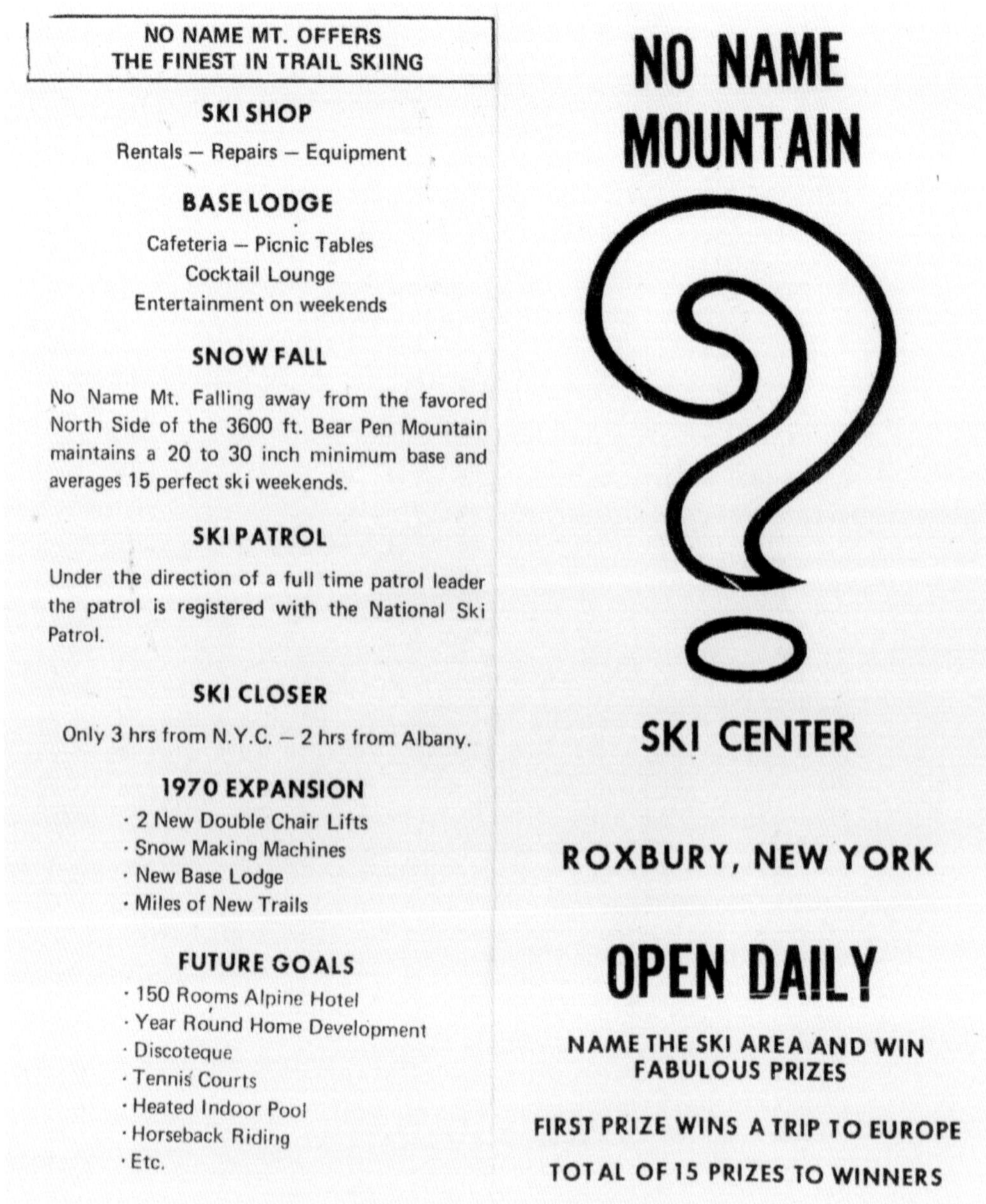

NO NAME MT. OFFERS
THE FINEST IN TRAIL SKIING

SKI SHOP

Rentals — Repairs — Equipment

BASE LODGE

Cafeteria — Picnic Tables
Cocktail Lounge
Entertainment on weekends

SNOW FALL

No Name Mt. Falling away from the favored North Side of the 3600 ft. Bear Pen Mountain maintains a 20 to 30 inch minimum base and averages 15 perfect ski weekends.

SKI PATROL

Under the direction of a full time patrol leader the patrol is registered with the National Ski Patrol.

SKI CLOSER

Only 3 hrs from N.Y.C. — 2 hrs from Albany.

1970 EXPANSION

- 2 New Double Chair Lifts
- Snow Making Machines
- New Base Lodge
- Miles of New Trails

FUTURE GOALS

- 150 Rooms Alpine Hotel
- Year Round Home Development
- Discoteque
- Tennis Courts
- Heated Indoor Pool
- Horseback Riding
- Etc.

NO NAME MOUNTAIN

?

SKI CENTER

ROXBURY, NEW YORK

OPEN DAILY

NAME THE SKI AREA AND WIN
FABULOUS PRIZES

FIRST PRIZE WINS A TRIP TO EUROPE

TOTAL OF 15 PRIZES TO WINNERS

A brochure for No Name Mountain entices viewers to come up with a suitable name for the area. Formerly known as Roxbury Ski Center, then Big Bear Ski Bowl, the ski area never got the chance for a new designation as it closed by the early 1970s. (Courtesy of Vic Wortman.)

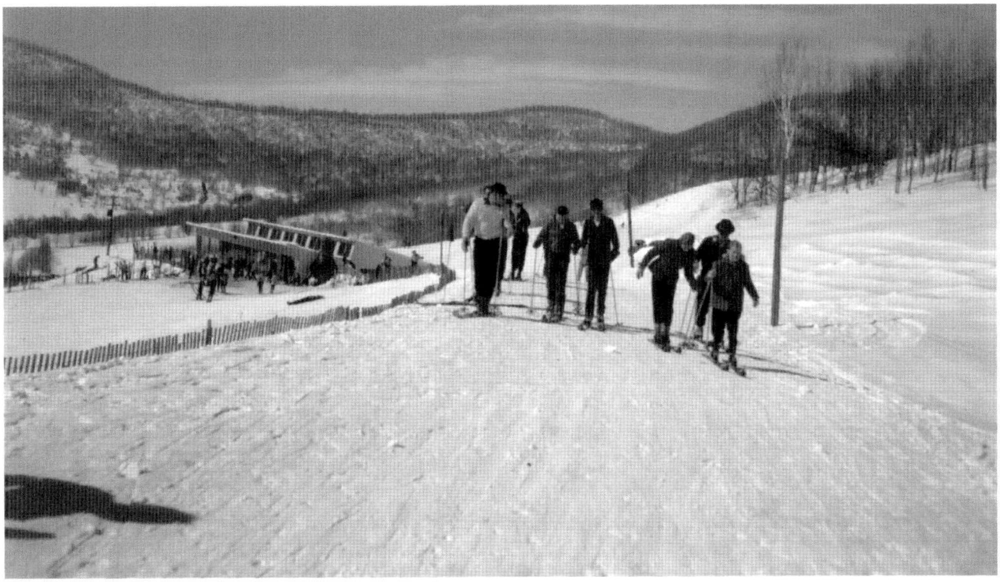

These skiers are seen making their way to the T-bar. Snow fences to the left were very important for trapping snow, and as in most areas at the time, there was not any snowmaking. The Roxbury ski area was at the end of bucolic Denver-Vega Valley on a section of Bearpen Mountain, although it did not reach the summit. (Courtesy of Delaware County Historical Association, Bob Wyer Collection.)

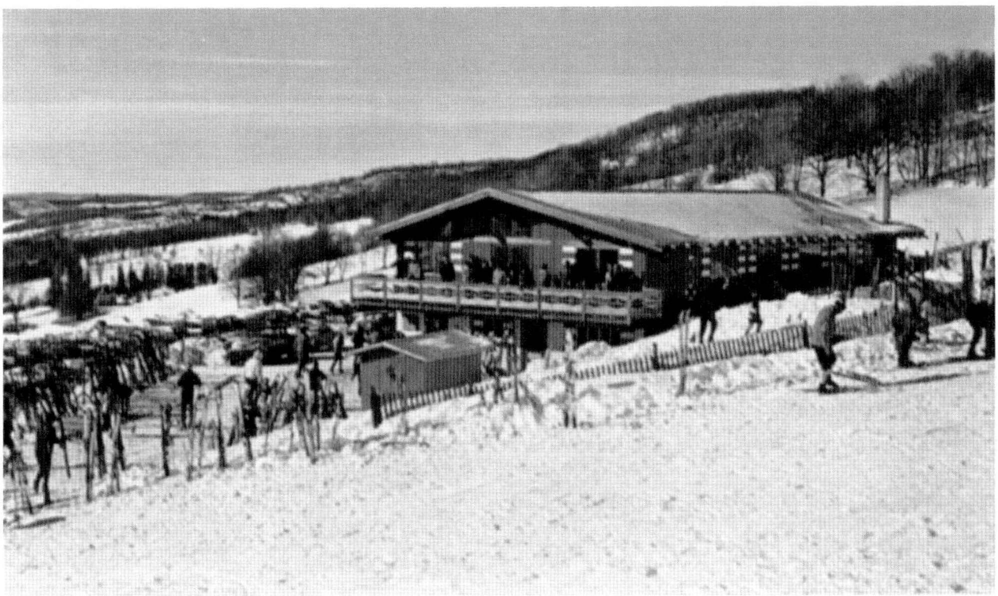

Bobcat, also called Catskill Ski Center in the earlier years, featured very wide slopes as well as narrow, woody expert trails. A long T-bar reached the summit, which offered fine views of the pastoral Andes valley. The base elevation was at 2,200 feet. On the southern flank of the same mountain, on New York Route 28, the Andes ski area operated with one chairlift and two rope tows for several years in the early 1960s.

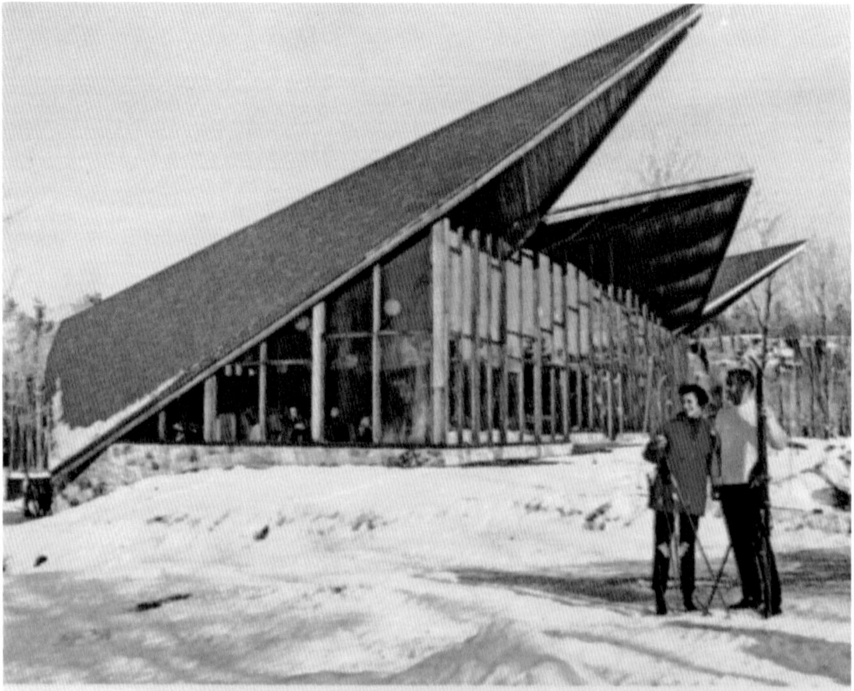

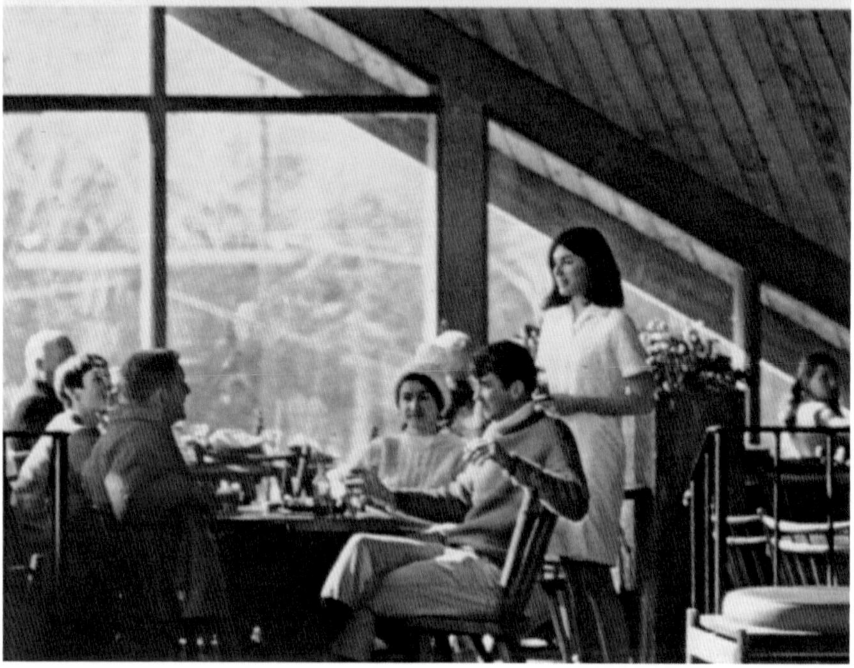

These photographs offer two views of the Ski Minne base lodge and restaurant, which opened in 1964. This large base lodge was out of proportion to the small ski area it served. The ski area had a T-bar and five slopes on a small vertical high on the Shawangunk ridge. The area also featured Swiss-style warming huts used by cross-country skiers. The ski area lasted until about 1978, and the remarkable lodge burned down in 1981.

Starting in 1962 in a region with good lake-effect snows, Scotch Valley prospered with day and night skiing. Its proximity to colleges in Oneonta and metropolitan Albany drew many students. A bowling alley and bar in the lodge was an extra incentive to get local residents out in the winter. The area closed in the late 1990s. (Courtesy of Milo Stewart Jr.)

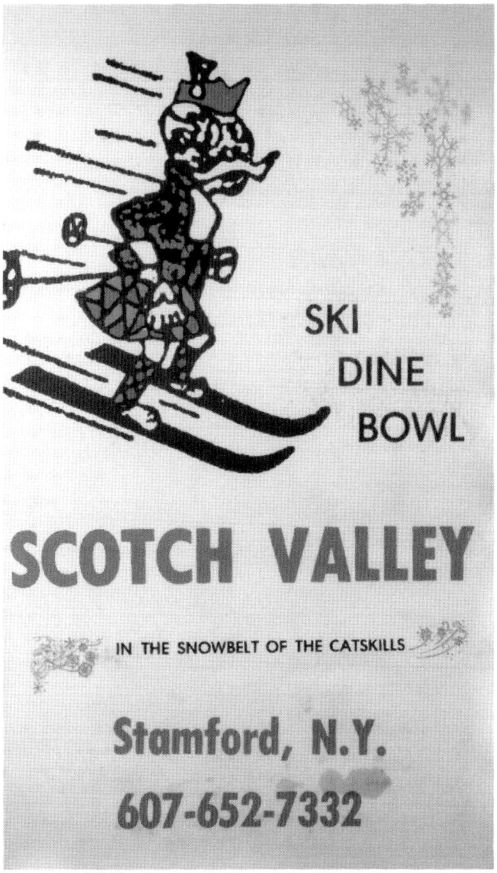

The view looking down into the valley near Stamford shows the twin double chairlifts from mid-station at Scotch Valley. Over the years, the area evolved into a large complex.

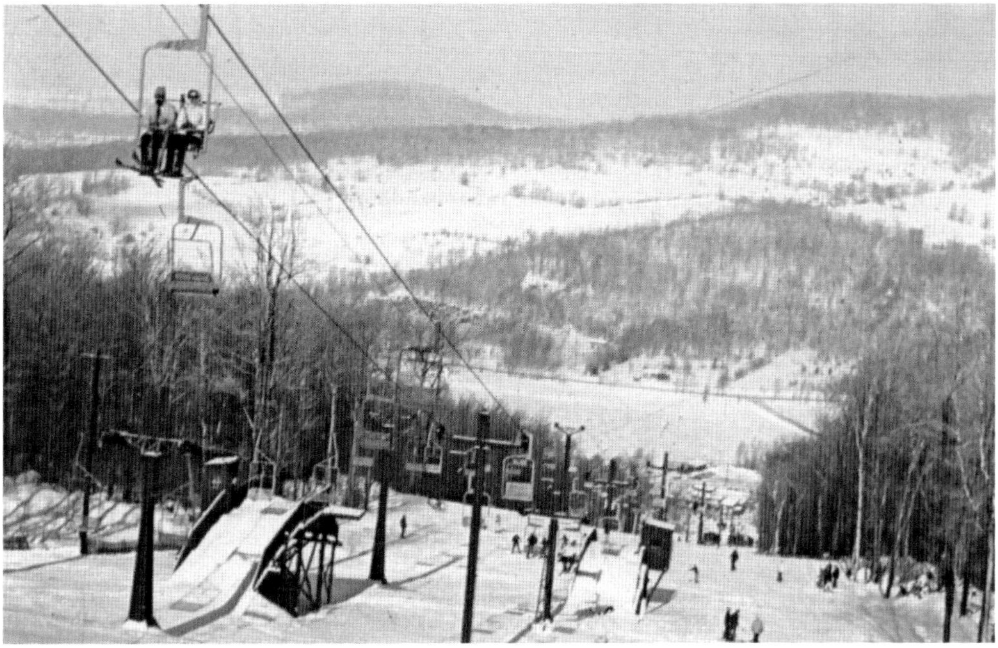

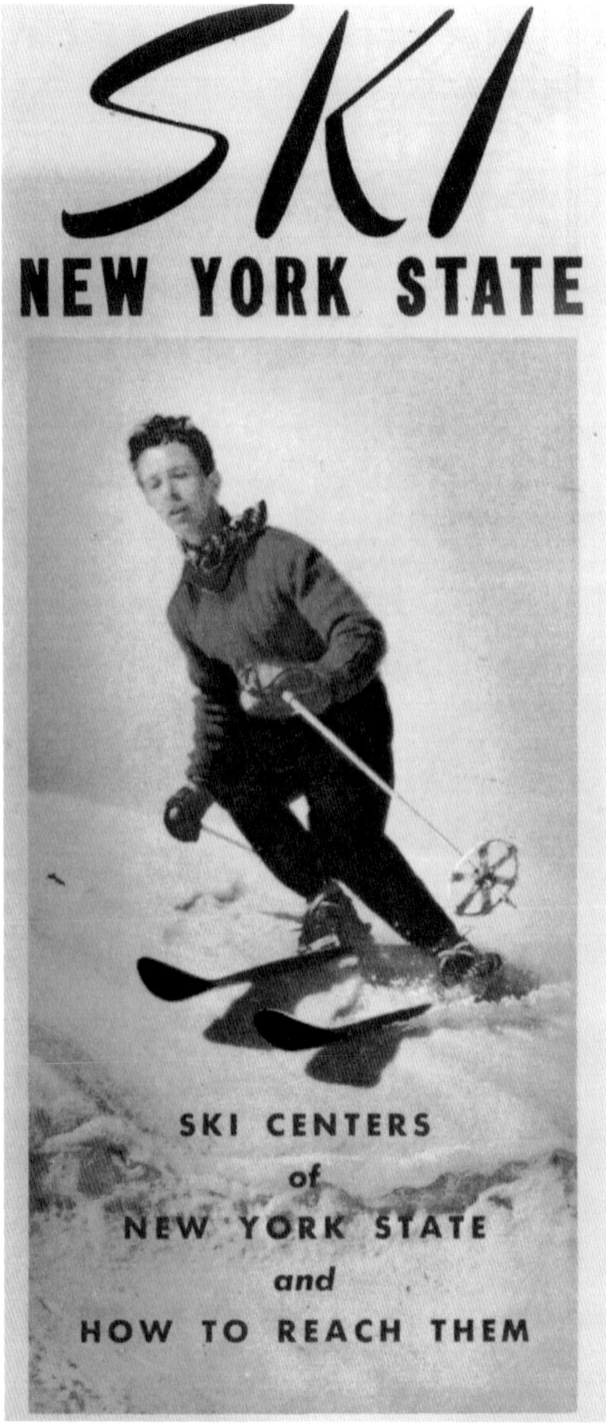

A New York State brochure from 1948 lists only four ski areas in the Central Catskills. A decade later, dozens sprang up over the Catskill hillsides, with up to eight on and around Belleayre Mountain.

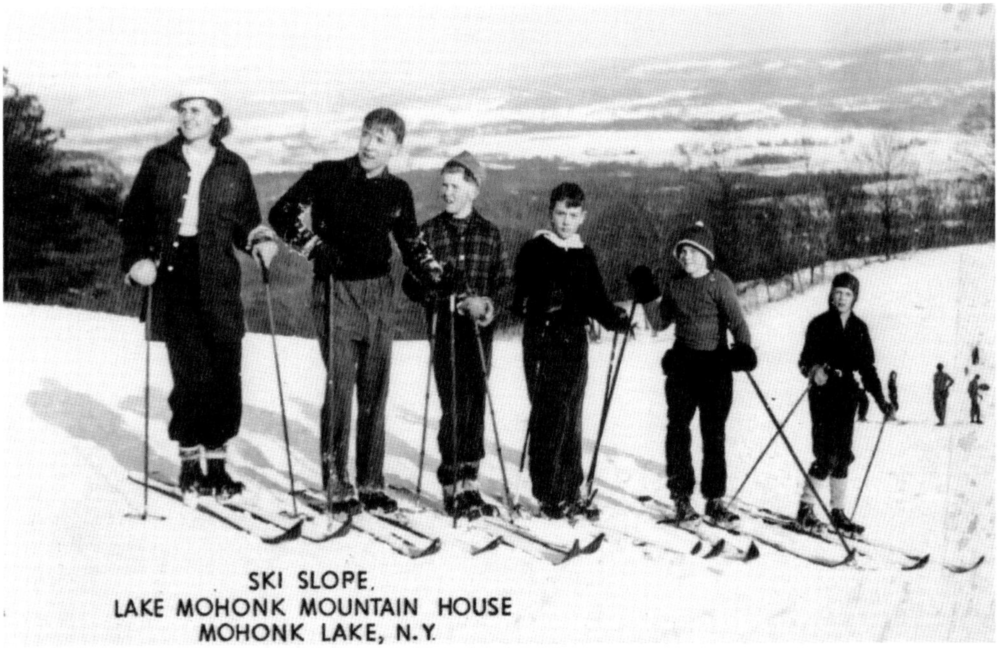

Ruth H. Smiley poses on Bonticou Hill with five Mohonk schoolboys. The fields in the valley are in the New Paltz area. The Bonticou ski area operated into the 1970s before closing.

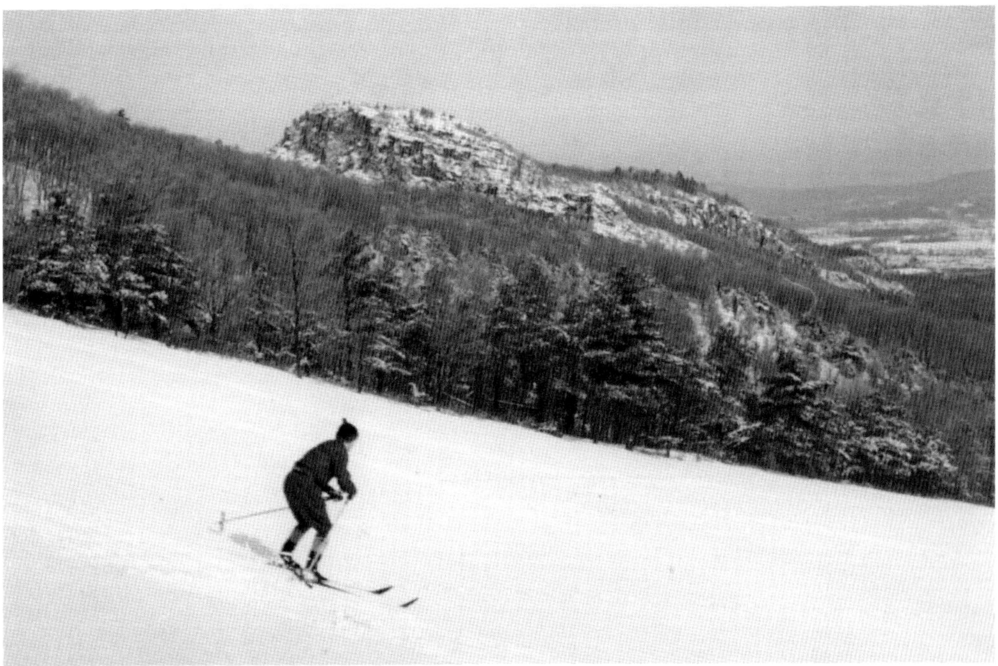

The Bonticou Run near New Paltz is pictured here in 1935. (Courtesy of MMHA.)

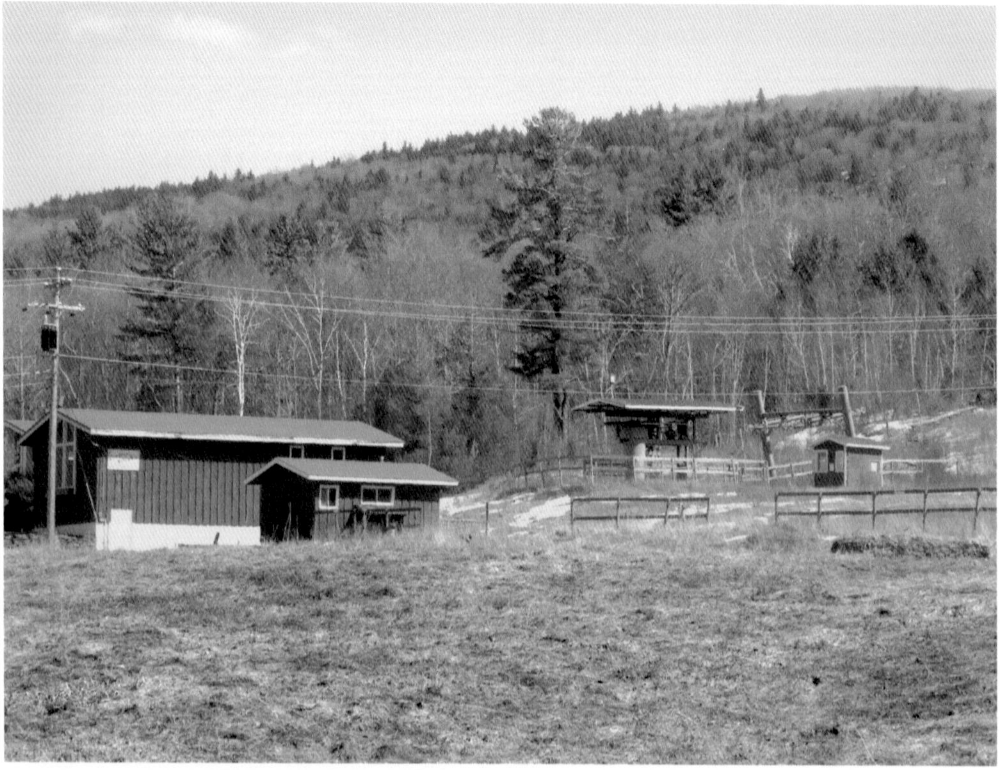

Cortina operated with two chairlifts, a Poma lift, and a Mighty lift in Tannersville, New York. Night skiing proved popular here. A high base of nearly 2,000 feet in elevation and a northern exposure made for good snowmaking.

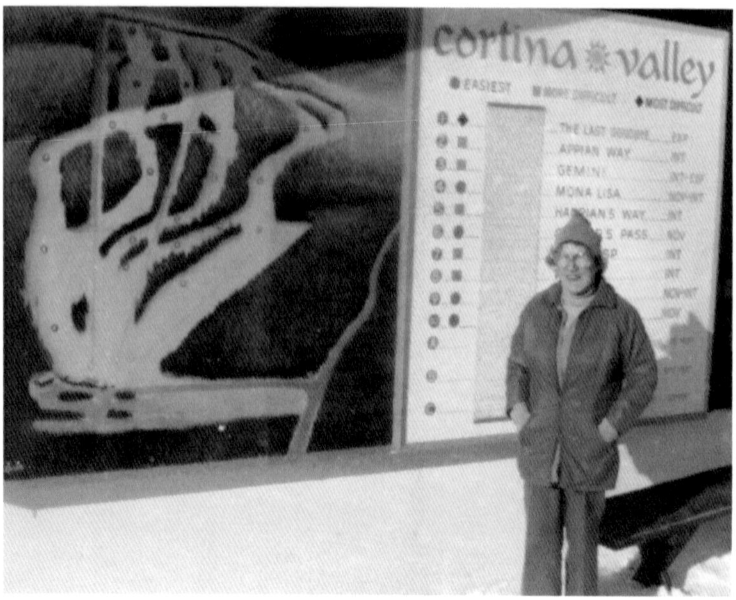

Elinor Lindemann stands in front of an Italian-themed trail map at Cortina Valley. (Courtesy of Howard Lindemann.)

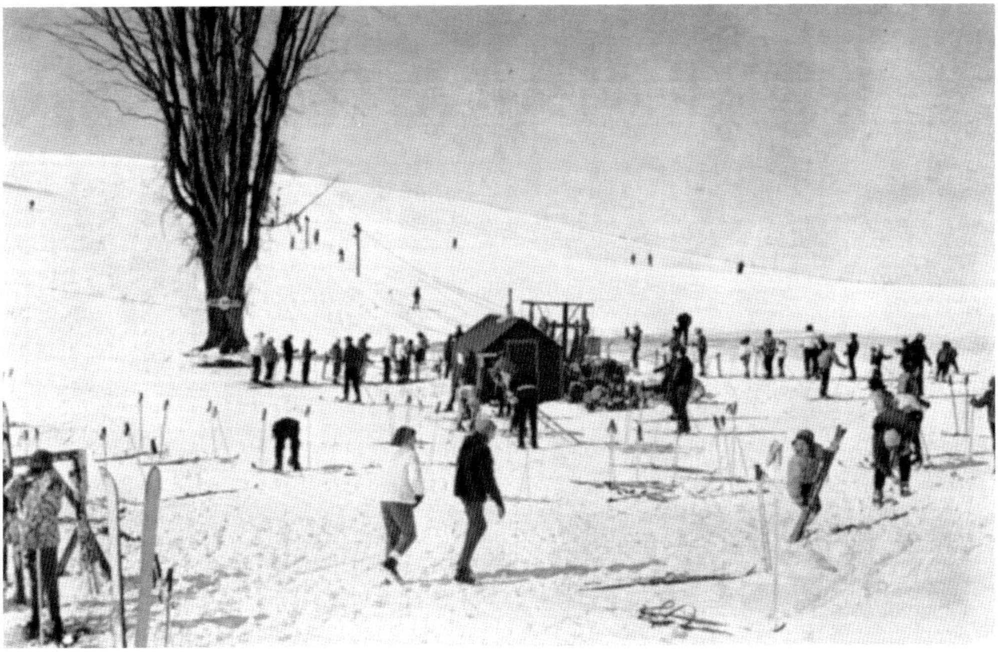

A lone maple tree that doubles as a ski school meeting place stands in the vast expanse of a white ski slope. Mount Otsego, north of Cooperstown, was representative of the terrain stretching from the northern Catskills to the Mohawk Valley. At the time of this photograph, it had two lifts and three tows.

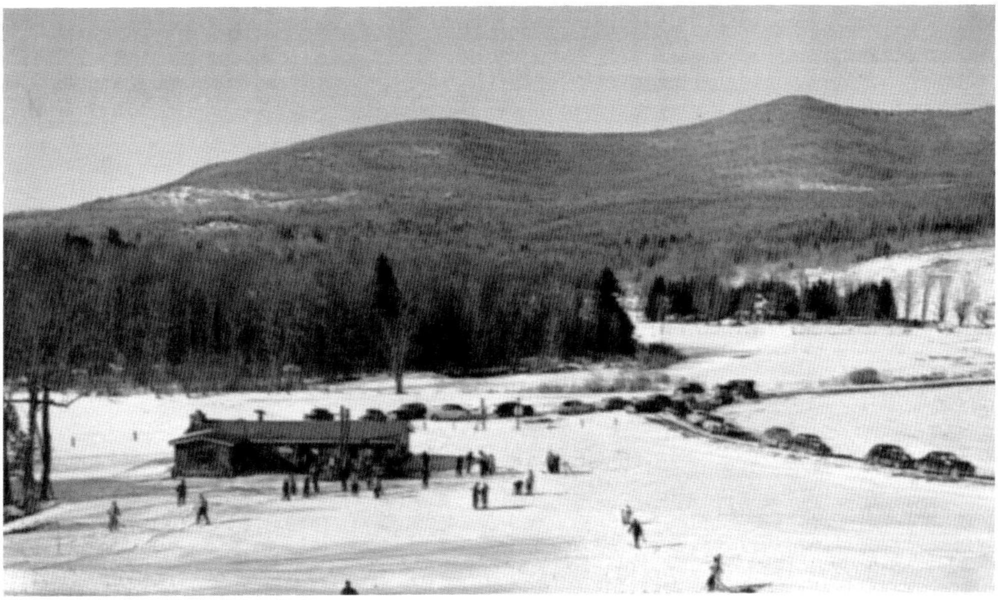

Timberlane Ski Ranch, located in East Jewett near Tannersville, had one mile of ski tows and billed itself as the "Sun Valley of the East" in the early 1950s. It also operated as a dude ranch later on. Entertainers such as Patti Page and Rosemary Clooney appeared here. Despite a high base elevation, the sunny exposure made skiing operations difficult.

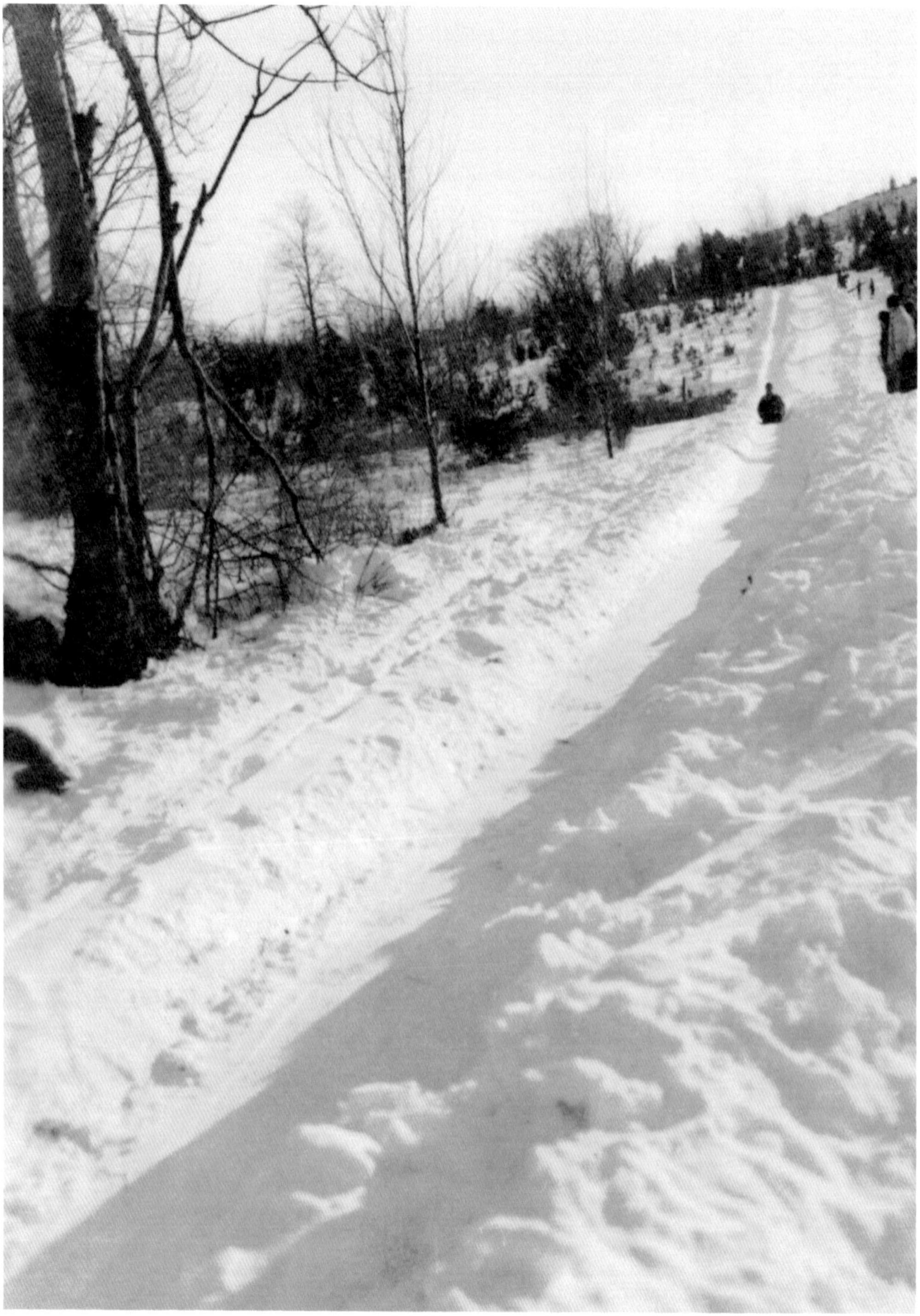

A small ski area and toboggan run was located on the north side of Ohayo Mountain just outside the village of Woodstock. In the upper right, a narrow ski trail with skiers hiking up can be seen. This picture is from 1938. (Courtesy of the Woodstock Historical Society.)

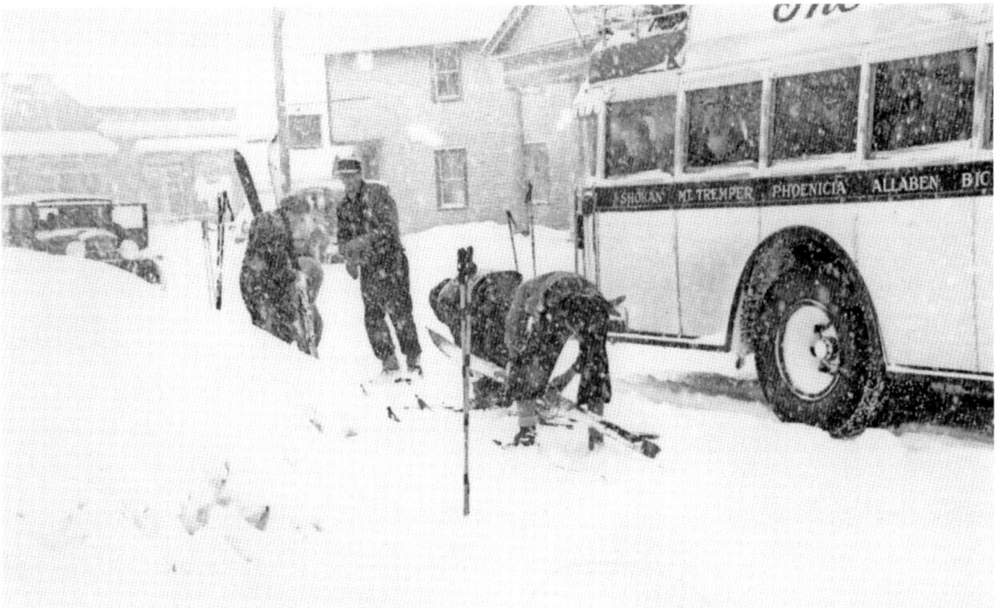

Valiant skiers brave a snowstorm in the center of Woodstock in 1938. They are getting off the bus that ran from Kingston to Pine Hill and are probably heading toward the Ohayo Mountain ski slope. This ski area disappeared from memory, and an attempt to build a ski area in the Wittenberg section of Woodstock in the 1970s was unsuccessful. (Courtesy of the Woodstock Historical Society.)

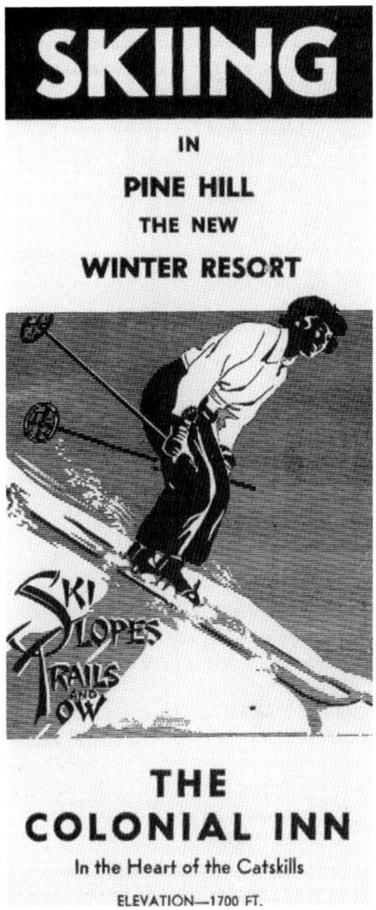

The Colonial Inn is still thriving to this day, although the small ski area behind the hotel is gone. (Courtesy of Phil Davenport.)

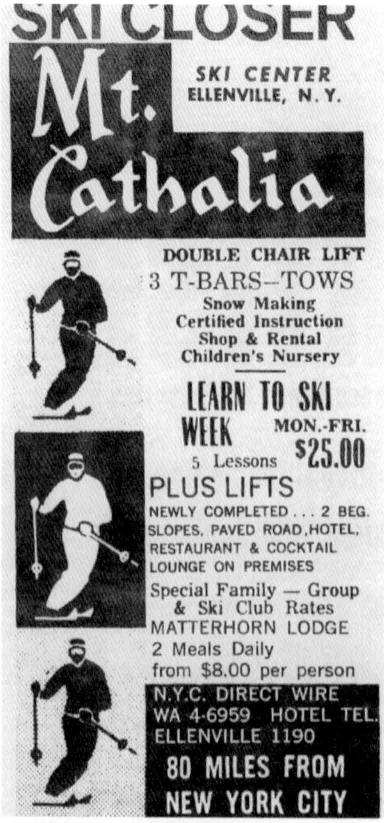

Mount Cathalia was located high on the Shawangunk Ridge near Ellenville. Down in the town, the Nevele Hotel had its own chairlift and a small ski area. The Davos ski area, located farther south, ran for many years as Big Vanilla at Davos. (Courtesy of Howard Lindemann.)

The trails at Highmount are reverting back to forest in this photograph taken in the late 1990s. The Friends' Chair Lift was a split double chair that was moved from another mountain to Highmount in the mid-1980s, ending an era of only feet-on-the-ground lifts. Till this day, there are controversial talks of annexing the ski area to the state-run Belleayre Mountain.

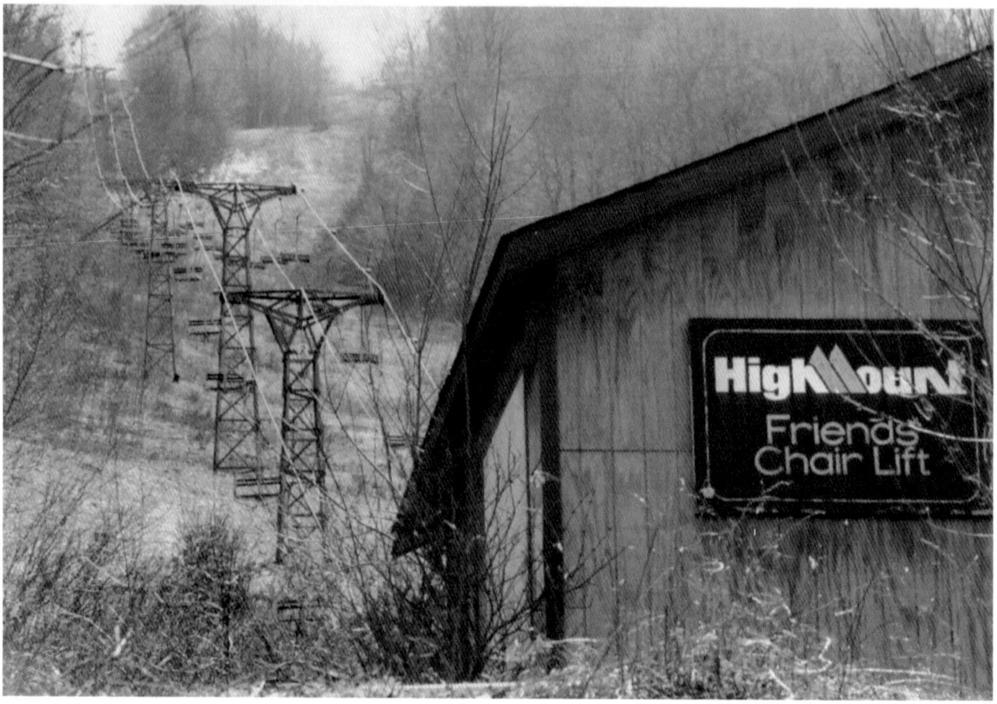

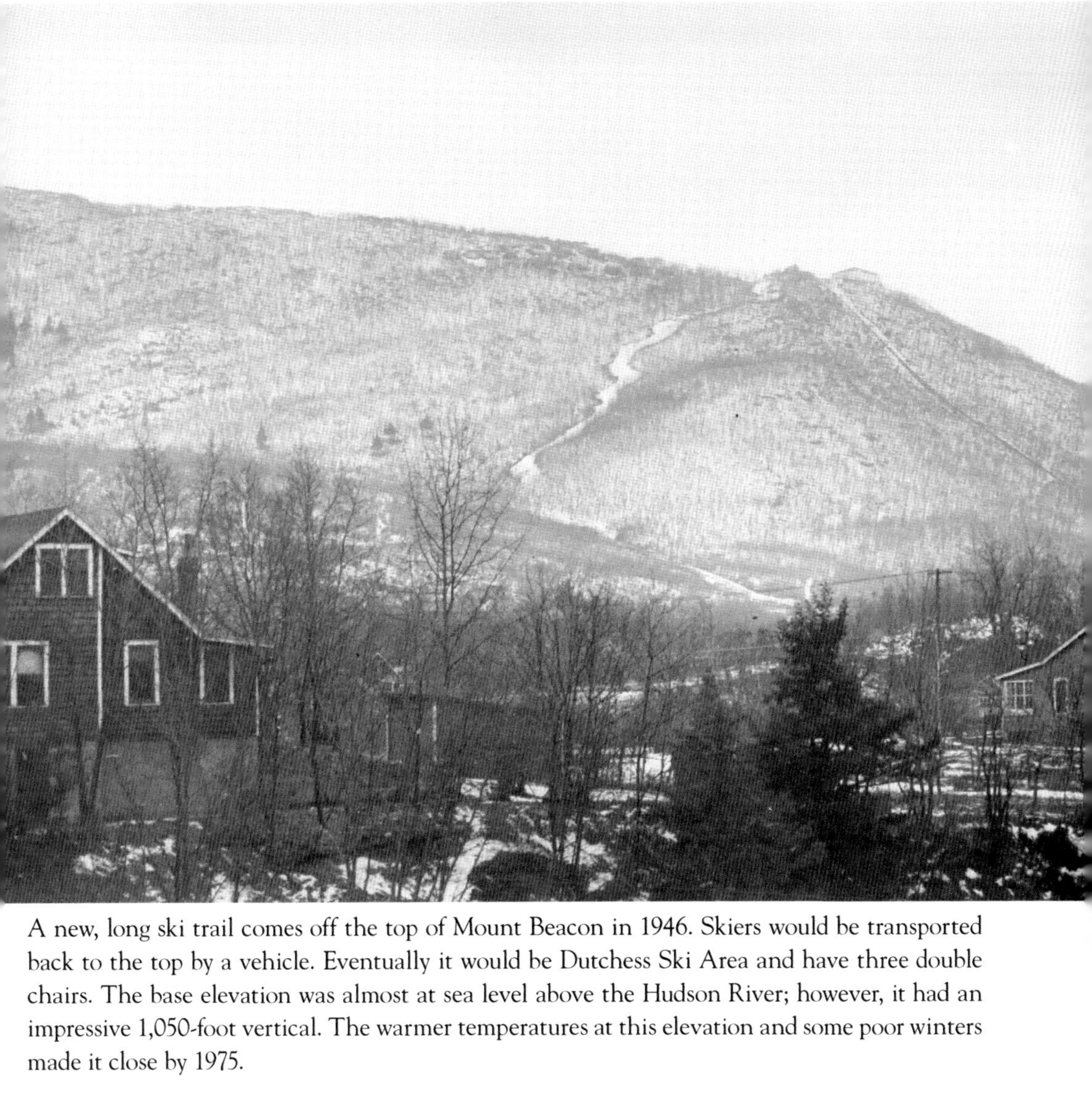

A new, long ski trail comes off the top of Mount Beacon in 1946. Skiers would be transported back to the top by a vehicle. Eventually it would be Dutchess Ski Area and have three double chairs. The base elevation was almost at sea level above the Hudson River; however, it had an impressive 1,050-foot vertical. The warmer temperatures at this elevation and some poor winters made it close by 1975.

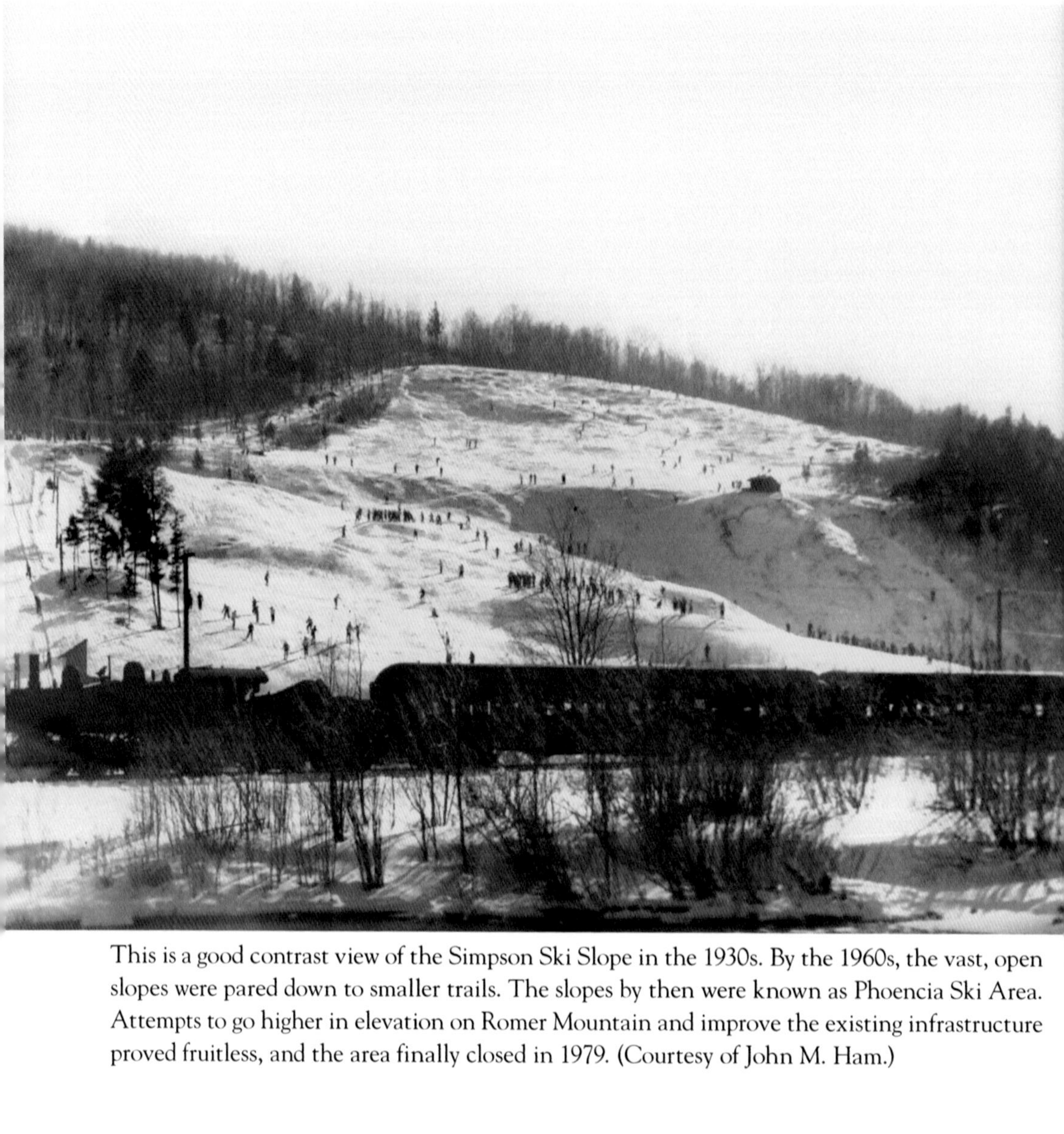

This is a good contrast view of the Simpson Ski Slope in the 1930s. By the 1960s, the vast, open slopes were pared down to smaller trails. The slopes by then were known as Phoencia Ski Area. Attempts to go higher in elevation on Romer Mountain and improve the existing infrastructure proved fruitless, and the area finally closed in 1979. (Courtesy of John M. Ham.)

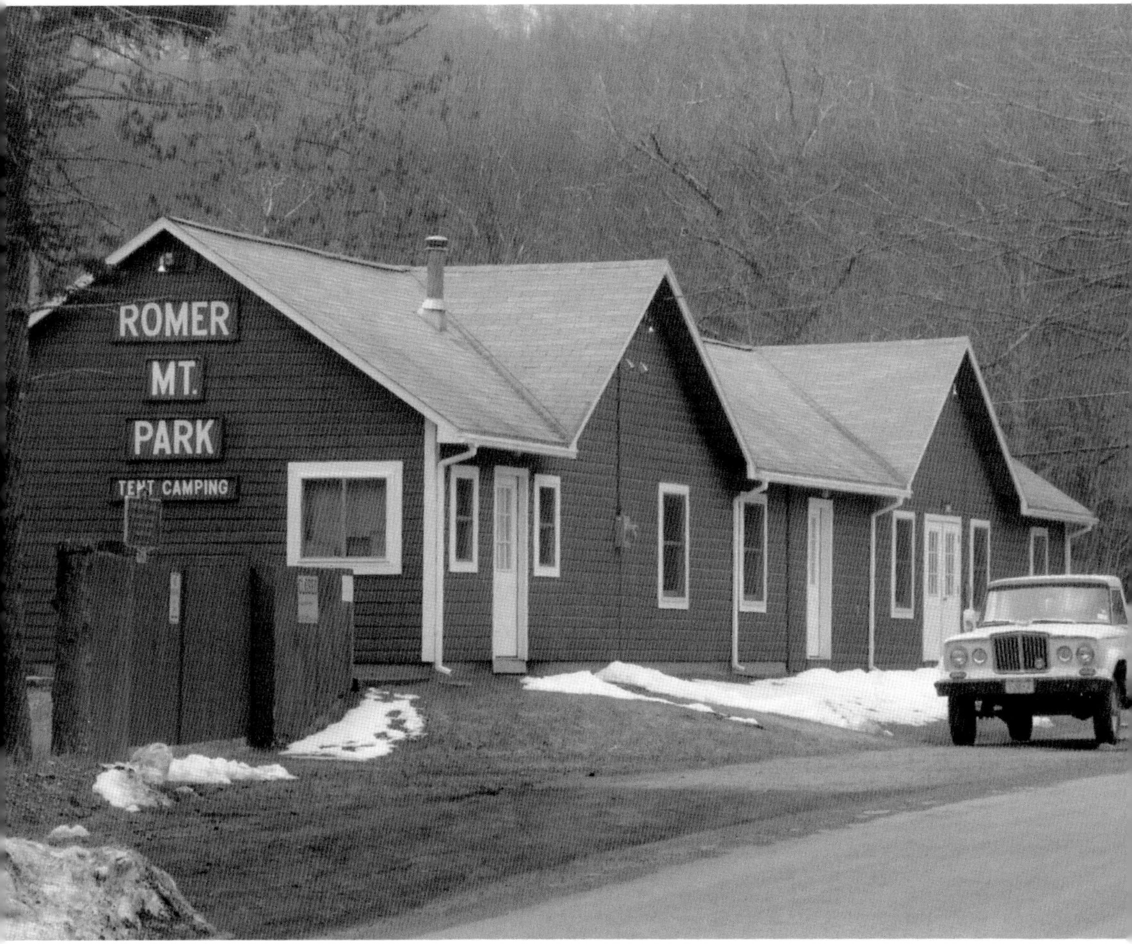

The Phoenicia ski lodge is shown here in more recent times. It still stands today at the entrance of Woodland Valley Road. Having been lovingly restored by local entrepreneur Harry Jameson, it hosts musical gatherings once a week.

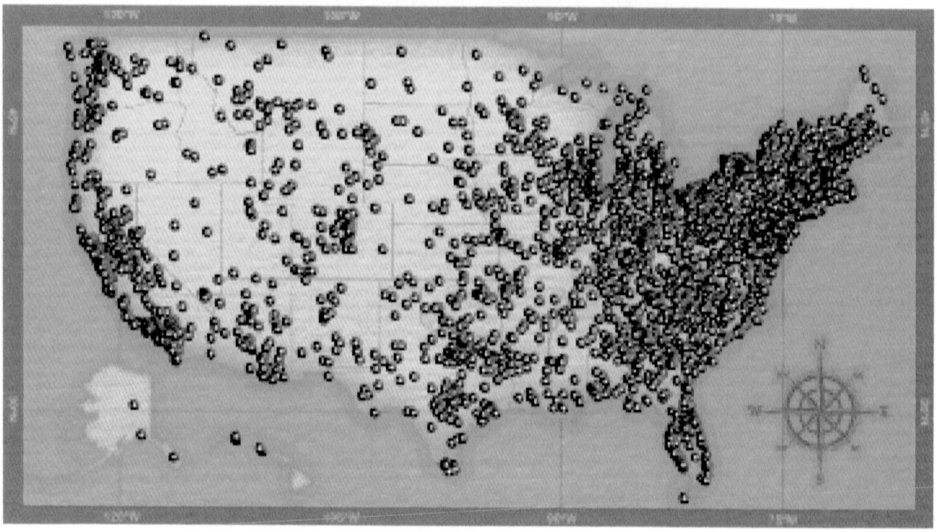